Abortion Politics, Mass Media, and Social Movements in America

Weaving together analyses of archival material, news coverage, and interviews conducted with journalists from mainstream and partisan outlets as well as with activists across the political spectrum, Deana A. Rohlinger reimagines how activists use a variety of mediums, sometimes simultaneously, to agitate for – and against – legal abortion. Rohlinger's in-depth portraits of four groups – the National Right to Life Committee, Planned Parenthood Federation of America, the National Organization for Women, and Concerned Women for America – illuminate when groups use mass media to forward their goals and why they might choose to avoid media attention altogether. Rohlinger expertly reveals why some activist groups are more desperate than others to attract media attention and sheds light on what this means for policy making and legal abortion in the twenty-first century.

Deana A. Rohlinger is an associate professor in the department of sociology and a research associate at the Pepper Institute of Aging and Public Policy at Florida State University. She is coeditor of the volumes *Media, Movements, and Political Change* and *Strategies for Social Change*. She is also the author of several book chapters and articles published in journals such as *Social Problems, Sociological Theory, Mobilization: An International Journal, The Sociological Quarterly, Sociological Spectrum, Research in Social Movements, Conflicts and Change, American Behavioral Scientist, the Journal of Women and Aging*, and *Social Movement Studies*. She is currently the editor for the Social Movements section of *Sociology Compass* and the book review editor for *Mobilization*. She also serves on the American Sociological Association's Collective Behavior Social Movement Council; the membership committee of the Society for the Study of Social Problems; and the editorial boards of *American Sociological Review, Social Problems*, and *American Behavioral Scientist*.

Abortion Politics, Mass Media, and Social Movements in America

DEANA A. ROHLINGER
Florida State University

CAMBRIDGE
UNIVERSITY PRESS

CAMBRIDGE
UNIVERSITY PRESS

32 Avenue of the Americas, New York NY 10013-2473, USA

Cambridge University Press is part of the University of Cambridge.

It furthers the University's mission by disseminating knowledge in the pursuit of education, learning and research at the highest international levels of excellence.

www.cambridge.org
Information on this title: www.cambridge.org/9781107069237

First published 2015

A catalogue record for this publication is available from the British Library

Library of Congress Cataloguing in Publication data
Rohlinger, Deana A.
Abortion politics, mass media, and social movements in America / Deana A. Rohlinger.
pages cm
ISBN 978-1-107-06923-7 (Hardback)
1. Abortion – Political aspects – United States. 2. Social media – Political aspects – United States. I. Title.
HQ767.5.U5R64 2015
362.1988′80973–dc23

2014021294

ISBN 978-1-107-06923-7 Hardback

Dedicated to
Jack, Noah, and Cole

Contents

Figures

Tables

Acknowledgments

Researching and writing this book has been the most rewarding experience of my career, and it would not have been possible without the generosity of colleagues, friends, and family.

This book started as a modest dissertation that benefited from the thoughtful feedback of Dave Snow, Cal Morrill, and Helen Ingram. As members of my dissertation committee, each of them played a special and important role in this project. Dave taught me how to be a scholar who contributes to an intellectual community. He showed me the value of discovering the roots of our ideas and writing in ways that respect the work of those preceding us. Cal introduced me to field theory and, at a critical time, helped me identify the heart and soul of my dissertation. Helen provided insightful critiques and continuous support for my ideas and work. I am thankful to many other scholars who provided friendship and support throughout this process, including Pat Martin, Tina Wright, Sandrine Szerbib, Dennis Downey, and Yvonne Braun. I am particularly thankful to Leslie Bunnage, who is an amazing friend and, when needed, an excellent cheerleader, and Tara Stamm, my charming and brilliant research assistant. I am grateful to Pam Oliver, Rod Benson, Judy Stepan-Norris, and Bill Hoynes, who provided invaluable feedback at various points in this project. I am especially grateful to Jill Quadagno, Suzanne Staggenborg, and Jennifer Earl, each of whom read various iterations of this and other projects and is a wonderful colleague and friend. I am indebted to Ed Amenta, Lee Ann Banaszak, Nancy Whittier, and Lew Bateman for pushing me to make the manuscript better and to Shaun Vigil for helping me get it into shape. I am thankful to each for their thoughtful, incisive, and supportive comments. I would like to express the deepest gratitude to my mentor, David S. Meyer. His intellectual curiosity, quick wit, enthusiasm, and unwavering support over the years have been invaluable. Without his guidance and insightful feedback, this project would not have been possible. He continues to be my intellectual inspiration.

A special thanks to all the librarians and scholars who helped me find the information for this book. I am particularly grateful to Sue Rumpf and Victoria Luong, for making the additional interviews with the National Organization for Women (NOW) activists possible, and Maryann Barasko, who generously shared some of her data on NOW with me. I also thank Bill Gamson, who shared transcripts from his own interviews with mainstream journalists and commented on an earlier version of this project. I am indebted to all of the activists, journalists, and editors who spoke with me (sometimes multiple times) over the years.

My family provided critical support to this project. My parents, Delaine and Adam Styborski, were instrumental in helping me travel across the country and collect much of the data for this research. I wish my father had lived to see the publication of this book. While he never understood my interest in media, movements, or the abortion issue, he did not waiver in his pride for his daughter. I also thank my in-laws, Dan Rohlinger and Chris Kemp, who provided countless hours of babysitting while I wrote the first draft of this book. This book would not have been possible without the love, understanding, and unending support of my wonderful husband, Jack. After twenty years of marriage, he still challenges me, inspires me, and makes me want to be a better person. I owe him everything.

This project benefited from several sources of financial support, including a National Science Foundation Dissertation Improvement Grant SES-0301835, a University of California Regents Dissertation Fellowship, a University of California Regents Summer Fellowship, and a Florida State University Council on Research and Creativity award. I am truly thankful to each of these organizations for their generous financial support.

INTRODUCTION

Dilemmas, choices, and consequences

Paul Hill picketed outside a Pensacola, Florida, abortion clinic every Friday for over year. Most of his signs bore messages such as "abortion is murder" and "abortion stops a beating heart," but occasionally his signs carried a more threatening message: "Execute Abortionists." Dr. John Britton, the clinic doctor, took precautions. He bought a flak jacket, hired bodyguards, and alerted the police to Hill's behavior. On Friday July 29, 1994, Hill shot Britton and one his bodyguards, killing both. Hill did not flee the scene or hide the shotgun he used to commit the crime. As the police led him away in handcuffs, Hill proclaimed, "Today there will be no more baby killings in this abortion clinic!"[1]

The reaction to the shooting was immediate and not just by pro-choice advocates. Wanda Franz, president of the mainstream, pro-life group National Right of Life Committee, argued that individuals who claimed murdering a clinic provider was justifiable in order to save unborn babies are "very much on the fringe of the pro-life movement." She added, "We feel as strongly about stopping this as we do about stopping the violence of abortion .... We're very concerned about the general population being encouraged to think that pro-lifers are violent."[2] This was not the first of such statements made by the National Right to Life Committee. The group was so concerned that violence was tarnishing the movement's image that it launched an "unending" campaign to counter this perception. The organization likened the pro-life movement to the civil rights movement, and compared moderate groups, such as itself, to the nonviolent Southern Christian Leadership Conference and violent pro-life "fanatics" to the Black Panthers.

Hill was convicted for two counts of murder and executed by the state of Florida in 2003. The execution received extensive coverage, and both pro-life

[1] James, Meg. "Abortion Doctor, Aide Are Slain in Pensacola." *Palm Beach Post*, July 30, 1994.
[2] Hall, Mimi. "Abortion Foes Deny There's a Conspiracy." *USA Today*, August 5, 1994.

and pro-choice advocates commented on the event. Hill supporters called him an "American martyr," insisting that "Paul Hill did exactly what was right according to the Bible. Think, twenty-five babies that day for the cost of two bullets. What a great deal."[3] Pro-choicers argued that these comments and continued violence at clinics only proved that the "anti-abortion" movement was comprised of extremists, who would kill to advance their anti-woman agenda. Eleanor Smeal, president of Feminist Majority, opined "There are hundreds of extremists out there. They don't believe in the ballot box or the judiciary, so they take it into their own hands and use bullets."[4]

I recount this tragic story not to reinforce stereotypes about activists mobilizing around the abortion issue. I do so because there is an important lesson to be learned in this example; one that is often missed by scholars. Social scientists focus on the ideas, individuals, and groups that are included in media coverage. This emphasis obscures analyses of who is *missing* from coverage and why. In the coverage of Hill's execution, the mainstream pro-life groups that were quick to condemn his actions were conspicuously absent. The National Right to Life Committee, which is the largest pro-life group in the United States, did not appear once in more than one hundred stories and editorials written on the execution nationwide.

The current stock of knowledge would suggest that mainstream groups were absent because they were not relevant, interesting, or strategic enough to get media attention. This is an inadequate explanation in the case of the National Right to Life Committee, which is highly regarded by journalists. A better explanation is that the organization *chose not* to comment on Hill's execution. After all, commenting on Hill's execution would not help the group bolster its image as a civil rights movement, nor would denouncing Hill effectively distance the organization from violent pro-lifers. The organization had nothing to gain from reminding the public that it was part of the very movement to which Hill claimed membership.

Scholars miss these strategic silences because they focus on the *coverage* of movement organizations rather than *the choices* groups make. This focus makes sense. Scholars try to connect strategy, or the link activists make "between the places, the times and ways" they deploy their resources in order to achieve a goal (Ganz 2000, 1010), to tangible outcomes. Naturally, scholars assess the effectiveness of group strategies relative to something that is amenable to analysis such as the mobilization of people (Snow, Rochford, Worden, and Benford 1986), the creation or maintenance of collective identity (Gamson 1997; Snow and Anderson 1987), and institutional change (Gamson 1990; Ganz 2000; Piven and Cloward 1977). Additionally, scholars presume that when media is involved

[3] Pinkham, Paul and Rachel Davis. "Abortion Doctor's Killer Executed by Injection." *Florida Times-Union*, September 4, 2003.

[4] Goddard, Jacqui. "Impending Florida Execution Piques Abortion Debate." *Christian Science Monitor*, September 2, 2003.

getting attention, rather than avoiding it, is the goal. Indeed, media coverage matters for groups. Organizations included in coverage can:

- Change the debate around an issue.
- Reach and mobilize a sympathetic public.
- Get recognition for their positions.
- Build their coffers.
- Buttress their legitimacy with politicians and the public.
- Create an opportunity for political change.

Given the potential rewards, it is easy to see why other aspects of media strategy, especially those that seemingly do not have such a large payoff, fall by the wayside.

The lack of scholarly acknowledgement of "strategic silence" points to a larger problem in the literature. Scholars examine how activists use different mediums to further their goals, but do not theorize about media strategy more generally. In the current stock of knowledge, media simply are a weapon in a group's arsenal which it wields with more or less success. As a result, scholars consider an organization's use of different mediums – such as mainstream, alternative, and online news media – separately. The problem with this piecemeal approach is that it obscures how groups *simultaneously* use different outlets to advance their goals. Likewise, this approach ultimately subordinates media strategy to political strategy, ignoring how activists align media and political strategies as well as when activists make tradeoffs between the two.

This book challenges conventional understandings of the movement–media relationship and offers a theoretical approach that elucidates how media strategy works and affects the trajectories of activist groups. Rather than focusing on whether a group gets mainstream attention, I consider the media field writ large and introduce a *strategic choice approach* that highlights what (and how) organizations regard and use media to forward their goals.

A STRATEGIC CHOICE APPROACH

Strategy is the heart of social movements. Activists make choices about how to deploy their resources in ways that seem likely to advance their goals. Strategy, however, is not simply a more or less effective means to an end. The choices activists make matter because they reflect the broader political environment as well as the actors operating in it. When an organization adopts an outrageous position or uses a shocking tactic to get attention for its ideas, allies and opponents alike must decide whether and how to respond. Strategic decision-making rarely is easy. Decision points often are rife with dilemmas, or "two or more options, each with a long list of risks, costs and potential benefits" (Jasper 2006), and the consequences of choosing one course of action over another are impossible to know (Jasper 2004). Like scholars, activists can only trace the course of a campaign and retrospectively examine the implications of past decisions in light of current organizational and political realities.

While scholars increasingly make dilemmas and tradeoffs central to their understanding of social movements (Downey and Rohlinger 2008; Jasper 2012; McCammon 2012), researchers studying the movement–media relationship have largely reduced decision-making to a handful of organizational variables that either help or hurt a group's efforts to get media attention. The literature on mainstream coverage of protest events, for example, typically codifies choice by categorizing a group according to its ability to respond to journalistic requests for information, its age, its overall repertoire of tactics, and the kinds of issues it represents.[5] On the one hand, this approach is practical and useful. In quantitative analyses, choices are variables that must be defined, and relatively big decisions (such as how to structure an organization so it reflects the values of its leaders) affect other choices down the line (such as how to attract media attention to a cause). This work sheds light on how certain kinds of choices shape the media outcomes of groups. On the other hand, treating choice as a set of variables that account for why some groups get media coverage and others do not ignores the reality that deciding whether or not to engage a news media outlet is a key organizational dilemma – and not all groups try to get mainstream attention. Qualitative scholars also are guilty of focusing on whether a group garners mainstream coverage. Researchers emphasize the tactics that activists use to overcome one or more organizational deficits and attract the media spotlight. While this work sheds light on how a group that chooses to engage mainstream media can build its credibility with journalists over time, it obscures when and why an organization may choose to *avoid* media attention.[6] The tendency of scholars to operationalize strategic choice narrowly, in short, is not a methodological flaw, but a conceptual one.

In order to expand how scholars think about media strategy, I outline three fundamental media dilemmas activist groups face.[7]

- Dilemma 1: whether to engage external media outlets.
- Dilemma 2: whether to respond to negative media attention.
- Dilemma 3: how to publicly deal with losing issues.

There are three important caveats. First, these dilemmas are not mutually exclusive, and resolving one dilemma may create another (Jasper 2006). Strategic choices are rarely discrete and a choice may involve two or more dilemmas simultaneously. Likewise, one strategic decision can create another

[5] See, for example, McCarthy, McPhail, and Smith (1996); Oliver and Maney (2000); Oliver and Myers (1999); Smith et al. (2001).

[6] For example, see the work of Gamson (1990), Gamson and Wolfsfeld (1993), Rohlinger (2002), Ryan (1991), Ryan, Anastario, and Jeffreys (2005), and Wolfsfeld (2004).

[7] Jasper (2006) offers an overview of dilemmas groups face across institutional arenas. The dilemmas outlined here are narrower and highlight the overlaps among institutional arenas as opposed to the similarities across them.

dilemma for an organization. A group that decides to engage external media outlets (Dilemma 1) may be immediately confronted with Dilemma 2 – whether to respond to negative coverage. Second, like other strategic choices, any given dilemma is discrete, but recurring. An activist group, for instance, will have to decide whether to engage external media outlets (Dilemma 1) throughout its organizational history.

Finally, most strategic choices require a group to make tradeoffs (Jasper 2006). This is particularly true as it relates to mass media. One reason that groups try to get coverage is because mass media overlap with and influence virtually every other American institution, including political institutions (Bourdieu 1998a). Groups try to employ this overlap to their advantage and use media attention as leverage in other institutional arenas (Gamson and Meyer 1996; Raeburn 2004). For example, groups routinely use mainstream media to "name and shame" corporations for discriminatory policies with high levels of success (King and Soule 2008). There are times when organizations have to choose how to deploy their finite resources. This may require groups to prioritize one institution over another and trade off gains in one institution for losses in another. I discuss below the basic media dilemmas and tradeoffs in more detail.

Dilemma 1: whether to engage external media outlets

There are two kinds of media: *direct media*, which are created by activists associated with a movement group, and *external media*, which use a particular set of norms and practices to create a media product that (ideally) generates profit from consumer sales and advertising. Direct media typically include newsletters, pamphlets, websites, listservs, forums, videos/documentaries, and songs or radio programming produced by group activists, while external media include mainstream and alternative news outlets (on- or off-line), radio stations, blogs, commercial documentaries, concerts, and social media. The distinction between direct and external media is important because while all movements may use mass media, not all groups choose to regularly engage media over which they have little to no control. This is because attracting media attention is rife with risk. Mainstream media professionals are quick to marginalize ideas that challenge the status quo, and this can have devastating consequences for organizations (Gamson 1990; Gitlin 1980). Negative attention can:

- Make a movement and organization appear unrealistic in its goals or dangerous to social mores and institutions.
- Cause constituents to withdrawal their support from an organization and cause.
- Prompt elites to distance themselves from an issue.
- Undermine the political inroads made by a movement.
- Provide opponents fodder in their efforts to derail movement progress.
- Disrupt an organization and undermine its ability to function effectively.

Given this, there are good reasons for activists to seriously consider whether or not to engage external media outlets – even when journalists call them for a quote.

There are several ways this dilemma may be resolved. A group may decide to engage external media and do its best to sidestep the potential pitfalls it entails. An organization that makes this decision will likely create a division dedicated to the media cause and designate a spokesperson to build credibility with media professionals. While these efforts can help a group get better coverage, it is far from a guarantee. There will be times when an organization wants media attention, but finds that its issue does not fit with the news of the day (Ferree et al. 2002). Likewise, there will be times when an issue or organization does get media attention, but the coverage is inconsistent with a group's agenda and goals. Both of these resultant dilemmas are addressed below.

An organization may also choose to focus its media efforts on outlets that are more sympathetic to its goals. While these enclaves of support may be relatively small, they provide a group an opportunity to mobilize consensus and action among its core constituents (Koopmans and Olzak 2004). Given that mobilization processes are rarely uncontested (Klandermans 1988), groups that target sympathetic venues may find it easier to move people to action when they require a quick response. Despite the potential benefits, the decision to focus its media efforts on sympathetic outlets may seem a foolhardy one. However, as I discuss in more detail later, the linkages among media outlets allow ideas to "cross over" from one venue to another (Bennett 2003). An organization may target ideologically like-minded outlets and find that as its ideas gain traction in sympathetic venues they are increasingly covered in mainstream ones (Rohlinger 2007). The potential for crossover is particularly high in the contemporary era where digital technologies put information at a citizen's fingertips in an instant; a development that has intensified competition among news outlets to report, "tweet," and post breaking news first. Like media coverage itself, crossover is not guaranteed. Organizations may find that they continually preach to the proverbial choir and do not expand their reach in any substantive way.

An organization may also decide to develop its own outlets so that it has control over how its issues are portrayed to the public. Activists can use a newsletter or a website to provide current and potential supporters information about the group, its cause, and current campaigns. Likewise, a group can create radio and public access programming, craft online videos, sponsor mediated events (such as community lectures and concerts), or craft advertisements that allow activists to sell its ideas to a broader public without interference. This choice is not without tradeoffs because the audience a group reaches via these venues may be fairly limited. Websites are great "brochures" for a group (Earl and Kimport 2011), but an individual has to be looking for the group or cause in order to be exposed to the information. Similarly, content circulated on niche media venues (such as public access stations) reaches small audiences. This is not to suggest that groups cannot find ways to increase their reach. The point is that an organization will have difficulty finding a mainstream audience if activists want to consistently control how its causes are represented.

Dilemma 2: whether to respond to negative media attention

At some point, a group will be unhappy with how it is represented and will have to decide whether (and how) it wants to respond to the coverage. The dilemma is how to respond to negative attention without making the organization look bad, or worse. The options available to an organization depend on the nature of the bad press. A group will respond differently to an opponent publicly bashing the organization than it will to a journalist who has written an unfavorable story, or to the actions of an ally.

Opponents come with the territory. Mainstream news thrives on conflict, which means opposing points of view and ad hominem attacks are part of most stories. Given this reality, a group can craft a response to their opponents and try to even the score the next time they issue a press release or give a quote to a journalist. When media professionals write stories that question the goals, tactics, or leaders of a movement, it is more difficult for a group to craft an effective response because they rarely have leverage with journalists. While organizations seek media coverage for their issues and events on a regular basis, journalists only occasionally need information from activists (Gamson and Wolfsfeld 1993). More importantly, there typically is no shortage of groups from which a journalist may get a quote, meaning there is an incentive for a group to grab the media opportunity if it arises – even when the outlook for the resulting coverage is less than desirable. An organization can respond to negative coverage, but the likelihood that it will result in different or better coverage in the short term is unlikely.

If a group decides to respond to the negative attention, it has several options it can pursue simultaneously. It can take on the outlet directly and try to get the offending journalist to write a correction or a follow-up piece which presents the organization in a more pleasing light. An organizational representative can write a letter to the editor to the offending outlet. If the letter is published, the group can publicly challenge the story and take the outlet to task for inaccurate reporting. An organizational leader can write an editorial and try to get another media outlet to run it. Alternatively, a group can issue a press release that refutes the coverage and challenges other outlets to report an issue accurately.

Again, the decision to pursue any of these options may seem foolhardy on its face. After all, a group must expend precious resources (time, money, and labor) to pursue these options and the media coverage payoff is low, at best. However, the tradeoff is not so simple. An organization can derive benefits from responding to bad press even if it does not get a chance to refute it. A response lets supporters know that the organization is engaged and fighting to educate the public, and provides an excellent opportunity for a group to ask supporters to fund an advertising campaign to counter misinformation. An organization also can use negative attention as a rationale for changing how its uses mass media. A group may argue that ongoing bad press requires it to cultivate relationships with alternative outlets or create its own venues.

Alternatively, a group may decide to ignore bad press altogether. Silence can have benefits. There are times when responding to negative media coverage creates other challenges for an organization. If a group denounces a tactic or campaign of its ally, it is by extension potentially criticizing its own supporters. Unless the tactic involves violence against people or property, there is little to be gained from alienating your allies or a pool of potential supporters. The beauty of a non-response is that silence can be interpreted different ways by different audiences (as censure or support), and all of these interpretations can favor a group. Silence also can effectively distance an organization from a rancorous debate or an undesirable association. It made sense for the National Right to Life Committee to remain silent on Hill's execution, particularly since Hill used his impending execution as a platform to validate violent tactics. Silence distanced the group from Hill's brand of pro-life politics. Not all forgone media opportunities are as clear cut because, while media coverage is sometimes an end in and of itself, it also is a means to influence political processes (Wolfsfeld 2004). Organizations operate in multiple institutional arenas simultaneously. Because institutions overlap, activist groups can use media attention to create opportunities to effect change (Armstrong and Bernstein 2008; Raeburn 2004). If given a choice, an organization will likely decide to exert influence in an institution over media attention.

These choices do arise. Social movements are composed of groups that may share a broad goal, but disagree on virtually everything else. Sometimes these disputes can have deleterious effects on a movement (Benford 1993). However, there are times when factionalism within a movement can benefit groups with moderate goals. The emergence of radical groups make moderate organizations more appealing to politicians, which may create an opportunity for moderates to advance their agenda (Haines 1988). This tradeoff has consequences. Radical groups can have a "tarring effect" on the entire movement by generating moral outrage toward (and negative publicity for) the movement as a whole (Rohlinger 2006). Groups must try to exploit the short-term benefits of the "radical flank effect" without significantly damaging the reputation of the organization or the movement.

Dilemma 3: how to publicly deal with losing issues

A group routinely frames – or ascribes meaning to – its issues (Benford and Snow 2000). While an organization frames issues in ways that reflect its mission and goals, even sympathetic politicians rarely adopt a group's interpretations of and solutions to a social problem wholesale. Generally speaking, framing an issue in a way that is amenable to organizational goals is a constant challenge with which a group must contend. This is particularly true when a group's opponents are on the offensive and have found a policy solution that is popular with a broad segment of the electorate, including some of the organization's own supporters. How a group publicly responds to these losing issues becomes important because it stands to lose the political battle and public support.

An organization has four options when it comes to losing issues. First, it can accept the predominant frame and challenge its merits. An organization acknowledges its opponent's position as valid and tries to quibble on the details in an effort to change public opinion and defang a policy before it passes. This option is the riskiest in terms of its potential to undermine broader public support. By challenging the particulars of a frame rather than the frame itself, the organization recognizes its opponent's position as legitimate and mainstream. Unless the points the group makes are as popular as the proffered frame, the organization may be marginalized for its positions and lose public support. Second, a group can try to co-opt its opponent's frame (Ellingson 1995; Noonan 1995). While this strategy may not win the day, it can confuse the audience and reduce support for the frame without reducing support for the organization.

Third, a group can try to reframe the debate in an effort to draw public attention to other resonant values that are relevant to understanding the issue at hand. This strategy also is unlikely to change a losing issue into a winning one. However, it allows a group to challenge popular positions without marginalizing itself in the process. In fact, an organization that successfully sidesteps rancorous debate and offers alternative ways to understand an issue can position itself as mainstream and garner additional support. Finally, a group can choose to avoid the debate altogether. Silence can be an organization's best option. However, a group is only likely to choose this option if its leaders decide the potential benefits of remaining silent outweigh the costs of taking a public stand on a losing issue. An organization may opt out of the public debate because it knows that a policy does not have the political support to pass. Likewise, a group may decide to skip one public battle in favor of another – one that it believes it can win.

How an organization approaches a losing issue will vary according to other strategic choices and tradeoffs it has made over the years. A group that has spent decades cultivating relationships with media professionals is more likely to avoid rancorous debate and losing issues than a group that does not have these connections because the former will have other media opportunities down the line. An organization, in contrast, that strategically avoids all but sympathetic media may see losing issues as *the* opportunity to move its ideas into new outlets precisely because its allies are not anxious to be cast as villains in a contentious debate. A group in this position may regard engaging external media on a losing issue (and getting bad press for it) as a winning prospect in the long run, particularly if it is able to find ways to reframe – or at least offer a viable alternative to – the current debate.

All organizations confront these three basic media dilemmas. Each of these dilemmas, the choices available, and potential tradeoffs organizations face are summarized in Table I.1. The table is not exhaustive. The purpose is to highlight the benefits of conceptualizing strategy in terms of the strategic choices a group makes, rather than the media coverage it gets. Here we see the potential tradeoffs associated with different choices as well as why the decision to avoid media attention makes sense in certain circumstances. For example, negative media attention can result from the actions of opponents *or* allies, or may simply be a poorly executed story. The source matters because the strategic options available to an activist group vary – as do the potential tradeoffs. Groups that opt out of a rancorous debate involving their opponents may lose public face, but may gain political leverage behind the scenes. The tradeoff involved when allies are the cause of negative media attention is different. As seen in the case of Hill's execution, silence distanced National Right to Life Committee from movement extremists. Of course, how a given group responds to these dilemmas is shaped by a number of factors including organizational, movement, and institutional dynamics. I take these issues up in the next chapter.

LESSONS LEARNED FROM A STRATEGIC CHOICE APPROACH

This book challenges conventional understandings of the movement–media relationship and explains how organizations use mass media to forward their goals in a rapidly changing political environment. To do so, I draw on tens of thousands of organizational and media documents, a content analysis of 1,424 media stories, and interviews with activists and journalists to comparatively analyze how four organizations mobilizing around the abortion issue used mass media to effect political change from 1980 to 2000. Here, I briefly highlight the conceptual benefits of a strategic choice approach.

First, a strategic choice approach's emphasis on decision-making elucidates the relationship between media and political strategies and highlights those moments when tradeoffs are likely to occur. In most cases, organizations take a hit to their public image in order to increase their influence with politicians. This important point is absent from the existing literature on the movement–media relationship which, given the emphasis on outcomes, often conflates political and media strategies. As Table I.1 makes clear, I do not treat media and political strategies as unrelated. Groups regularly create campaigns whose success depends on the effective use of media. The point is that the relationship between the two needs to be analyzed so that we understand how media and political strategies work in tandem and when they diverge.

Second, a strategic choice approach sheds light on how organizations think about mass media, which helps us understand what media venues activist groups use and to what end. A flaw in much of the current scholarship is the assumption that groups want mainstream attention because it will increase their political clout. This is true for some, but not all, organizations. A group that regards

TABLE 1.1. *Media dilemmas, choices, and tradeoffs*

Dilemma	Potential strategic options	Potential tradeoffs
Whether to engage external media		
	Create a division within the organization to deal with media professionals	Resources for the potential to reach a broader audience
	Focus media efforts on outlets that target sympathetic audiences	Ability to reach a general audience for control over messaging
	Develop programming and try to get outlets to circulate it	Ability to reach a general audience for control over messaging
	Pay for advertising space or other direct media efforts	Resources for the potential to reach a broader audience
	Decide not to engage external media	Ability to reach a broader public for control over messaging
Whether to respond to negative attention		
Source: journalists	Request a correction	Resources for potentially better coverage and new/continued member support
	Write/submit a letter to the editor	Resources for potentially better coverage and new/continued member support
	Write/submit an editorial	Resources for potentially better coverage and new/continued member support
	Issue a press release chastising an outlet	Resources for potentially better coverage and new/continued member support
	Ignore bad press	Public image for resources and evidence of media bias
Source: opponents	Denounce opponents	Resources for media coverage
	Try to reframe the debate	Resources for a potential shift in the political conversation
	Remain silent on the debate	Public support for political influence or the potential to diminish an issue

(continued)

TABLE I.1 (*continued*)

Dilemma	Potential strategic options	Potential tradeoffs
Source: allies	Denounce ally	Broader movement support for organizational support
	Try to reframe the debate	Resources for a potential shift in the political conversation
	Remain silent on the debate	Potential to shape a debate for distance from "extreme" groups
How to publicly respond to losing issues		
	Challenge the merits of opponent's frame	Resources for the potential to slow public support
	Try to co-opt opponent's frame	Resources for the opportunity to confuse public debate
	Try to reframe the debate	Resources for a potential shift in the political conversation
	Remain silent on the debate	Potential political losses for the ability to protect an organization's public image

mainstream media with suspicion may not try to get its ideas in these venues. Instead, it might target alternative news outlets and other mediums that enable it to mobilize sympathetic audiences quickly and build its credibility as representative of a particular constituency – both of which can help an organization build its political clout. While this strategy may have limitations over the long haul, it is a *choice* available to groups.

Third, a strategic choice approach highlights that not all groups have the same standing in an institution and that differences in reputation have real consequences for decision-making. Institutional actors assess the extent to which the logic of an organization corresponds with the logic of the field as well as their own more particularistic goals (Rindova, Williamson, and Petkova 2005). If there is a match, the organization will have a strong reputation in the field and more opportunities to access a range of media outlets for its own purposes (Rohlinger and Brown 2013). Reputation, in short, directly affects the strategic choices available to an organization. A group with a strong reputation can decide to opt out of a contentious media debate because it will have other opportunities to showcase its point of view. A group with a relatively weaker reputation is unlikely to make the same choice, particularly if they want media coverage and opportunities to get it are few and far between.

Fourth, a strategic choice approach recognizes that organizations make decisions that potentially improve (or stymie) their ability to use media to forward their goals over time. For instance, organizations that develop a brand for their group will have a better reputation in the media field and more opportunities than those that do not. Most groups that want to engage media craft a public image (or a representation of the organization) for external consumption. A savvy group will play up those aspects of its identity that appeal to broader audiences and are likely to enhance its credibility with media targets. Some groups will sink considerable resources into crafting a brand which establishes an emotional and symbolic connection between the organization and its target audience (Aaker 1991). Brands have benefits. A brand gives a group cultural cache, which it can use to frame and reframe controversial debates. Alternatively, an organization can use its brand to shield itself from debates in which it would rather not participate – even as the group works behind the political scenes to effect change on the issue.

Fifth, a strategic choice approach shows that media strategy is shaped by the broader political environment and other actors operating in it. Activists have agency insofar as they have a range of options available to them, including inaction. The circumstances in which activists find themselves, however, are seldom of their own making. While scholars have developed understandings of how institutional change as well as allies and opponents influence an organization's political strategy (Amenta 2006; Andrews 2004; McCammon 2012), this insight is rarely applied to the movement–media relationship. This gap is a significant one because the larger political environment, and the actions of those operating in it, helps explain how groups choose their media targets and tactics.

As mentioned above, the National Right to Life Committee initiated an unending, mainstream media campaign to counter the rhetoric of individuals committing violence in the name of the pro-life cause. This campaign would have been unnecessary otherwise.

Finally, a strategic choice approach provides a comprehensive framework for understanding the relationship between strategy and outcomes. Conceptualizing the success and failures of a strategy in terms of a group's media coverage obscures the fact that the line between strategy and outcomes is not always a direct one, nor is a strategy always immediately effective. The National Right to Life Committee's decision to remain silent on Hill's execution is a good example. While the organization's silence did not prevent outlets from covering Hill's execution, it removed mainstream pro-life voices from the debate, which helped reinforce the group's point that violence was advocated by extremists alone. Additionally, as I detail in Chapter 4, the ways that the National Right to Life Committee responded to its more radical allies may not have gotten the group mainstream media coverage, but were effective over time. A strategic choice approach moves scholars away from linear conceptualizations of the relationship between strategy and outcomes.

OUTLINE OF THE BOOK

Chapter 1 outlines the organizational, institutional, and movement dynamics that influence the strategic choices available to a group and its response to media dilemmas. Chapter 2 conceptualizes the "mass media field" and discusses how field dynamics affect an organization's reputation and its strategic choices. Here, I use new institutionalists' and Pierre Bourdieu's understandings of "field" to reconceptualize mass media as a strategic action field that includes social media, organizational websites, talk radio, art, and concerts. This reconceptualization is beneficial for two reasons. First, it recognizes that different kinds of media venues may not be direct economic competitors, but do take cues from one another – a reality that activist organizations can exploit for their own purposes. Second, it highlights the permeability of media boundaries and allows scholars to better understand how organizations use a range of outlets (sometimes simultaneously) to forward their goals.

Chapter 3 provides an overview of the political context in which the war over legal abortion has been waged. I focus on three different arenas in which pro-choice and pro-life forces engage and highlight how the movements have worked to advance their causes. The purpose of this summary is to outline the ongoing tensions and contests in abortion politics so that the media strategies of particular groups can be understood within the broader political context in which they were devised. Then, I introduce the study and the four organizations – the National Right to Life Committee, National Organization for Women, Planned Parenthood Federation of America, and Concerned Women for America – included in the research. Because organizational dynamics are integral to strategic decision-making, each chapter features a group and illustrates the utility of a strategic choice approach for understanding how organizations respond to the media dilemmas they face as well as the tradeoffs they make along the way.

Chapter 4 examines how intramovement dynamics affected the strategic decision-making of the National Right to Life Committee (NRLC) during a moment ripe for political change. Moderate groups that opposed NRLC's support for pro-life legislation that permitted abortion to save the life of the mother posed the biggest political challenge. If moderate pro-lifers could not agree on a position, conflict would reign and meaningful policy change would be difficult to achieve. NRLC responded to this conflict by working to build a consensus among the moderate pro-life core. Its efforts in this regard ultimately played an important public relations role because it directly challenged oppositional claims that the movement did not care about women's rights and health. Radical allies, in contrast, presented both a media and political challenge for NRLC. While NRLC found that not commenting on the activities of some of its radical allies had financial and political advantages, strategic silence was not always possible. This was particularly true when allies either tried to build their membership and coffers by attacking the strategies and political legitimacy of NRLC or advocated violence against abortion clinics and personnel.

Chapter 5 illustrates the long-term consequences of organizational choices for reputation in the mass media field. I show how organizational decision-making, coupled with changes in the broader political climate, weakened the reputation of the National Organization for Women (NOW) with news outlets and altered the group's response to media dilemmas. When leaders engaged radical pro-life groups outside of clinics, they diminished their reputation with journalists. Its reputation weakened further after it moved its battle with pro-life extremists from the street to the courtroom. The court battle, which spanned two decades, made it difficult for NOW to distance itself from its colorful opponents and respond to a rapidly changing political environment – one that pushed back against feminism and feminist organizations. NOW struggled to remain relevant and, ultimately, changed what outlets it used and how it used them in its political efforts.

Chapter 6 shows that groups can navigate the political and media worlds with relative ease by crafting a brand that cultivates (and then represents) middle-of-the-road opinions and policies. Through an analysis of the Planned Parenthood Federation of America (PPFA) I illustrate how a brand can be used to mitigate many media dilemmas, particularly the dilemma of losing issues. Branding an organization is not a panacea. Crafting an effective brand is resource intensive, as is maintaining a brand over time. Likewise, even organizations with successful brands will encounter moments of crisis. For PPFA this crisis came when pro-choice ally, Bill Clinton, took office and made universal health care his priority. While access to abortion was part of Clinton's plan, it provided a dramatically different framework for understanding legal abortion. Because PPFA clinics received federal funding, leaders worried that if PPFA did not alter its message and structure it would become obsolete in the new era of managed care. National PPFA leaders began to distance the group from the abortion issue and beat the drum of health care reform, which sparked a revolution within the organization.

Chapter 7 illustrates that there are alternative ways for organizations to use mass media to effect political change. Through an analysis of Concerned Women for America (CWA), an organization that barely registers in mainstream coverage of the abortion issue, I show that groups can use sympathetic media to build political connections and clout. This media strategy, which relied heavily on the celebrity status of its founder, allowed CWA to both mobilize Christian conservatives around specific campaigns and build the organization's political reputation with Republican politicians, candidates, and presidents. CWA eventually set its sights on mainstream outlets, but found itself unable to get coverage on the abortion issue and, later, on the receiving end of negative coverage that lambasted the organization for its opposition to gay rights. Over time, CWA reframed its position in the debate and focused public attention on its right to express a different perspective on an issue in a democratic society. This experience was transformative insofar as CWA began to view mainstream outlets as a means to advance its political goals and made efforts to use mainstream news venues for this end.

In the final chapter, I revisit the strategic choice approach and highlight its utility for understanding how organizations use mass media to forward their goals and the dynamics that can enhance (or impede) their ability to do so. In the final part of the book, I revisit the pro-life and pro-choice movements and discuss their prospects in the twenty-first century.

1

Constraints on strategic choice

Movement groups make strategic choices, but the circumstances in which they make them are rarely of their own design. Decisions regarding how to respond to media dilemmas are shaped by three overlapping dynamics: organizational, movement, and institutional. I begin the chapter by outlining how organizational dynamics shape the media opportunities available to a group and how it responds to media dilemmas. Then, I show how institutional and movement dynamics – specifically elites, movement allies, and opponents – affect an organization's response to media dilemmas and influence the tradeoffs that a group makes. I conclude the chapter with a summary of how these dynamics constrain the strategic choices of organizations.

ORGANIZATIONAL DYNAMICS AND STRATEGIC CHOICE

Organizations provide a foundation for collective challenges. They enable activists to aggregate and coordinate resources and deploy these resources in their strategic efforts (McCarthy and Zald 1977). Scholars pay a fair amount of attention to the structural characteristics that help groups successfully navigate political and media institutions. Organizations that are bureaucratic and hierarchically structured with a centralized leadership, a professional staff, and a clear division of labor are better positioned to respond to breaking than are informally organized groups that rely on volunteers who engage in activism during their free time (Staggenborg 1991). Likewise, professional organizations have an easier time building credibility with journalists because they can quickly respond to requests for information, issue statements in the wake of political events, and maintain regular contact with media professionals (Gamson and Wolfsfeld 1993); all of these can give a group more influence over how its issues are presented to the public (Ryan, Anastario, and Jeffreys 2005).

While structure matters, it is not the only factor that shapes media strategy. *Resources* are extraordinarily important to strategy because they determine whether an organization has the ability to staff a media position, craft a campaign, publish a newsletter, create a website, buy advertising space, sponsor a concert, or reasonably respond to emerging issues. Resources are not simply financial. The right personnel can help an organization effectively push forward its goals. Leaders are important in this regard. Effective leaders can mitigate internal conflicts, unite the membership under a common banner, and frame issues in ways that appeal to a broader public (Curtis and Zurcher 1974). Leader effectiveness and organizational structure are related. Structures that facilitate open communication among group leadership and supporters, hold leaders accountable to constituents, and provide a foundation for broad-based networks can increase the ability of leaders to move forward a political agenda (Ganz 2000). In short, financial and human resources circumscribe organizational decision-making.

Organizational identity also determines how a group responds to media dilemmas. Organizational identity refers to a group's self-definition project (Whetten and Mackey 2002) and serves three core functions. First, it communicates the purpose and goals of an organization to the broader public, which includes institutional authorities, bystander audiences, and opponents. Second, it provides a template for relationships within an organization as well as a set of "scripts" that outline the goals of a group and the means through which these goals may be accomplished. Finally, it provides a common language that leaders and members employ when they act or speak on behalf of a group (Clemens 1997; Whetten 2006; Whetten and Mackey 2002). Organizational identity provides a conceptual base for a group's agenda and goals and constrains decision-making insofar as it rules in some kinds of strategies and tactics and rules out others (Clemens 1996; Rohlinger 2002).

Structure and identity are related. In fact, the choice of organizational identity and structure are "parallel if not identical" projects (Whetten 2006), which means that the form a group adopts reflects aspects of its identity (Clemens 1993). Activists who want to effect change through institutional processes will adopt structures that enable them to do so. Likewise, activists who want to circumvent, disrupt, or destroy institutions will assume organizational forms that allow them to communicate with one another without making them vulnerable to detection or repression by authorities (Meyer and Staggenborg 2012). Organizational identity is important to consider apart from structure because it provides scaffolding for group decision-making and, consequently, influences strategy and how a group responds to media dilemmas.

Organizational identity shapes media strategy in two related ways. *First, it affects an organization's public image, or the representation of the group that leaders craft for an external audience.* Public image and organizational identity are related, but may be understood as being associated with the "front stage" and "back stage" respectively. Erving Goffman (1959) used a theatre as a metaphor for understanding how an individual presents him/herself to others. He argued that individuals engage in performances on the "front stage" that are based on cultural values, norms, and expectations. The goal of these performances is acceptance, meaning if the individual succeeds, the audience will view her/him as s/he wants to be viewed. Performances, in essence, are manipulations in which individuals craft versions of themselves for public presentation that gain acceptance from audiences. The "back stage" is where performers are present but the audience is not. Here, performers can step out of character and be themselves.

Goffman's observations can be applied to movement organizations. A group may strategically craft a representation of itself that highlights those aspects of its identity that are appealing to broader audiences and are likely to enhance the organization's credibility with media targets. This "front stage" presentation, or public image, is a deliberate construction of the group that is designed to maximize its appeal with a population. While a group will not act fundamentally differently "back stage," members and leaders will engage in conversations and activities that the broader public is not privy to. For example, a group may publicly denounce the tactics of an ally, while offering it encouragement behind closed doors. Similarly, an organization may take a strong public stance on a policy and privately bemoan the fact that it has been dragged into the debate at all. Public image is a marketing tool that groups use to attract support to their cause and to navigate a changing political environment. Organizations trying to grow and maintain support for their groups will make distinctions between the "front" and "back" stages and tailor ideas to each.

The extent to which a group's public image will be used as a marketing tool varies by organization. Some groups may not be overly concerned with their public image and do very little to construct a version of themselves that might give them broader appeal. This may be particularly true of groups that have an "elaborated" organizational identity, meaning that institutionally and culturally resonant themes are integral to their mission and goals.[1] As I discuss in the next chapter, groups with elaborated identities can fit better with the institutional norms of the news media (mainstream media in particular) and have more and better opportunities to get coverage. In contrast, organizations that have "restricted" identities, meaning they define themselves and their issues, solutions, and goals in more particularistic ways, may have difficulty marketing their ideas and themselves to a mass audience. These groups may pay more attention to their public image and try to highlight the aspects of their identity that have the broadest appeal.

The extent to which a group's public image is used as a marketing tool can also vary over time. While some organizations recognize the potential utility of marketing themselves from their origin, others may make this determination later in their histories. In other words, unlike organizational identity, public

[1] See Rohlinger (2002) for a discussion on elaborated and restricted identity.

image is relatively fluid, meaning the extent to which an organization develops and deploys a public image can change over time. The relative development of a public image also varies according to an organization's resources. Having an experienced professional at the helm of a media department, for example, can help an organization craft a public image that builds credibility with journalists. Money also matters. Financially flush activist groups can put more resources into their public image and craft a "brand" for their organization. At the most basic level, a brand may be thought of as a well-developed public image. However, the two are distinct from one another insofar as a brand deemphasizes an organization's agenda or goals and, instead, pulls at the heart strings of the public by imbuing the group with symbolic meanings and cultivating an emotional connection between the public and the group (Feldwick 2009). Crafting and maintaining a brand is a resource-intensive affair and not an option available to all groups.

Second, organizational identity affects how a group frames – or ascribes meaning to – its issues and its campaigns. An organization must craft frames that effectively sell its ideas and campaigns to the public. In order to do so, the proffered frame must be consistent with the beliefs, claims, and actions of the organization (Benford and Snow 2000). A group that engages in tactics that harm people and property, but tries to frame its activities as nonviolent civil disobedience, will be regarded as inconsistent by the broader public, which will negatively affect its ability to generate support (Johnson 1997). Organizational identity determines the kind of ideas and themes a group's frame can champion with legitimacy.

Organizational identity can either broaden or limit the resonance of a group's frames during a given historical moment. Effective frames are empirically credible, which means that the arguments contained within are consistent with (and visible in) political reality. The more evidence there is for an organization's frame in the political world, the more support it will generate among the citizenry (Benford and Snow 2000). A group with an elaborated identity will be best positioned to craft credible frames because it has a broader repertoire of cultural language from which to draw, making it easier for the group to match its interpretation of political moments with an observable reality. In contrast, an organization with a restricted identity will have difficulty crafting frames that generate widespread support. A group with a particularistic understanding of its issues, solutions, and goals often has difficulty "stretching" its linguistic repertoire to reflect historical contingencies, which, ultimately, limits the resonance of its frames and its potential support (Rohlinger 2002).

It is important to remember that a group will create different frames for different audiences in the hope of mobilizing different kinds of support (such as money or political muscle) for its position and goals. A group may frame its opposition to a policy very differently to politicians than it does to the broader public. Similarly, an organization will be mindful of its media target when packaging its ideas. A group with an elaborated identity will craft frames that reflect moderate points of view for mainstream media outlets because these are the most likely to get picked up and broadcast to a larger audience. The same group, however, may draw on more particularistic ideas and arguments when addressing outlets that target more sympathetic audiences. Organizational identity circumscribes a group's framing efforts, which affects how it sells its ideas and campaigns to a broader public.

Organizational dynamics and media dilemmas

Organizational dynamics, or how structure, resources, and identity interact, shape a group's response to media dilemmas. Structure and resources provide a foundation for a group's foray into mass media and determine who engages media professionals (e.g., a volunteer on a cell phone or a professionally trained activist), how, and with what frequency (Dilemma 1). A paid activist whose job is to establish and maintain a media profile for the organization will be able to target media easier (and more often) than a volunteer engaging in activism during his/her free time. Likewise, the professional activist will be better positioned to use direct and social media to circulate a group's ideas more consistently. Having a structural foundation that makes media efforts part of the organization's daily routine also is useful when a group wants to respond to bad press or tries to reframe a losing issue (Dilemmas 2 and 3). It is easier for a professional activist to craft and disseminate press releases, hold press conferences, commission and place advertising campaigns, and circulate relevant research findings when s/he has contacts and examples from which to draw.

Organizational identity also affects how a group responds to media dilemmas. Assuming an organization decides to target external media outlets (Dilemma 1), organizational identity winnows down the list of venues likely to help a group forward its goals. A conservative group will not see much point in targeting ideologically progressive media venues with its messages and will focus its resources elsewhere. Likewise, groups that seek to fundamentally alter social structure and institutions may perceive mainstream media as hostile to their causes and avoid these outlets altogether. Organizational identity shapes the options available to a group responding to bad press and losing issues (Dilemmas 2 and 3). Organizations with elaborated identities as well as credibility with (and access to) journalists are far more likely to remain silent on an issue than groups fighting to get into the mainstream. While the former will have other opportunities to influence media coverage, the latter may not. Similarly, direct action groups that want to use media attention to document their campaigns are unlikely to remain silent when an opportunity to get media attention arises – regardless of its quality.

Figure 1.1 summarizes how organizational dynamics shape a group's response to media dilemmas. First, organizational dynamics affect how a group thinks about mass media and their utility for achieving organizational goals. This determines the number and type of resources a group invests in engaging

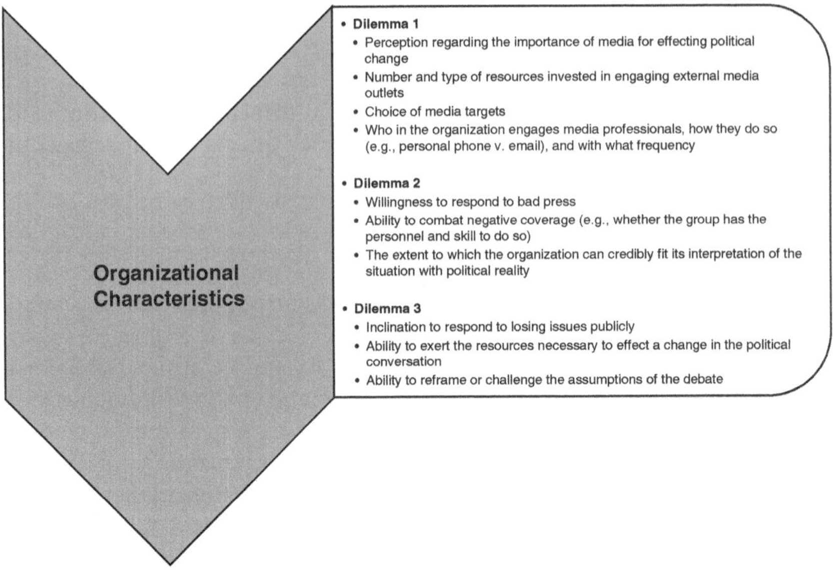

FIGURE 1.1. Organizational dynamics and responses to media dilemmas

external media, its choice of targets, and how it goes about dealing with these targets. Structure, resource, and identity are key to determining whether a group targets an external media venue as well as *when* and *how* they do so. Second, organizational dynamics affect a group's inclination to respond to negative coverage. An organization may want to respond to bad press in mainstream outlets, but may not have the financial resources, personnel, or media connections to do so. Likewise, a group may want to refute negative coverage, but lack the ability to credibly craft an argument that would be convincing to media professionals or a broader public. In these instances, a group may choose to target sympathetic media outlets or simply post its response on organization-controlled venues (such as its website and email lists). Organizations that have the required resources, skills, and messaging may still decide to ignore negative coverage. These groups may decide that the resource expenditure is too high or use it as evidence to justify changing their media approach. Finally, organizational dynamics shape a group's inclination to respond to losing issues publicly. A group may not have the resources necessary to alter the political conversation directly (through an advertising campaign) or indirectly (by moving ideas from sympathetic to more mainstream outlets). Similarly, a group may decide that silence is its best option because it cannot reasonably engage in the debate without potentially undermining support for the organization. These are only a few examples of the strategic options available to a group facing media dilemmas. The point here is that organizational dynamics circumscribe how they do so.

It is important to remember that organizations can change – and their media strategy may change with it. Leaders may leave and resources fluctuate widely from year to year – changes that can dramatically alter how groups use media. Additionally, organizational perceptions regarding the costs and benefits of using external media outlets to promote issues and campaigns can change over time. A group, which has long regarded mainstream media as hostile, may decide that even a hostile outlet with a broad audience is an outlet worth targeting.

INSTITUTIONAL DYNAMICS AND STRATEGIC CHOICE

Organizations do not make strategic decisions in isolation. Groups have allies and opponents, who are trying to use media for their own purposes. When and how a group engages mass media is shaped by the larger political context. Scholars typically conceptualize this context as the structure of political opportunity, which refers to the "consistent – but not necessarily formal or permanent – dimensions of the political environment that provide incentives for collective action" (Tarrow 1998, 77). The opportunity structure may be more or less "open" to movement claims. One factor that determines whether a "window" of opportunity exists is the configuration of state actors. When a movement has sympathetic elites in positions of power, activists have more access to political processes (McAdam, McCarthy, and Zald 1996). The structure of political opportunity, and the presence or absence of elites more specifically, has implications for the strategic decision-making of movement actors. When a movement has sympathetic allies in office, organizations may primarily choose institutional tactics, such as writing drafts of legislation and lobbying, to push forward their goals. In contrast, when the window of political opportunity is closed, organizations may rely more heavily on extrainstitutional strategies (such as direct action campaigns) to get their issues onto the political agenda (Meyer and Staggenborg 2012).

Political elites not only choose what issues are worthy of governmental attention but affect how these issues are framed. Elites provide narratives regarding political problems that proffer some kinds of solutions and dismiss others. These frames determine what kinds of actors will have authority in the political process and who will have an opportunity to shape policy proposals (Wolfsfeld 2004). Generally, movement organizations that want to influence policy processes will, if possible, craft strategies that are consistent with the narratives being offered by their political allies. This does not mean that an organization completely agrees with the agenda or policy proposals offered by elites. Groups, however, will try to take advantage of elite allies' willingness to act on an issue and will work to shape policy proposals in ways that are consistent with organizational goals (Rohlinger and Quadagno 2009). Of course, opposing organizations will simply attack elite frames and policy proposals and, when possible, the political process for not being open to alternative points of view.

Elites influence media strategy as well. Because journalists primarily draw on institutional sources when "catching" the news of the day (Tuchman 1978), elites can shine the media spotlight on an issue and propose policy changes. Movement organizations develop strategies to contend with elite opposition to their goals. Groups can activate the "balance norm" (Gans 1979) by offering an opposing point of view on events and policies. Likewise, organizations can try to take advantage of elite support or opposition to their issues. For example, organizations can support the claims and policy proposals of elite allies by providing journalists with relevant human interest stories that illustrate the hardships existing policies create for individuals. Alternatively, organizations may decide media silence is the best course of action. This option may be particularly appealing when there is great deal of controversy over a policy and elites willing to engage in the battle in their stead.

The media choices an organization makes also are shaped by the actions of its opponents. Opposing groups seek to advance their goals, and adopt strategies that are likely to succeed within a given political context. When institutional channels are largely closed, opponents may take to the streets or employ other tactics that enable them to reframe debates and push their position back into the political limelight. These activities rarely go unanswered for fear that oppositional arguments may gain traction and bring about political change. Organizations, in other words, craft strategies to stymie their opponents' progress (Lo 1982). This rarely is an easy task. An organization is not always equipped to confront its foes in a given venue (Meyer and Staggenborg 1996). A group with strong grassroots chapters, for instance, may initiate state-level lobbying programs in an effort to push through legislation. Unless they have similar grassroots strength, opposing groups may find it difficult to disrupt their adversaries' efforts. Additionally, opposing groups can espouse similar values, making it difficult for an organization to strategically attack the ideological foundations of its foes (Turner and Killian 1987). Groups, in short, must find strategies that simultaneously forward their goals and undermine the efforts of their opponents.

Opponents affect *how* and *when* groups talk about movement issues. Because journalists often report conflict, an organization may use dramatic rhetoric to describe its opponents or choose to publicly engage an opponent in an effort to attract media attention. Groups routinely "piggyback" on their opponents' conventions, events, or press conferences in order to generate an atmosphere of controversy – and find that their activities and ideas are covered in the news (Rohlinger 2002). Controversy and conflict with opponents is beneficial insofar as it provides an opportunity for organizations representing different points of view on an issue to get media attention. Strategic silence, then, can undercut an opponent's efforts to get coverage for their cause. A group can downplay conflict by strategically remaining silent on its opponent's campaigns and rhetoric. This can diminish the newsworthiness of an event and make it less likely to get covered.

Finally, an organization's strategy is influenced by allied groups, who want to advance shared social and political goals (Curtis and Zurcher 1973). Generally speaking, relationships with allies are shaped by two dynamics – competition and cooperation. Allied organizations compete with one another for resources (such as members, money, and support) in order to increase their political legitimacy and ensure their survival (Zald and McCarthy 1987). That said, there are good reasons for allies to cooperate. Cooperation allows allies to combine their resources and push forward their goals more effectively. Additionally, groups that work together may find it easier to divide and conquer their shared opponents.

Cooperation is rife with complications. Organizations may agree on a broad agenda and little else, making common ground difficult to find. Likewise, because groups often have very different identities, organizations may struggle to find ways to work together without compromising their core values and goals (Hathaway and Meyer 1997; VanDyke and McCammon 2010). The emergence of political opportunities and threats make coalition work relatively harder or easier (McCammon and Campbell 2002). During political opportunities, competition often dominates intramovement dynamics as allies work to push forward their own particularistic agendas at the movement's expense. The opposite is true when political threats emerge. During these moments, allies quickly set their ideological differences aside and band together in order to stave off political losses or defeat a common foe (Staggenborg 1986).

The competitive dynamics among allied organizations are featured prominently in research on the movement-media relationship. Like-minded organizations are considered competitors in a zero sum game for the media spotlight in which winners are catapulted to political legitimacy and losers fall into relative obscurity. There is some truth to this understanding. The space available for movement actors in the news is limited. More importantly, the rewards associated with media attention mean that there are not a lot of incentives for allies to cooperate with one another (Bob 2005). Competition, in short, shapes an organization's media strategy.

Competitive dynamics may be particularly relevant to organizationally dense and diverse movements. Scholars have long emphasized the importance of movement-level characteristics to the strategies and outcomes of social movements (Gerlach and Hine 1970; Minkoff 1997; Olzak and Ryo 2007). Organizational density and diversity, for example, can help forward a movement's goals (Armstrong 2002; Minkoff 1993; Minkoff 1999). In the media arena, organizational density and diversity may simply mean that a group has more competitors to contend with when it wants media attention. Groups in organizationally diverse and dense movements, consequently, may employ media strategies that groups in less populated movements would not (or could not) consider. For instance, organizations looking to use mass media to build their coffers, membership, and influence may do so by attacking established and politically respected allies, arguing that they better represent movement goals and are poised to bring about political change. Other movement groups, particularly ones that already have credibility with media professionals and the citizenry, may publicly distance themselves from their allies, casting themselves as mainstream and politically effective and their allies as radical and emphasizing rhetoric over meaningful change.

Competition can influence media strategy even as a group cooperates with its allies. Organizations that participate in coalitions may still try to promote themselves and their goals. While self-promotion is to be expected, efforts to monopolize the public face of the coalition may be more or less overt. Groups negotiate how many human and financial resources each organization will supply, as well as who will get credit for the coalition's efforts. Competition plays prominently in these negotiations as organizations determine which group should get top billing in campaign ads and events. Because it is generally assumed that viewers will only remember the first coalition member listed, these negotiations are often only settled by developing a "neutral" name for the coalition. Self-promotion may be covert as well. A single organization can quietly dominate the coalition and use its media standing to drown out messages with which it does not agree (Rohlinger 2004, 2006).

Cooperation among groups is not always contentious, nor is it always formal. Allied organizations, particularly ones that disagree on strategy and goals, may cooperate informally by sharing information on issues, campaigns, and tactics. These informal arrangements can have several benefits. Moderate groups benefit politically from the presence of radical allies. Radical organizations offer politicians and the public a comprehensive vision of a problem and more drastic solutions than their moderate counterparts. As a result, the incremental changes suggested by moderate groups appear reasonable and politicians are more inclined to invite them into the political process (Haines 1988). It is easy to imagine allies using mass media to exploit this dynamic for their own purposes. Radical organizations use extreme rhetoric and dramatic tactics to attract media attention to their cause and draw new adherents into the movement, while moderate groups use their political legitimacy to push legislative proposals that are consistent with movement goals. Informal cooperation also can protect a movement from its opposition. Organizations often try to undermine the strength and support of their opponents by creating rifts among groups that employ very different strategies to effect political change. This "divide and conquer" approach can weaken a movement as allies battle one another in addition to their opponents (Downey and Rohlinger 2008). Informal cooperation provides some defense against this because it allows diverse groups to work toward a common goal outside the view of the public and, sometimes, without the knowledge of their opponents.

Institutional Dynamics, Movement Dynamics, and Media Dilemmas

Elites, allies, and opponents affect how an organization responds to media dilemmas. Figure 1.2 summarizes the potential effect of institutional and movement dynamics on strategic decision-making. Elite allies allow a group to deal

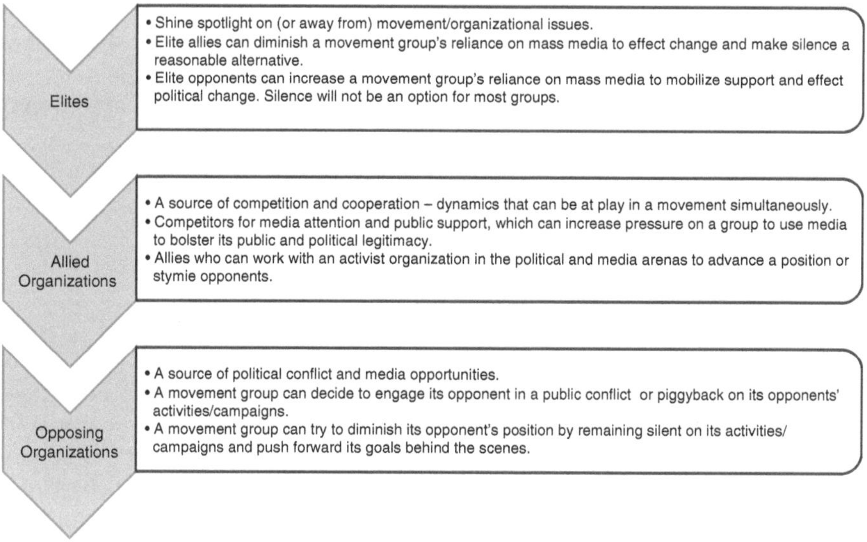

FIGURE 1.2. How institutional and movement dynamics shape media dilemmas

with dilemmas differently than elite opponents. When a movement group has a person with power on its side, it can be selective in its external media efforts (Dilemma 1), particularly if it can shape political decision-making. This is not true when an opponent holds office and media coverage becomes the primary mechanism through which a group can voice its dissatisfaction with the political process. While having friends in high places does not get rid of Dilemma 2 (negative coverage), it does make it easier for a group to deal with losing issues (Dilemma 3). An organization can opt to remain silent during controversial debates and let elected officials carry the water in their stead; an option that disappears once an opponent takes office. A group, however, may be unwilling to cede a media opportunity to its allies, particularly if it wants to shape public debate and the policy options under consideration (Dilemma 1). Again, this is not to suggest that allies always compete for media attention. When an ally generates bad press for an issue or movement or takes an outrageous position on a losing issue (Dilemmas 2 and 3), a group may avoid media coverage in an effort to preserve its public image or, perhaps, try to capitalize on the drama in the political arena and outside the public's view.

Opposing movements also influence how an organization contends with media dilemmas. Opponents can make it easier for a movement group to get media attention because mainstream news media highlight the conflict between various points of view (Dilemma 1). Engaging one's enemies in the nightly news, consequently, is not always an ideal way for a group to showcase its arguments or goals. In fact, these conflicts may be a source of negative attention for an organization (Dilemma 2). A group, however, can ignore media opportunities involving their opponents in the hope that silence will diminish the conflict and make their enemies less newsworthy. Opponents pose the biggest problem when it comes to losing issues (Dilemma 3). In these situations, opponents already have the political upper hand and are well positioned to use media attention to try to further diminish support for a movement. This limits the strategic choices available to an organization, which may enter the fray on its opponent's terms, try to reframe the debate, or remain as silent as possible on the issue.

CONCLUSION

Organizational, institutional, and movement dynamics all affect the strategic decision-making of a group. Figures 1.3 and 1.4 summarize how different kinds of organizations generally approach media dilemmas and outline how these dynamics affect an organization's media opportunities and strategic decision-making. The organizations depicted in the figures are professional, which, as previously discussed, matters because informal groups face different challenges than formal ones. Additionally, I use news media as a reference point for both figures in order to underscore a key advantage of a strategic choice approach – recognition that avoiding media attention is just as important as getting media attention.

Figure 1.3 illustrates the general orientation of movement groups with restricted identities to media dilemmas. These groups will find it difficult to stand apart from their allies, particularly in established movements, and will be reliant on mass media to build their public and political legitimacy. Even

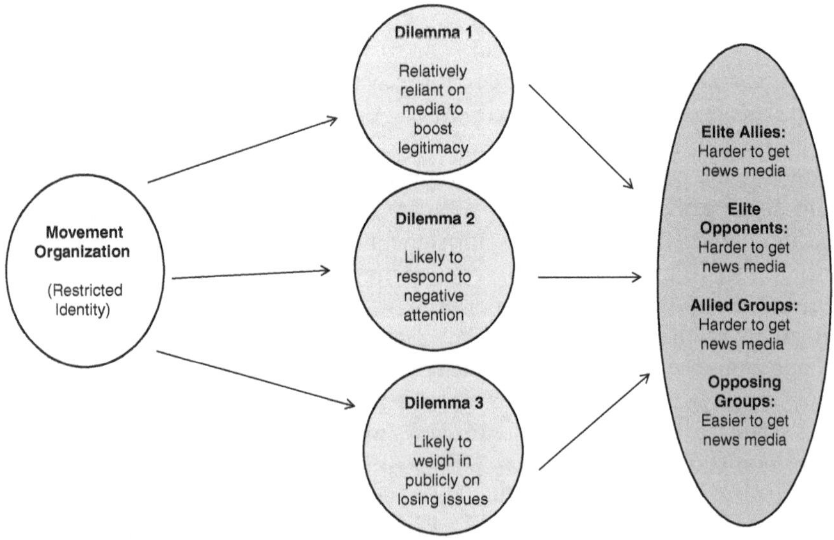

FIGURE 1.3. Restricted identity, media dilemmas, and media opportunity

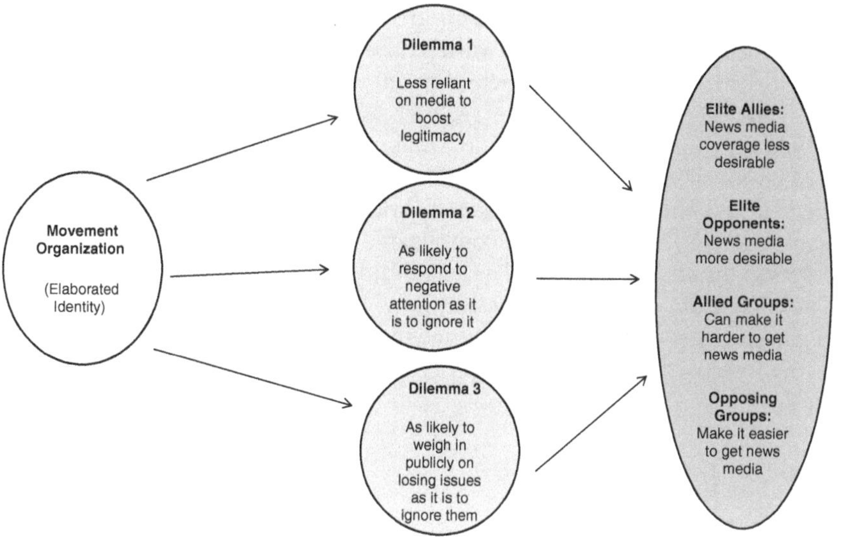

FIGURE 1.4. Elaborated identity, media dilemmas, and media opportunity

groups that decide to avoid mainstream media will find it necessary to sell their ideas to sympathetic audiences in order to generate the funds needed to keep their doors open and build political clout. Because of their relative reliance on media, groups with a restricted identity rarely remain silent when it comes to negative media coverage and losing issues. Likewise, these organizations are fairly vulnerable to movement and institutional dynamics. Elite allies and opponents and allied organizations (particularly those with more elaborated identities) can all make it more difficult for these groups to attract media attention. Their best opportunities to get media coverage are on losing issues where the quality of coverage may be less than desirable.

Figure 1.4 shows the general orientation of movement groups with elaborated identities to media dilemmas. These groups will find it easier to position themselves relative to (and ultimately stand apart from) their allies. Groups with elaborated organizational identities have an easier time crafting campaigns that distinguish them from allies. Thus, while these groups still need mass media to communicate with sympathetic and general audiences, they are less reliant on news coverage to build their legitimacy and have more options when it comes to negative media coverage and losing issues. Most notably, these organizations can remain silent on an issue or debate. Institutional and movement dynamics play an important role in these organizations' strategic decision-making. While the presence of elite opponents makes it nearly impossible to stay out of a debate, groups with elaborated identities can remain silent when they have elite allies willing to champion their shared position. Similarly, these organizations may refrain from commenting on issues in which opponents have public opinion on their side. Allies can be the trickiest for groups to contend with publicly. Groups with elaborated identities do not want to alienate their supporters and must find ways to deal with their allies while maintaining their position in a broader movement.

While a group has agency, decision-making processes and the potential trade-offs of choosing one option over another are constrained by previous choices, movement dynamics, and the broader political environment in which it operates. Organizational choices also are complicated by the fact that a group typically operates in multiple institutional arenas simultaneously and that each institution has its own logic regarding what and how groups can effectively achieve their goals. In the following chapter, I outline the contours of mass media and discuss how the logic of the field affects an organization's decision-making and media strategy.

2

The mass media field

News media are often referred to as the "fourth estate" of the U.S. constitutional democracy. News media are charged with the responsibility of providing the public information on a range of issues, actions, and events, as well as reporting on elected officials. Not surprisingly, there is a voluminous literature analyzing news media and assessing how well they perform their duties (for example, see Baker 2002; Bennett, Lawrence, and Livingston 2007). Rather than rehash these arguments, I examine how institutional dynamics affect the reputation and media opportunities of an activist organization as well as its strategic choices. I begin the chapter by outlining field theory as conceptualized by new institutionalists and Pierre Bourdieu. I maintain scholarly focus on the "journalistic field," or news outlets, and discuss how an organization's reputation in the field affects strategic decision-making. Then, I reconceptualize the journalistic field as a broader "mass media field" in order to include social and direct media outlets. This reconceptualization is useful for two reasons. First, it recognizes that different kinds of media take content cues from one another – a reality that activists can exploit for their own purposes. Second, it underscores the permeability of media boundaries and allows scholars to better understand how organizations use a range of outlets (sometimes simultaneously) to forward their goals. I classify different kinds of media into three categories – moderated, social, and direct – and outline how this reconceptualization sheds light on the strategic decision-making of groups. I conclude the chapter by discussing how an organization's reputation affects its response to media dilemmas.

REPUTATION AND STRATEGIC CHOICE IN THE JOURNALISTIC FIELD

There are two variants of field theory relevant for understanding the movement–media relationship: the organizational fields discussed by new institutionalists, which often implicitly inform research conducted by media scholars, and field theory as discussed by Pierre Bourdieu. These variants of field theory are complementary. Both perspectives explain the regularities in individual or organizational action by situating actors within a larger field of action; conceptualize a field as a structured social space that is comprised of a network of relationships among actors with more or less power; argue that fields are relatively coherent because the actors operating in a given field are oriented toward a particular value or prize and agree on the "rules of the game" by which these values are accumulated; and suggest that forces external to the field can influence the rules and field output (Benson 2006; Bourdieu 1998b; DiMaggio and Powell 1983; Martin 2003). The theoretical and empirical emphases of the perspectives are different, however.

New institutionalists define an organizational field as "organizations that, in the aggregate, constitute a recognized area of institutional life" (DiMaggio and Powell 1983, 148). Actors are guided by an institutional logic, or "a set of material practices and symbolic constructions" (Friedland and Alford 1991, 248), which provides the organizing principles of the field. New institutionalists often highlight the processes through which actors in a field come to resemble one another, or isomorphism (Scott 2001; Zucker 1987). There are three forms of institutional isomorphism: coercive isomorphism, which results from organizations exerting pressure on more dependent organizations; mimetic isomorphism, which is the result of organizations employing similar responses to ambiguity; and normative isomorphism, which is the result of occupational professionalization (DiMaggio and Powell 1983). Because of isomorphism, fields are structured, meaning they have clear relational networks that constrain any one organization's actions and choices. Thus, while organizations are strategic actors and may alter their goals and/or practices, the rules of the field circumscribe what organizations do and their ability to change (Fligstein 2001; Hensmans 2003; Rao, Morrill, and Zald 2000).

New institutionalism highlights how both forces external and internal to the journalistic field systematically narrow and homogenize media coverage. Specifically, scholars examine how journalistic professionalization, news production processes, market pressures, and state intervention shape mainstream coverage. Journalists currently uphold the doctrine of objectivity and employ practices designed to inform the masses through fact-driven and politically-neutral reporting (Schudson 2003; Sigelman 1973; Tuchman 1972). Journalistic practices also are influenced by pressures external to the "journalistic field" – mainly economics (market imperatives to generate profits) and the state (issues of national security) (Benson and Saguy 2005; McManus 1994). Journalists, who consistently deal with scarce resources, tight deadlines, and limited space for the news, use "news nets" to "catch" the big stories (Tuchman 1978), rely heavily on "insider" sources (such as government officials), and look to prominent outlets (such as *The New York Times*) to provide the news of the day (Gans 1979; Tuchman 1987). Together, these pressures create a consensus regarding the day's news and have a homogenizing effect on coverage (Gamson, Croteau, Hoynes, and Sasson 1992).

The focus on isomorphism, however, obscures the fact that institutional fields are fairly heterogeneous. An actor situates itself relative to other players in a field and, in doing so, establishes how it is similar to and different from other actors (Deephouse 1999; Whetten 2006). In the "journalistic field," which is comprised of a broad spectrum of news outlets including mainstream and partisan news venues, news blogs, local newspapers, and community news sites, outlets strategically situate themselves relative to one another in an effort to attract an audience (Benson and Neveu 2005; Bourdieu 1998a; Rohlinger 2007). In practical terms this means that while outlets in the field try to balance the dual demands of informing the citizenry and making a profit, how they do so varies widely.

Pierre Bourdieu explains heterogeneity by focusing on the differential pressures that come to bear on outlets in the journalistic field (Bourdieu 1998a, 2005). He argues that the social world is structured around two opposing forms of power, or economic and cultural capital (Bourdieu 1998a, 1998b, 2005). While the forms of economic and cultural capital vary by field, economic capital is represented by circulation/ratings as well as advertising dollars, and cultural capital by professional honors that result from peer recognition such as the Pulitzer Prize in the journalistic field (Benson 2006; Bourdieu 1998a). The field itself is structured around two poles: the "heteronomous pole," which represents forces that are external to the field (the market), and the "autonomous pole," which represents the specific form of capital valued within the field (intellectual reporting). Because a field is a structured space between these two poles, an actor's location within the field indicates the kinds of internal and external pressures that come to bear on an actor and the amount of cultural capital it wields (Bourdieu 1998a). Commercial, mainstream media outlets are located near the heteronomous pole because they are disproportionately influenced by economic considerations, while "serious" media are situated near the autonomous pole. Outlets, at either extreme or located anywhere in between, strive to build legitimacy in the field through the accumulation of economic or cultural capital. At the same time, outlets espouse the superiority of their particular form of capital relative to the other, which accounts for field heterogeneity (Benson 2006).

Over the last decade, scholars have used Bourdieu's ideas regarding field to analyze how heterogeneity generates differences in what (and how) issues get covered within and across nations (Benson 2005; Benson and Hallin 2007; Benson and Saguy 2005; Duval 2005; Marchetti 2005; Rohlinger 2007). I argue that field theory is useful for understanding strategic choice because it also highlights how institutional norms and dynamics shape the *organizational reputation* of a given movement actor, which affects its media opportunities and how a group responds to media dilemmas. My conceptualization of the field varies from that of new institutionalists and proponents of Bourdieu, which are primarily interested in how actors in a field orient their actions in relation to one another. I too am interested in field norms and dynamics, *but only insofar as they affect the strategic choices of actors trying to operate within a field.* In this way, my conceptualization of field is closer to that of Neil Fligstein and Doug McAdam (2012), who focus on how fields are socially constructed and how they change. The former is important because it helps explain the standing of a field actor during a given historical moment, the factors that lead to a boost or decline in an actor's standing in a field, and how outside actors (movement groups) looking to navigate a field might exploit field dynamics (or changes) for their own purposes.

Organizational reputation is central to understanding the strategic decisions of groups. Organizational reputation refers to an external assessment of an organization's identity by an actor in an institutional field. Actors assess the extent to which an organization's identity corresponds with the logic of the field and their own, more particularistic goals (Rindova, Williamson, and Petkova 2005). These assessments matter because they determine an organization's ability to access an institutional arena (Clemens 1997). An actor's reputation may be strong or weak. If there is a match between an organization's identity and the logic of a field and actor, then the group will have a strong reputation. If the organization's identity does not match the demands of the field or actor on one or more dimensions, then the group will have a relatively weak reputation.

Mainstream news outlets dominate the journalistic field (Bourdieu 1998a) and reach a broad, general audience. Not surprisingly, these venues are the primary target of many organizations. A group's reputation relative to these outlets often shapes how an organization uses mass media to forward its goals. There are at least four aspects of an organization's identity that are relevant to reputation in mainstream outlets: the group's media structure, the presence of a credentialed spokesperson, the scope of the organization's goals, and the extent to which the organization draws on resonant values to frame its issue.

Structure shapes an organization's reputation in mainstream media. Mainstream journalists rely on "legitimate" sources of information when crafting their stories. If a movement organization wants mainstream media attention, it must mimic the structure and practices of institutional sources on which journalists regularly rely. A group can establish a minimal reputation with mainstream media professionals by calibrating their media efforts to fit journalistic routines, producing information and events for journalistic consumption (press releases, press conferences, and research reports), and having a designated spokesperson whose primary job is to communicate with media professionals. An actor can bolster its reputation further if its spokesperson (or leader) is credentialed, meaning one or more activists are professionally recognized for their expertise in a given area, or are publicly recognizable figures (e.g. a celebrity).[1] While the latter can give a group media cache (Meyer and Gamson 1995), institutionally

[1] This is different from the credentialing process discussed by Gitlin (1980).

credentialed activists give a group a professional veneer. Rather than simply being seen as an activist organization, journalists regard groups with credentialed activists as a legitimate and engaged actor on an issue (Rohlinger and Brown 2013). Credentials must be maintained if they are to provide an effective boost to an organization's reputation. A spokesperson can only leverage their institutional status on behalf of an organization if s/he is practicing or otherwise professionally engaged.

An organization whose goals suggest incremental changes to the status quo will have a better reputation in mainstream media than a group that proposes dramatic overhauls to an institution. Mainstream outlets are designed to attract a broad, general audience. Not surprisingly, journalists prefer to include moderate views in their stories because these are more representative of (and appealing to) a broad public (Gamson 1990). A group that challenges an institution in relatively small ways, then, fits better into the logic of mainstream outlets than groups proposing institutional overhauls. Similarly, whether an organization has an elaborated or restricted identity affects its reputation in the journalistic field. Mainstream journalists prefer not only groups with moderate goals, but also actors whose ideas resonate with widely held norms and values (Benford and Snow 2000; Ferree 2003). Groups with an elaborated identity will find this easier to do than organizations with restricted identities. An organization with an elaborated identity that uses constitutional principles and rights as a conceptual basis for action, for example, is more likely to champion ideas that resonate with culturally relevant frameworks than actors who draw on more particularistic points of view (such as religious doctrine). The former fit better with the institutional logic of mainstream media, which translates into more access to journalists and more media attention. In short, the more an organization's identity aligns with the logic of mainstream media, the stronger its reputation will be. A group that has a media structure, boasts a credentialed or publicly recognized spokesperson, advocates for incremental change, and possesses an elaborated identity will have a relatively strong reputation in mainstream media, and will have more and better opportunities to shape how its issues are presented to the public.

There are two additional points worth making about reputation. First, reputation is different from an organization's relevance during a given historical moment. The latter has been emphasized in research as scholars try to explain what groups appear in news coverage (Amenta et al. 2009; Sobieraj 2010). Scholars typically refer to this as "standing," which is a measure of how much "voice" a particular group has in mainstream media coverage (Ferree et al. 2002). Standing is tied almost completely to the political environment and is relatively volatile. A radical group that attracts media attention using dramatic tactics can have as much (and likely more) standing than a moderate group during a given political moment because they are the source of story. Reputation, in contrast, reflects the correspondence between the characteristics of a movement actor and the dynamics of the field, which are relatively stable. *In other words, reputation is more enduring and focuses on movement–media interactions over time rather than at a specific point in history.*

Second, the composition of a movement has implications for reputation. Reputational evaluations are made comparatively (Whetten and Mackey 2002). Journalists determine the reputation of one organization in part through their evaluations of its allies. As a result, an organization may have a more difficult time establishing and maintaining a strong reputation in the journalistic field if it is part of a movement that is dense with organizations that also fit the institutional bill. This is true even for an organization whose identity generally fits with the demands of the field. In situations where journalists have lots of sources from which to choose, they can be finicky and shift their preferences from one group to another. This is not true of sparsely populated movements. If a journalist needs a quote and there are few organizational sources from which s/he can choose, s/he will go with the best option available.

Mainstream media outlets are not the only venues available to carry movement ideas and, more importantly, a group's reputation can vary across the journalistic field. Although journalists in mainstream and alternative news outlets share a broad occupational goal, how they achieve this goal is quite different. Mainstream journalists use "objective" reporting and emphasize conflict and drama in their stories in an effort to attract large, general audiences (Gans 1979; Schudson 2003; Tuchman 1972). This is not true of alternative venues, which target audience niches with ideological interpretations of – and political perspectives on – the news of the day (Atton and Wickenden 2006; Harcup 2003; Lievrouw 2011). The emphasis on cultural over economic capital shapes how journalists working in alternative news outlets evaluate issue newsworthiness, source credibility (Atton 2001), and, ultimately, an organization's reputation with an outlet. Media professionals in alternative news outlets such as *The Nation* and *National Review* are less concerned with whether a group looks and acts like institutional sources and more interested in whether an organization's position on and solution to a social problem will be compelling to their audience. Consequently, a broader range of organizations get covered in alternative news venues than in mainstream outlets (Rohlinger et al. 2012). For groups with a weak reputation in mainstream outlets, coverage in alternative venues may be invaluable because it simultaneously allows them to build support for their goals among a generally sympathetic audience and potentially build a reputation via these outlets with political (rather than media) targets.

Conceptualizing mass media as a field of action highlights how the correspondence between organizational identity and the institutional logic of a field (and actor) shape a group's reputation, which influences how an organization deals with media dilemmas and the tradeoffs it is forced to make. An organization with a relatively strong reputation will have more and better media opportunities, which means that strategic silence is an option. During moments of rancorous debate, the tradeoff for the group is simple: it trades the ability to weigh in on a debate for the option to avoid the negative attention that can accompany controversial issues. A group with a weak reputation may want to get its ideas in mainstream news outlets, but may have difficulty doing so. As such, it is unlikely to turn away mainstream media opportunities when they are available, even when these opportunities promise to reflect the organization and the issue in an unfavorable light. A group with a weak organizational reputation trades media attention for favorable media attention, which can create other media dilemmas. For instance, if an organization receives negative coverage, activists must then decide whether or not (and how) to respond to the bad press. Dealing with negative coverage will be particularly tricky if the group finds itself engaged in a heated and long-term political battle. News space is limited and journalists are likely to move on to other issues and events relatively quickly. An organization, then, might find itself locked in a high-stakes political battle about which the broader public has limited knowledge.

TOWARD A CHOICE-CENTERED UNDERSTANDING OF MASS MEDIA

The current conceptualization of the "journalistic field" emphasizes the importance of economics to output, which ignores the fact that different kinds of venues may take cues from one another without being in direct competition (Rohlinger et al. forthcoming). Mainstream journalists pay attention to stories circulating in the "Twittersphere" and incorporate the ideas they read into their work (Hermida 2010; Lasorsa, Lewis, and Holton 2012). While journalists are not in direct competition with individuals who witness and report news on the ground, scholars should not ignore that journalists increasingly take cues from diverse sources when putting together their stories. Scholars, in short, cannot simply focus on traditional news (and their online companions) if they want to understand news processes in the twenty-first century.

Likewise, if social scientists want to understand how individuals or groups use mass media to bring about change, they must look beyond the front page (or homepage) of mainstream outlets. After all, activist groups do not have to rely on "earned" media coverage to make an appearance in the mainstream. Organizations with the financial means to do so can buy media space and take their message directly to the people through advertisements. Moreover, news outlets are not the only venues that groups can use to achieve their goals. This is particularly true in the contemporary communications environment where there are numerous venues on- and off-line available to carry movement ideas, including books, talk radio, music, social media, and organizational websites (Atton and Wickenden 2006; Eyerman and Jamison 1998). News media is but one type of outlet activist groups can use in a broader *mass media field*.

Figure 2.1 shows a cross section of the media field with the heteronomous and autonomous poles labeled at the top and bottom of the field respectively. The outermost layer of the field (A) is composed of moderated media. In these venues, actors use institutional and organizational norms to determine whether

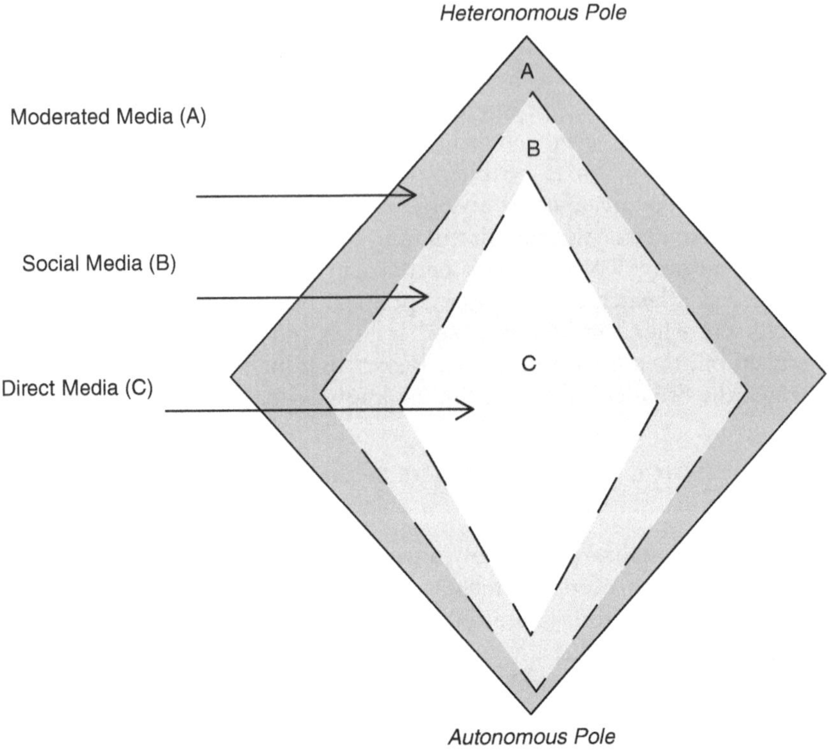

FIGURE 2.1. The mass media field

(and how) movement ideas will be included in their stories. Concerns over whether and how to include movement perspectives may be more or less central to the decision-making process of actors working in these venues. News outlets are far more likely to consider the relevance of movements than a music radio station, which is more concerned with profit-making at the heteronomous pole and "music purity" at the autonomous pole.

Reputation still matters to non-news outlets; however, it is evaluated differently. Artists are under no obligation to be neutral and, as long as they are profitable, can use their work (concerts and art exhibits) to advocate on behalf of movement causes. There have been several concerts over the last thirty years (opposing apartheid, raising AIDS awareness, promoting cleaner oceans, and advocating debt relief for developing countries) that brought artists together to advocate on behalf of an issue. In these endeavors, movement organizations team with sympathetic artists in an effort to raise money for the group as well as to educate a broader public (Eyerman and Jamison 1998). While the rules governing the music world are quite different from those governing the news, both are oriented to survival, which means that nonjournalistic venues are just as likely to carefully consider an activist partner – even if profitability is more central to their assessments.

The next layer (B) consists of social media such as Twitter, Facebook, Tumblr, Snapchat, Instagram, YouTube, and the numerous other outlets that allow movement leaders, supporters, and opponents to communicate with a broader audience directly. Organizations can use social media to bypass moderated outlets and get their ideas to a broader public, but so can individuals and entities not necessarily affiliated with (or supportive of) the group. Moreover, social media are not an open forum. Many social media outlets are oriented toward profit-making, which means that movement messages are often crowded next to advertisements pushing related products. On Facebook, it is not uncommon to see a post by a local farm co-op next to an advertisement for a company that sends all the ingredients for a meal directly to your door. Likewise, the terms and conditions of a social media platform may allow the company to censor some ideas. Facebook has been criticized for removing the pages of breastfeeding activist and anarchist groups, while allowing white supremacists to use its group page function to organize without interruption. Using social media to disseminate movement messages, in short, presents its own sets of challenges.

The innermost layer of the field (C) is direct media. Unlike social media, groups have control over (and assume the cost of producing) both the medium and the content. Organizational websites, newsletters, pamphlets, blogs, radio stations, and films are all examples of direct media. While direct media are available to all groups, an organization's ability to use them will vary with its resources as well as its media priorities. Websites are a good example in this regard. Some organizations offer visitors little more than an online brochure of their issue, while others create content (e.g., movies, games, and links to signup sheets) designed to engage and mobilize visitors (Earl 2006). Both kinds of websites require money and skill to develop and maintain, and some activist groups may find themselves short on both. Thus, even though direct media are fairly far away from the heteronomous and autonomous poles, whether and how movement organizations use these venues are still shaped by economic (and other) considerations.

Reputation influences the ability of a group to use social and direct media effectively. Organizations that have a strong reputation with some moderated media outlets will have some name recognition and get some foot traffic via social and direct media. Likewise, groups that have strong reputations may have the opportunity to embed invitations into its moderated media appearances. A group may be able to invite listeners or viewers to visit its website at the end of a program, or a news outlet may include an organization's information at the end of a news story, particularly in its online edition. Reputation not only affects the media opportunities available to a group, but also shapes how an organization moves its ideas across the media field. Organizations with a relatively weak reputation may find that they need to build support for their ideas on social media before they are picked up by moderated outlets. Groups with a relatively strong reputation, in contrast, are better positioned to target different outlets with different messages. For example, they may post unedited footage of a recent event on their website (direct media), put together a short film that they circulate on their YouTube channel (social media), and get the event covered in a variety of news outlets (moderated media).

REPUTATION AND RESPONDING TO MEDIA DILEMMAS

The media field comprises a range of outlets that take cues from one another, but differ in their form, function, and the extent to which they are oriented to the heteronomous and autonomous poles. I conceptualize the media field as a diamond-shaped prism for two reasons. First, it underscores the basic differences between outlets. Moderated media vary by *outlet type* (e.g., a news outlet is different from talk radio and music), *outlet purpose* (which may be more or less oriented toward profitability), and *target audience* (which may be more or less particularistic). Second, it emphasizes the permeability of boundaries between different kinds of media, particularly from the perspective of actors looking to use media to forward their goals. Different media have different advantages and disadvantages, and a group can use a range of venues (sometimes simultaneously) to achieve different goals.

Not all groups have the same opportunities in the media field. Reputation helps explain the kinds of opportunities available to a group, which shapes how it uses media to forward its goals. Organizations with strong reputations in the media field have more opportunities to use moderated media to their advantage and are less reliant on social and direct media to move their ideas across the media field. This is not true for groups with weak reputations, which have fewer opportunities to use moderated media and need social and direct media to market their ideas (and themselves) to sympathetic audiences. Organizations with weak reputations rely on social and direct media to generate enough support to move their ideas into moderated media.

Reputation has implications for how a group responds to media dilemmas. Table 2.1 summarizes how organizations with strong and weak reputations are likely to respond to each dilemma. An organization with a strong reputation is likely to be selective when engaging external media (Dilemma 1) because it has more opportunities to access a range of outlets, including moderated media. A group with a strong reputation may decide to opt out of a television interview that includes an opponent, reasoning that it has little to gain by engaging in a heated debate with an enemy. A group with a weak reputation will not be so selective and may see the same interview as an opportunity to show a sympathetic public that it is confronting its opponents directly and is worthy of support. The same is true of Dilemma 2, whether to respond to negative media

TABLE 2.1. *How groups with strong and weak reputations respond to media dilemmas*

	Strong Reputation	Weak Reputation
Dilemma 1		
	Selectively	Less Selectively
Dilemma 2		
	Only in extreme cases	If it is likely to result in coverage
Dilemma 3		
	Avoid a public response and work behind the scenes	Try to disrupt or reframe the public conversation

attention. An organization with a strong reputation is likely to be selective about when and how it responds to bad press, while a group with a relatively weak reputation will engage moderated media in hopes of receiving more (and potentially better) coverage.

The strategic options available to groups with stronger and weaker reputations vary when faced with Dilemma 3, how to publicly respond to losing issues. An organization with a strong reputation may offer its assessment of losing issues in social or direct media, but generally avoid taking up the cause in moderated media, where its name and ideas will be contrasted directly to the more popular ideas of its opponents. This is less true of a group with a weak reputation, which may use direct and social media to outline how it is fighting for the rights of an aggrieved population and moderated media to offer an alternative understanding of a popular issue.

CONCLUSION

How an organization uses media is shaped by four dynamics – organizational, movement, institutional, and field dynamics. As the last two chapters make clear, these dynamics do not operate independently. A group is nested in a larger movement comprised of other organizations trying to respond to (or change) the broader political environment in ways that will make it more hospitable to their goals. Media plays an important role in this regard because organizations use different kinds of outlets to promote their causes and demand action from the citizenry and politicians. How a group uses media varies according to its reputation and the dilemmas to which it is responding. These dynamics and dilemmas, in short, interact with one another and affect how an organization navigates the political world and uses mass media to forward its agenda. These dynamics are summarized in Figure 2.2, which is labeled a strategic choice approach to the movement–media relationship.

A strategic choice approach underscores relational dynamics and the importance of movement, environmental, and institutional dynamics to

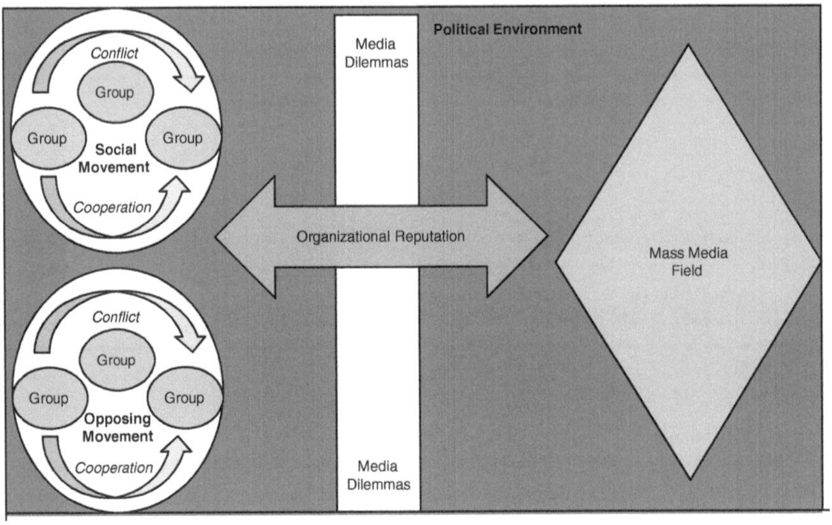

FIGURE 2.2. A strategic choice approach to the movement–media relationship

organizational decision-making. While organizations never have perfect information, they use what information they do have about elite positions, the positions and activities of allies and opponents, and how the media field works (and their reputation in it) to decide whether, when, and how to use mass media to their advantage. The remainder of this book illustrates how these dynamics work and affect how four movement organizations mobilize around the abortion issue and respond to media dilemmas over time.

3

Abortion, social movements, and mass media

Legalized abortion is a contentious issue in contemporary American politics. This was not always the case. Initially, abortion was a medical concern and physicians were the arbiters of its administration. This "medicalization" of abortion largely was the result of a campaign by physicians to professionalize medicine. Throughout most of the nineteenth century, there were no licensing laws regulating who could practice medicine. This, coupled with the lack of a traditional guild structure, meant that physicians had to compete directly with other medical sects (such as homeopaths) for patients. Physicians saw abortion as an issue through which they could distinguish themselves from other practitioners and push for industry regulation. They argued that their scientific-based training gave them superior knowledge regarding if and when a woman should have an abortion. The campaign was a success. All but "therapeutic" abortions were outlawed and licensed professionals were charged with deciding whether an abortion was performed (Luker 1984; Mohr 1978).

In the late 1940s and early 1950s, physicians, activists, and clergy pushed state legislators to repeal abortion laws and expand the circumstances in which physicians could administer abortions, including in cases of rape, incest, and fetal deformity. These efforts were both successful and largely uncontroversial, in part because of how the abortion issue was framed. Advocates argued that the state should expand physicians' authority regarding the medical circumstances in which an abortion could be administered; an approach that focused on medical practice rather than women's rights (Burns 2005; Staggenborg 1991). However, the framework for understanding abortion changed in the 1960s as a result of two controversies that focused public attention on women's authority in reproductive decision-making. The first case involved Sherri Finkbine, a teacher in the popular television series *Romper Room*, who sought an abortion in 1962 after learning that she had ingested a drug known to cause fetal deformity. Finkbine used her celebrity status and connections with journalists to raise public awareness regarding the issue. While Finkbine's story generated a lot of press, the publicity scared hospital officials, who refused to give her an abortion. Finkbine traveled to Sweden for the procedure, where her physician informed her that the fetus was severely deformed and would not have survived outside of the womb (Luker 1984). The rubella measles epidemic also served as a lightning rod for abortion controversy. When contracted by a pregnant woman, the disease could cause fetal malformations. After this link was made visible via the evening news, thousands of pregnant women who contracted the disease sought abortions.

These controversies provided a new framework for understanding the abortion issue – a woman's right to choose whether she had an abortion – and spurred the growth of the pro-choice movement, which explicitly argued that women have a constitutionally protected right to an abortion. For instance, the National Association for the Repeal of Abortion Laws (now known as NARAL Pro-Choice America) formed in 1969 and began organizing repeal campaigns countrywide. Likewise, dozens of grassroots groups emerged and used direct action tactics and street theatre to raise awareness regarding the importance of safe and legal abortion to women's health (Staggenborg 1988). The controversies also highlighted how great the differences of opinion regarding legalized abortion were in America. Pro-life activists began organizing at the state level with the goal of protecting "unborn children." The stage for the contemporary battle over abortion was set with two Supreme Court decisions decided on January 22, 1973. In *Roe v. Wade* the Court ruled that a woman has a constitutionally protected right to an abortion and that the state could not prohibit abortion during the first trimester or before viability. Viability was defined as the potential for a fetus to live outside of the womb in *Doe v. Bolton*.

Pro-choice advocates believed that the Supreme Court decisions resolved the issue. The composition of the pro-choice movement changed dramatically in the following decade. With abortion legal, there was limited need for direct action tactics and many of the radical organizations fell into obscurity. The movement became one of highly professional, national organizations with federated chapters throughout the United States (Staggenborg 1991). The movement between 1980 and 2000 predominantly consisted of groups that focused on research, shaping abortion policy, and ensuring access to reproductive services. The pro-life movement changed as well. Before 1973, the movement was largely spearheaded by the Catholic Church and pro-life groups that emerged locally in opposition to liberalizing abortion laws (Burns 2005). However, in the wake of the decisions, pro-life advocates quickly mobilized inside and outside of government and began to challenge the new status quo. The movement developed organizations supporting three distinct foci: changing abortion policy, providing alternatives to abortion, and politicizing abortion clinics (through sidewalk counseling, prayer vigils, and direct action against clinics and its personnel). The compositions of the opposing movements, in short, are quite different.

The Supreme Court decisions not only influenced how the movements took shape, but also affected the contours of the battle. Most pro-life groups either looked for ways to limit legal abortion and its availability or to shut down abortion clinics. In both regards, the pro-choice movement found itself on the defensive. Here, I offer a brief overview of the political context in which the war over abortion has been waged. I focus on three different arenas – inside state legislatures and the Supreme Court, on Capitol Hill, and outside of abortion clinics – in which pro-choice and pro-life forces engage and discuss how they have tried to advance their interests since the *Roe* and *Doe* decisions. The purpose is not to provide a comprehensive account of abortion politics, but to give an overview of how the movements have worked to advance their causes so that the strategic decisions of particular groups can be understood within the broader context in which they were made. After this historical summary, I introduce the study and the organizations included in the research. I conclude the chapter by situating these organizations within a broader media context. I document the visibility of movement groups relative to other actors that are included in abortion coverage and highlight where the organizations included in this research rank relative to their allies over a twenty-year time frame. While media coverage does not reflect an organization's media strategy, it provides a useful baseline for assessing an actor's reputation in the media field as well as its use of mass media.

ABORTION POLITICS AFTER *ROE* AND *DOE*

There are three different arenas in which the battle over abortion has been fought: at the state level (state legislatures and the Supreme Court); at the federal level (on Capitol Hill); and on the streets (outside of abortion clinics). I discuss each and pay particular attention to how pro-choice and pro-life advocates have worked to advance their interests after *Roe* and *Doe*. This background is relevant to the discussion of organizational media strategy insofar as it provides the context in which groups make decisions about how to use mass media to forward their goals.

Restricting abortion within the state

After the *Roe* and *Doe* Supreme Court decisions, the pro-life movement introduced legislation that would restrict abortion access in states across the United States. The pro-choice movement was not nearly as organized as their opponents at the state level and found it difficult to stave off pro-life legislation. Therefore, after a state passed legislation restricting abortion, pro-choice groups challenged the constitutionality of the law in the judicial system. Generally speaking, pro-lifers advocated for legislation that acknowledged the rights of other parties (the parents of minor women and the fathers of the unborn child) in abortion decisions, discouraged women from getting abortions by making them more difficult to access, and recognized the life and rights of unborn babies. For instance, pro-life advocates successfully passed parental involvement laws for underage women seeking the abortion procedure, and most of these requirements have been affirmed by the Supreme Court. In *Planned Parenthood of Kansas City v. Ashcroft* (1983) the Court upheld a Missouri provision that required minors to obtain consent from a parent before obtaining an abortion. The ability of the state to restrict access to abortion was stipulated in a broader set of legal principles in *Planned Parenthood of Southeastern Pennsylvania v. Casey* (1992), where the Supreme Court ruled that regulating abortion was constitutional as long as the requirements did not place an "undue burden" on a woman's ability to obtain an abortion.[1] As I discuss in the Afterword, testing what does or does not constitute an undue burden on women animates much of the pro-life movement's contemporary legislative efforts.

Pro-lifers also successfully passed, and defended the constitutionality of, laws designed to discourage women from getting abortions and make the procedure less accessible. Informed consent laws, for example, mandate that women seeking an elective abortion undergo counseling and be given information about fetal development, the abortion procedure, their legal rights, and abortion alternatives.[2] Additionally, pro-lifers passed dozens of TRAP (Targeted Regulation of Abortion Providers) laws that reduced the availability of the abortion by limiting where the procedure can be done and who can perform the procedure. Again, many of these provisions have withstood the scrutiny of the courts and, in fact, forty-four states and the District of Columbia currently have TRAP laws on their books.

The pro-life movement also made some headway in shifting the legislative emphasis away from women's rights to those of the fetus. Initially, pro-lifers focused on passing fetal viability testing requirements before a woman could obtain an abortion. In Missouri, legislators passed a law declaring that life began at conception and that unborn children have "protectable interests." The statute, among other things, prohibited government-employed doctors from aborting a fetus that they believed viable and required fetal viability testing after the twentieth week of pregnancy. The Supreme Court upheld the provision, noting that the state had the right to protect "potential life." This spurred other states to pass viability legislation as well. As of 2014, twenty-one states have laws that prohibit abortion if the fetus is viable, except in cases of life or health endangerment of the woman.

The battle over abortion on Capitol Hill

The *Roe* and *Doe* decisions made the abortion issue a political one. This politicization, and eventual partisanship on abortion, began in the 1980 election

[1] As of February 2014, thirty-nine states require parental involvement in a minor's abortion decision.

[2] As of February 2014, twenty-six states require a waiting period before a woman can obtain an abortion, seventeen states mandate counseling, and 43 states allow institutions to refuse to provide the procedure to women.

when Ronald Reagan inserted a pro-life position into the Republican platform. While Reagan believed in the pro-life plank, he also saw the potential to draw evangelicals away from the Democratic Party; a constituency that Jimmy Carter made visible during his presidential bid. Throughout the 1980s and early 1990s, the abortion issue became ingrained in party politics with Democrats favoring legal abortion and Republicans opposing it. Not surprisingly, the makeup of Congress affects the number of allies a given bill has and whether it comes to fruition. Although activists and legislators often work together crafting policy proposals, a relatively small number of bills get congressional attention and an up-down vote. Here, I briefly discuss some of the most significant policy proposals advanced by pro-life and pro-choice advocates since the *Roe* and *Doe* decisions.

The pro-life movement initiated two federal challenges on abortion. First, they questioned the use of tax dollars to pay for a procedure that many citizens vehemently opposed. Despite pro-choice arguments that such restrictions discriminated against poor women and women of color (Sillman et al. 2004), this line of attack proved successful. In 1976, the Hyde amendment passed and prohibited the use of federal funds for the abortion procedure. In 1979, funding restrictions were extended to military health care coverage, banning the use of federal funds for abortion services at overseas military hospitals. In 1995, pro-lifers passed a Department of Defense appropriations bill that restricted women from obtaining privately funded abortion services at overseas military facilities except in cases of rape or incest.

Second, pro-lifers tried to overturn the *Roe* decision. However, as I discuss in the next chapter, there was not a consensus among groups regarding whether pro-life proposals should include an exception to save the life of the woman. While mainstream groups argued that an exception was necessary and supported the passage of the Human Life Amendment, which would reverse *Roe* and prevent states from making abortion legal at a later date, more radical pro-lifers regarded the exception an unacceptable compromise. Other pro-life advocates, who also advocated for states' rights to make policy decisions, argued that the passage of a Constitutional Amendment was unlikely and advocated for the Human Life Bill, which declared that unborn humans were legal persons and restricted the power of lower federal courts to interfere with laws restricting abortion passed by the state. All of these efforts ultimately failed.

More recently, an important win for the pro-life movement has been the debate over partial-birth abortion; a phrase that refers to a particular abortion procedure (medically known as the intact dilation and extraction procedure) performed late in a woman's pregnancy. Pro-lifers coined the term partial-birth abortion in 1995 and launched a national campaign calling for its ban. Congress answered the call and passed three bans on the procedure. The first two were vetoed by President Clinton, who refused to sign the bill because it did not include an exception to protect a woman's health, in 1996 and 1997. President George W. Bush, Jr., however, signed the Federal Abortion Ban into law in 2003.

The Supreme Court upheld the law in *Gonzales v. Carhart* (2006), ruling that an exception to protect women's health was not necessary because there were other medical procedures available.

The pro-choice movement has introduced its share of legislation. Once it became clear that the Supreme Court would permit restrictions on abortion access, pro-choicers pushed for the passage of the Freedom of Choice Act (FOCA), which gave every woman the right to choose to terminate a pregnancy before viability and after viability if it is necessary to protect her life or health. FOCA would codify the *Roe* and *Doe* decisions and nullify existing state laws restricting abortion. The bill was introduced in 1989, 1993, and 2004, but languished in Congress. Pro-choice politicians, with the support of several pro-choice organizations, introduced FOCA again in Congress the day after the *Gonzales* decision. To date there has been no progress on the bill. Pro-choicers were successful at passing legislation that protects reproductive health clinics and its clients. Most notably, they passed the Freedom to Access Clinic Entrances Bill (FACE), a law that makes it a federal crime to use force, the threat of force, or physical obstruction to prevent individuals from obtaining or providing reproductive health care services. FACE was a response to rising clinic blockades and violence in the 1980s and 1990s.

The battle at abortion clinics

In the 1980s, pro-life activists, who felt that President Reagan had done little more than give lip-service to movement goals, decided to stop abortion by counseling women regarding other options, disrupting clinic operations, and using violence to close clinics. These activists share a moral abhorrence to abortion and regard the clinic as a location where they can effectively end the practice. Direct action groups differ in terms of whether they believe violence against clinic facilities and personnel is a justified and effective tactic. Those opposed to violence argue that sidewalk counseling outside of clinics is the best way to provide women the support and information necessary to prevent abortion. Those that use violence regard it as a legitimate way to defend the life of the unborn.

The pro-choice movement responded to efforts to close clinics in four ways. First, pro-choicers engaged in clinic defense and mobilized volunteers to escort women into abortion clinics. Second, pro-choice advocates passed state-level "buffer zones," which required protestors to stay a specified distance away from clinic entrances and walkways. Third, pro-choice leaders publicly called on the president and Department of Justice to take steps to curb clinic violence. Pro-choicers contended that the incidents of clinic violence were part of a larger campaign designed to reduce women's access to the abortion procedure. This line of argument fell on deaf ears until Clinton took office and asked Attorney General Janet Reno to investigate the incidents. Finally, as I discuss in Chapter 5, the National Organization for Women (NOW) along with two clinics sued pro-life activists under federal antitrust laws and charged the defendants with a "nationwide criminal conspiracy to close women's health clinics."

In short, the battle over abortion is a long and contentious one that is not reserved to political institutions alone. Likewise, while their composition varies, the pro-life and pro-choice movements consist of vibrant organizations that adopt a range of orientations, practices, and goals as they relate to the abortion issue. Both of these realities make the abortion case an excellent one for examining how activist groups use mass media to forward their goals over time and in response to larger movement and institutional dynamics.

OVERVIEW OF THE STUDY AND ORGANIZATIONS

I analyze four organizations over a twenty-year period: the Planned Parenthood Federation of America (PPFA), the National Organization for Women (NOW), the National Right to Life Committee (NRLC), and Concerned Women for America (CWA). PPFA and NOW are pro-choice organizations that support legal abortion, while NRLC and CWA are pro-life organizations that advocate for limited abortion availability. Because each of the groups is discussed in detail in the subsequent chapters, I give only an overview of them here.

Table 3.1 summarizes the basic characteristics of each organization. There are several general differences and similarities among the organizations worth mentioning. The organizations differ in their orientation to the abortion issue and goals. Both PPFA and NRLC are single-issue organizations, meaning they represent a limited set of grievances and work to achieve policy change on a fairly narrow set of issues. PPFA mobilizes around reproductive issues more broadly and NRLC focuses on protecting life "from womb to tomb." NOW and CWA, in contrast, are multiple-issue organizations that seek policy change on a broad range of women's public policy issues. As a conservative, Judeo-Christian women's organization, CWA mobilizes around issues of reproduction, welfare, education, national security, and religious expression. NOW, which is a liberal feminist group, mobilizes around reproductive, economic justice, lesbian rights, and sexual discrimination. It also is clear from Table 3.1 that the organizations vary in size and general structure. While all of the groups have a formalized organizational structure and rely on a membership to fund organizational activities and campaigns, PPFA's structure is more elaborate than those of the other groups; it has multiple national offices and affiliates, which offer reproductive health services in addition to engaging in activism, instead of chapters.

These groups were included in the study for three reasons. First, they have different organizational identities and, therefore, appeal to different constituencies within their respective social movements. PPFA and NRLC have more elaborated identities than NOW and CWA insofar as they explicitly try to appeal to a broad segment of the population. NOW and CWA, in contrast, organize around more particularistic points of view (feminism and Christianity, respectively) and,

TABLE 3.1. *Overview of the organizations, 1980–2001**

	NRLC	PPFA	NOW	CWA
Founded	1973	1942	1966	1979
Membership	10,909,091	Not Reported	316,818	600,019
Abortion position	Pro-life	Pro-choice	Pro-choice	Pro-life
Average budget	Not Reported	$28,786,000 (US)	$6,774,253 (US)	$5,836,364 (US)
Organizational structure	Formal, with a national office in Washington, D.C. and chapters across the U.S.	Formal, with national offices in NYC, D.C., and San Francisco and chapters/affiliates across the U.S.	Formal, with a national office in Washington, D.C. and chapters across the U.S.	Formal, with a national office in Washington, D.C. and chapters/prayer groups across the U.S.
Organizational identity	Elaborated	Elaborated	Restricted	Restricted
Number of chapters/affiliates	2,560	179	1,699	2,515

* *Note:* The membership and budget information presented above represent the average totals for the years in which data could be obtained between 1980 and 2001. NRLC only reported its membership from 1980 to1990 and it never reported its budget information. It did report chapter and state information for all the years. I combined the numbers to derive the average. PPFA did not report its membership and only reported its budget from 1987 to 2001. I used the information provided in the Encyclopedia of Associations and figures from the PPFA archives for 1980, 1981, 1984, 1985, 1986, 1987, and 1988 to derive the average. NOW reported membership and chapter information for all years between 1980 and 2001. It did report chapter, state, and region information separately, which I have combined to derive the average. The budget figures represent the following years: 1980, 1983, 1984, 1985, 1986, 1988, 1989, 1990, 1991, and 1992. CWA did not begin reporting information until 1983. Additionally, it reported budget information only for the years 1988 to 1998 and chapter information for 1984 to 1998. The averages, then, reflect only the years that information was reported.

consequently, appeal to narrower segments of the population. As discussed in Chapter 1, these variations should have implications for each organization's reputation in the media field and influence how each uses media to forward its goals. Second, the groups are fairly comparable (CWA and NOW, and NRLC and PPFA), which permits an analysis of how movement composition affects the reputation and media strategy of an organization. Groups mobilizing around legal abortion may find it more difficult to maintain their reputation in the media field than a similarly situated pro-life group because there are more reputable competitors with whom they must compete for the media spotlight. Finally, the groups identified one another as a clear threat to their goals, which allows an analysis of how opposition affects media strategy.

The organizational analysis is based on several data sources. I read all of the newsletters for each of the organizations from 1980 to 2000 (approximately 2,000 pages for each group). Newsletters are an important data source because they document the strategies and campaigns of a group as well as clearly identify opponents and allies during a given historical moment. Likewise, newsletters provide accounts of group actions *as they occur* and, therefore, are useful for tracking how strategies and perceptions of mass media change over time. I also conducted archival research, which provided another way to assess how the groups, their strategies, and perceptions of mass media change over time. Archival records are particularly useful for uncovering strategies that are intentionally designed to not undergo public scrutiny and provide important insight into how structure as well as resource availability and allocation affect strategy.[3]

Additionally, I conducted interviews with current and past activists working with the organizations; many were interviewed on multiple occasions. The number of interviews varied and ran from thirty minutes to three hours. I conducted a total of twenty interviews: six with activists from CWA, ten with activists from NRLC, two with activists from PPFA, and two with activists from NOW. I also conducted fifteen interviews with journalists from a range of news media outlets including *The New York Times*, *Time* magazine, *The Nation*, *Human Events*, *National Review*, *Ms.* magazine, and media professionals working for ABC, CBS, and NBC news, in order to assess each group's reputation on the abortion issue. Finally, I read historical accounts on each organization as well as *all* of the available newspaper, radio, magazine, and television media coverage mentioning each group from 1980 to 2000. The analysis is therefore based on tens of thousands of documents and a number of interviews by activists and media professionals.

[3] PPFA documents are available through the Sophia Smith Collection at Smith College and at the Katherine Dexter McCormick library in New York City. NOW documents are available at the Radcliffe Institute for Advanced Study at Harvard University. Neither CWA or NRLC have formal archives. I was granted access to NRLC's documents stored at the Greater Cincinnati Right to Life office and CWA's documents at their Washington, D.C. office.

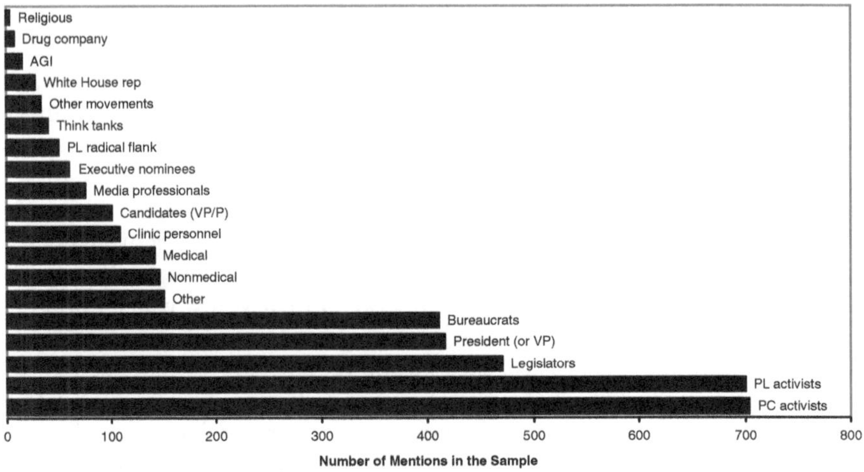

FIGURE 3.1. Overview of the kinds of actors mentioned in media coverage
Note: The categories of actors mentioned include religious actors, individuals representing companies that make drugs (e.g., the pill), the Alan Guttmacher Institute, White House representatives, leaders from other social movements, think tank spokespeople, radical pro-life organizations (such as Army of God), executive nominees, media professionals (e.g., other journalists), presidential and vice presidential candidates, medical professionals, non-medical academics (e.g., lawyers), other actors (e.g., unaffiliated individuals), bureaucrats, the current President or Vice President, pro-life activists, and pro-choice activists.

OVERVIEW OF MEDIA ATTENTION ON THE ABORTION ISSUE

While scholars should be careful to disaggregate media coverage from media strategy, examining what kinds of actors get coverage can provide a baseline assessment of an organization's reputation in the mass media field. Because organizations with a strong reputation will have more media opportunities and get more and higher quality media coverage over time, it is visible (to some extent) in coverage. Figure 3.1 shows the results of a content analysis of 1,424 media stories on the abortion issue in which all the actors mentioned in the news story were coded.[4] Here, we see that activist voices often are included in abortion coverage. While this does not indicate the quality of coverage, pro-life and pro-choice organizations are included in more stories than any other category of actor. It is worth noting that pro-choice and pro-life groups are included in coverage at

[4] I sampled media coverage during thirty-six critical discourse moments in the abortion debate. I chose critical discourse moments that were (1) identified as important by scholars and activists and (2) represented wins and losses for both sides over time. Using Lexis-Nexis, indexes, abstracts, and manual inspection, I coded *all* media stories discussing the abortion issue during specified time frames. For anticipated events (such as legislative votes, presidential elections, executive nominations, and the *Roe v. Wade* anniversary), I coded media stories about abortion occurring before and after the event. For unanticipated events (such as clinic violence and the murder of Dr. Gunn), I coded media stories about abortion the date of and after the event. A detailed account of the sampling time frames for each critical discourse moment for each of the outlets is available in the methodological appendix on my website.

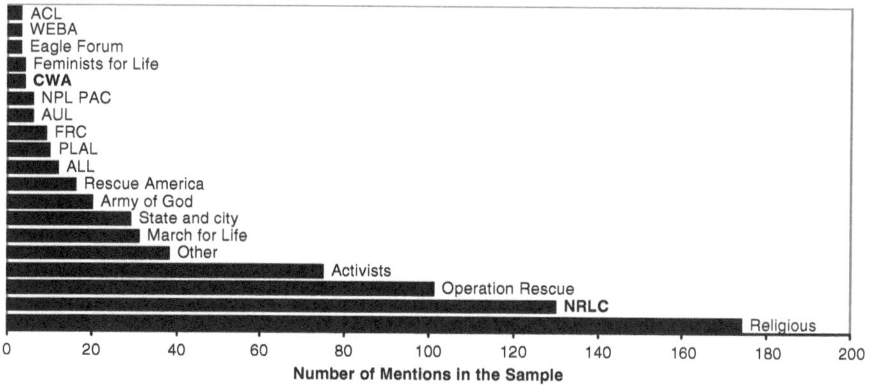

FIGURE 3.2. Overview of the pro-life actors mentioned in media coverage
Note: The "other" category consists of organizations that received two or fewer mentions in the sample. The "state and city" groups category consists of all state, county, and city level organizations in the sample. The most mentions one of these organizations received was three. The acronyms listed above stand for the following organizations: American Coalition of Life (ACL), Women Exploited by Abortion (WEBA), Concerned Women for America (CWA), National Pro-Life PAC (NPL PAC), Americans United for Life (AUL), Family Research Council (FRC), Pro-Life Action League (PLAL), American Life League (ALL), and National Right to Life Committee (NRLC).

nearly identical rates. Again, while this does not provide insight into how various groups are covered, it is clear that journalists are presenting arguments that represent both sides of the abortion debate (also see Rohlinger 2002, 2007).

Figure 3.2 notes all of the pro-life organizations that were mentioned or quoted in coverage and highlights how much media attention NRLC and CWA received relative to other actors. The figure makes clear the diversity of the pro-life movement. In addition to national level organizations, the movement consists of state- and city-level pro-life groups, direct action organizations, and a vast contingent of denominationally diverse religious figures who routinely speak out against abortion. NRLC appears to have a strong reputation in the media field. NRLC, which is the organization with the most coverage, gets 130 mentions. Operation Rescue is second with 101 mentions and the March for Life a distant third with only thirty-one mentions. Only religious actors, a composite category that consists of all religious figures who spoke out against legal abortion in the sample, get more coverage. CWA gets very little media attention on the abortion issue. This does not seem to be a function of intramovement competition to represent women's perspectives on abortion to the broader public. None of the other pro-life women's groups, including Eagle Forum, Feminists for Life, or Women Exploited by Abortion, get much attention either. Instead, this seems to be a function of movement-level competition, suggesting that CWA does not have a strong reputation relative to other pro-life actors.

There are fewer pro-choice actors mentioned within the context of abortion coverage, and nearly all of the actors are professional organizations (Figure 3.3). Compared to the pro-life movement, there are very few state- and city-level

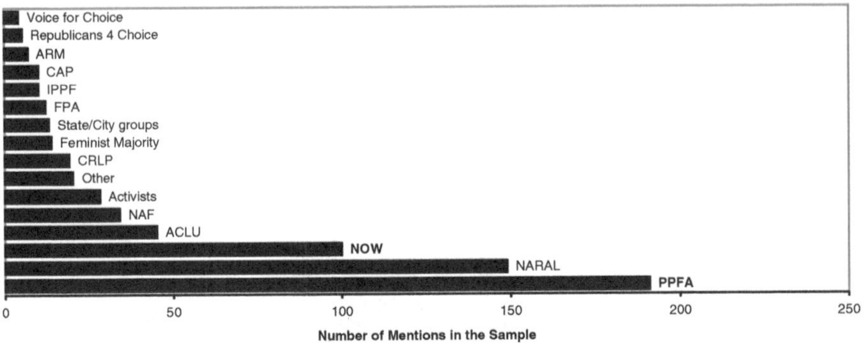

FIGURE 3.3. Overview of the pro-choice actors mentioned in media coverage
Note: The "other" category consists of organizations that received two or fewer mentions in the sample. The "state and city" groups category consists of all state, county, and city level organizations in the sample. The most mentions one of these organizations received was three. The acronyms listed above stand for the following organizations: Abortion Rights Mobilization (ARM), Coalition of Abortion Providers (CAP), International Planned Parenthood Federation (IPPF), Family Planning Association (FPA), Center for Reproductive Law and Policy (CRL&P), National Abortion Federation (NAF), American Civil Liberties Union (ACLU), National Organization for Women (NOW), National Abortion Rights Action League (NARAL), and Planned Parenthood Federation of America (PPFA).

groups or unaffiliated actors included in the stories. Interestingly, the distribution of mentions in media coverage is skewed in favor of three groups: PPFA was mentioned in 191 stories, National Abortion Rights Action League in 149 stories, and NOW in one hundred stories. On its face, then, PPFA and NOW both appear to have relatively strong reputations in the mass media field, with PPFA leading the pack. In short, the compositions of the pro-life and pro-choice movements are quite different and this likely influences how individual groups use mass media to forward their goals.

Figures 3.4 and 3.5 provide additional context for understanding each organization's reputation on the abortion issue. Figure 3.4 shows the total number of mentions for each organization (regardless of the issue) in English newspapers for every year between 1980 and 2000, while Figure 3.5 plots the number of mentions each group received during the abortion events sampled during the same period.[5] Figures 3.4 and 3.5 show that PPFA's media coverage climbed steadily over the twenty-year period and that it remained a prominent player in abortion coverage. This is true of NRLC as well, which also increased the amount of media attention it received over time. NOW and CWA, however, have a different pattern. While both organizations experienced an uptick in coverage in the late 1980s and early 1990s, by the late 1990s both groups encountered declines in coverage. NOW garners less attention on the abortion

[5] These data were obtained using LexisNexis, which includes 2,500 newspapers worldwide.

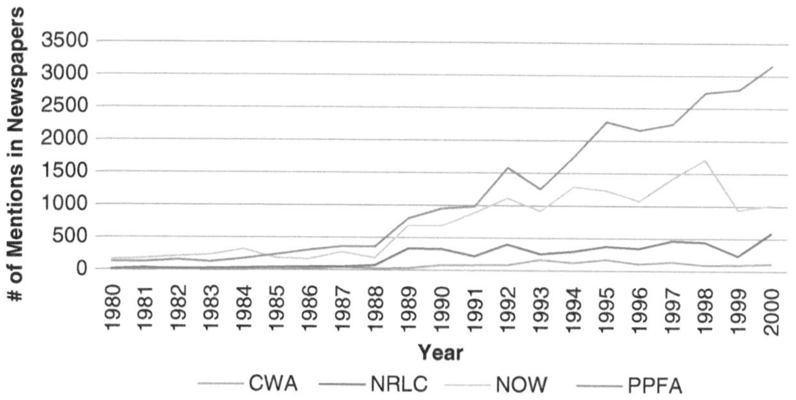

FIGURE 3.4. Number of mentions in American newspapers, 1980–2000

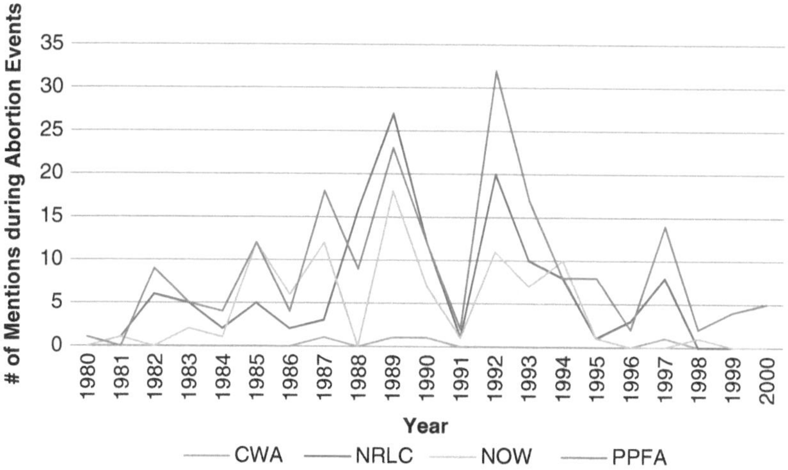

FIGURE 3.5. Number of mentions and quotes on the abortion issue, 1980–2000

issue over time and CWA gets next to no coverage. This trend suggests that NOW experienced a decline in its reputation over time and that CWA's uptick in coverage was not on the abortion issue. Reputation, in other words, may vary by issue. Although CWA did not get much coverage on the abortion issue, clearly it became a player on another cause. The remainder of the book examines media strategy in more detail and analyzes how NRLC, PPFA, NOW, and CWA respond to different media dilemmas over time. In doing so, I illuminate the factors that can lead to reputational decline and examine how actors can establish a reputation in new issue areas.

4

Media, politics, and the National Right to Life Committee

Attracting media attention is full of challenges, almost all of which are beyond the control of an organization. An issue's currency in the political arena can change relatively quickly and, with it, the ability of a group to get media attention. Elections, for instance, can dramatically change the configuration of elites and the issues that become a political priority. This was true of the abortion issue in 1981, the year Ronald Reagan took office. Making good on his campaign promise, Reagan made abortion a priority. Two days after his inauguration, Reagan met with six national pro-life leaders, including John Willke, M.D., president of the National Right to Life Committee (NRLC), to reaffirm his commitment to the cause.[1]

The ways in which Reagan championed a pro-life agenda often differed from the expectations of pro-lifers. While Reagan made abortion less accessible during his tenure, most organizations expected him to champion legislation that would overturn *Roe* and block states from making abortion legal at a later date. When Reagan did not, pro-life groups tried to plot a reasonable course that would enable them to influence abortion practices and policy. Unable to agree on a single course of action, organizations advocated for reform both inside and outside the political system.

How a given pro-life group approached the political opportunity created by the Reagan presidency varied according to its organizational identity. Direct action groups such as Operation Rescue that wanted to end abortion immediately argued that the political process was too slow and targeted abortion clinics instead. Extremists operating under the pro-life banner upped the ante by targeting clinics and clinic personnel with violence. While moderate groups uniformly opposed violence and advocated for legislative reform, they often agreed on little else. Conflict arose over the political course the movement should pursue.

[1] Press release, January 22, 1981. Greater Cincinnati Right to Life (GCRTL), Folder: 1980–1981.

The emergence of conflict during a time of political opportunity is not surprising. Recall that like-minded organizations often compete with one another for constituents and political access (Benford 1993; McCarthy and Zald 1977). Competition can get particularly fierce when a movement has access to institutional politics and elites appear poised to effect change. During these times, the differences among groups become more pronounced and organizations vie to advance their own particularistic policy goals (McCammon and Campbell 2002; Staggenborg 1986). These divisions, in fact, can become so pronounced that groups spend their time fighting over acceptable compromises and miss a political opportunity completely. Additionally, intramovement conflict rarely occurs behind closed doors. Divisions among allied organizations quickly become apparent to movement supporters through organizational newsletters, e-mails, and websites, and are often broadcast to a larger public via mainstream media. As groups call on adherents to back their political strategies and renounce those of other movement organizations, intramovement divisions can deepen and make it vulnerable to an attack. Savvy opponents will capitalize on these internal conflicts by drawing attention to the most extreme ideas with the hope of generating enough public pressure to stymie legislative change. Intramovement conflict, in short, creates media dilemmas with which a group must contend.

This chapter shows how intramovement conflict affected the strategic choices of NRLC during an era of political opportunity. I begin the chapter by situating NRLC in the pro-life movement, detailing how NRLC leaders crafted a mainstream public image and established the group as the leader of the movement. The remainder of the chapter outlines the dilemmas posed by NRLC's allies, the strategies NRLC employed in response to these challenges, and the tradeoffs NRLC made along the way. When possible, NRLC built consensus among the movement's moderate middle. Consensus-building was an important political strategy because, in order to pass legislation that could withstand legal challenge, the moderate middle needed to embrace policies that would permit abortions to save the life of the mother. Consensus-building also played a public relations function because it challenged opponents' claims that pro-lifers did not care about women's rights and health. Consensus-building was not always a viable strategy. One pro-life organization in particular, American Life League (ALL), publicly attacked NRLC's strategies and goals in an effort to build its own political clout. NRLC initially did not respond to these attacks, fearing that it would tarnish its public image as a voice of reason in an otherwise heated debate. However, as ALL's rhetoric became more virulent, NRLC retaliated. While it dueled with ALL in a range of media venues, NRLC informally cooperated with its more radical ally, Operation Rescue (OR). NRLC quickly learned that the political benefits derived from cooperation exacted a public relations cost. The dramatic tactics used by OR to attract media attention reinforced old stereotypes regarding the pro-life movement – stereotypes that NRLC had worked hard to dismantle – and effectively pushed NRLC out of the media spotlight. Staying the course paid off for NRLC in the long run; OR crumbled under legal and political pressure and NRLC reclaimed the mainstream spotlight for its own.

MAINSTREAMING THE PRO-LIFE CAUSE

NRLC supports the protection of life from natural birth to natural death. NRLC argues that the "unborn" have a right to life, meaning the "preborn" should have the same legal protections afforded to every other human being. The organization emerged in a nascent form in 1971 after pro-life leaders from around the country met in Chicago O'Hare International Airport to discuss the formation of a national group to help coordinate state-level actions. The activists formed a board of directors and appointed a five-member executive committee to hash out the goals of the movement at the national level and determine the level of resources needed to accomplish these goals.[2] After much debate the NRLC, which is a federation of the fifty largest state pro-life groups, was officially founded in June 1973 with the following purpose:

1. To promote respect for the worth and dignity of all human life, including the life of the unborn child from the moment of conception.
2. To promote, encourage, and sponsor such amendatory and statutory measures which will provide protection for human life before and after birth, particularly for the defenseless, the incompetent, and the impaired and the incapacitated.[3]

It was the first nondenominational and nonpartisan national pro-life organization in the United States.

The decision to make NRLC a secular organization was intentional. Activists believed that avoiding religion would allow diverse individuals, who may agree on little else, to work together to end legal abortion in the United States. As one of NRLC's founders explained, adopting an explicitly Christian perspective would likely discourage pro-life Jews, Muslims, and atheists from joining the organization. Avoiding religion also allowed NRLC to distance the organization from stereotypes, particularly that of the white, male, pro-life fanatic preaching about the immorality of abortion. Instead, NRLC crafted a public image based on medical expertise, which allowed activists to focus on the scientific aspects of abortion such as medical explanations of when life begins.

This approach worked largely because NRLC's president, who also serves as the primary spokesperson, has generally held credentials as a lawyer, medical

[2] Letter, Michael Taylor to the NRLC board of directors, November 1, 1972, GCRTL, Folder: 1972.

[3] Bylaws, GCRTL, Folder: 1973.

doctor, or Ph.D. in a medical field.[4] Credentials carry weight for two reasons. First, credentials are widely recognized, socially respected, and, consequently, the individuals who hold them do not require additional vetting by journalists. This saves journalists time and energy. Second, having a credentialed leader lends a level of credibility to an organization that a group otherwise may have difficulty acquiring on its own. Credentials give an organization a professional veneer, which positions the group as a legitimate and engaged actor (rather than activist) on an issue. Because activism is often understood as an emotional response to an issue or event by movement outsiders (Einwohner 2002), and journalists fuel this perception by emphasizing rhetoric and spectacle over deliberative discourse (Sobieraj 2011), the borrowed legitimacy of credentials is a useful resource. Organizations can use this legitimacy to challenge stereotypes of activists, reframe debates on movement issues, and establish the organization's reputation with journalists.

In the case of NRLC, credentials allowed activists to emphasize scientific research on the question of when life begins and to talk more authoritatively about the rights of the unborn. NRLC argues that human life begins at fertilization because all the necessary chromosomes are present. In their view, if fertilization constitutes the beginning of a human life, it also marks the moment that an individual's protected civil liberties begin. These scientific assumptions provide scaffolding for the NRLC argument that opposition to abortion is fundamentally a civil rights issue and that the pro-life movement is a civil rights movement. NRLC newsletters and documents routinely compare the pro-life movement to both the abolition and civil rights movements. Joesph Hitselberger, a NRLC lawyer, argued in 1980:

> It is not correct to say that because infants are not persons (in the constitutional sense) that they do not have rights. Slaves were not persons in the constitutional sense until the 13th Amendment was passed. Until then, slaves were regarded as property only. Nevertheless, a slave was entitled to be free from assault . . . To argue that the lives of unborn babies can be taken because it is "legal" is an argument which would approve Hitler's gassing of Jews in World War II. That too was a legal taking of life.[5]

Despite NRLC's efforts to carefully position itself in the movement, its leadership was suspicious of mainstream news outlets (Dilemma 1). Leaders regarded mainstream media an "enemy" of the movement, arguing that journalists were "solidly pro-abortion."[6] That said, NRLC also recognized the potential power of media to shape public opinion and policy debates. Burke Balch, a long-time NRLC activist, noted that the battle over abortion is fought on two tracks: "On one is the battle for public opinion, on the other is the

[4] NRLC did not have a credentialed spokesperson in 1973–1974, 1983–1984, or 2011–2014.

[5] "Rights of Unborn Argued During Sit-in Trial." *NRTL News*, February 1980.

[6] Interview with a NRLC founder and former president.

legislative and electoral struggle."[7] A former NRLC president agreed, "Before you can change people's mind and influence policy, you have to change the terms [used in the debate]."[8] Not surprisingly, its initial media efforts were modest and the group largely targeted sympathetic audiences. NRLC began by publishing a newsletter called the *National Right to Life (NRLT) News*, which it circulated to members and sympathetic politicians. The decision to provide politicians the newsletter was a good one. The *NRTL News* quickly gained national recognition as *the* source for pro-life news and commentary on Capitol Hill and in state legislatures throughout the country. Taking advantage of this momentum, NRLC leaders transformed the newsletter into a pro-life news service, which it provided to mainstream journalists free of charge.[9]

NRLC's decision to focus its efforts on developing direct media was not just a function of its reservations regarding mainstream venues (Dilemma 1). In its early years, NRLC almost exclusively relied on volunteers and, consequently, getting media attention was not a priority. In 1980, the organization had five employees, several volunteers, and a US$ 400,000 budget. A decade later, the organization employed fifty-five activists and had a US$ 15 million budget.[10] As the organization grew, so did its media ambitions. In 1984, NRLC took steps to increase its visibility with a broader audience and establish a mainstream public image by highlighting the secular, non-partisan orientation of the organization. The group formalized its media department and ran its first, professionally produced advertisement in *Time* magazine. The ad catapulted the organization into the national spotlight and hundreds of individuals joined the organization. NRLC capitalized on this unexpected financial boon and quickly expanded its media efforts. The group launched a Media Impact Campaign placing similar pro-life ads, which used "dramatic photos of the unborn child to prove human life begins long before birth," in seven markets across the country.[11] By 1985, its efforts to disseminate the pro-life message had expanded exponentially. NRLC's communications department produced and distributed a daily five-minute pro-life radio broadcast to more than 300 stations in virtually every state, spearheaded media campaigns in markets throughout the country, and maintained regular contact with mainstream journalists.[12]

7 Balz, Dan. "Antiabortion Forces Seek to Shift Focus of Debate." *The Washington Post*, September 10, 1989.

8 Interview with an NRLC founder and former president.

9 Annual Report, July 3, 1985, GCRTL, Folder: 1984–1985.

10 Interview with an NRLC founder and former president.

11 Unknown. "NRLC Ed. Trust Fund Launches Media Impact Campaign." *NRTL News*, August 1984; Annual Report, August 14, 1986, GCRTL, Folder: 1986–1988.

12 Proposed 1982 Budget, GCRTL, Folder: 1982–1983; Annual Report, August 14, 1986, GCRTL; Also see *NRTL News* in 1982, 1984, and 1985.

NRLC's efforts to establish itself as a mainstream organization and credible source of sound medical and political information has paid off. NRLC has an excellent reputation with mainstream and conservative journalists alike and garners praise that is not extended to other pro-life groups that rely on passion alone. A reporter at *The New York Times* noted, "The National Right to Life Committee is a very good source of information ... because they collect a lot of different information, they have very strong-focus lobby arm, and they just have been involved in the news for a long time."[13] An executive producer of *NBC Nightly News* agreed: "NRLC is a perfect example of a group that has established itself as credible."[14] Conservative journalists also hold the group in high regard. A journalist at *Human Events* described the vast amounts of material he receives from conservative organizations and how much of it ends up in the trash can.

> There's some groups that tend to send superior material.... When I see their emails come in, I'll scan through them to see basically what they're talking about, if they have new perspective on it, [or] some new information I haven't seen.[15]

NRLC was among the groups he paid attention to. An editor at *National Review* concurred, "I find NRLC's [materials] better than other organizations'."[16]

This mainstream public image has had political benefits. Members of Congress and presidential candidates regularly attend the NRLC annual convention to tout their pro-life credentials. In 1986, President Reagan wrote a letter to the NRLC membership praising their "selfless efforts" to end legal abortion.[17] Its political credentials are buttressed by the organization's pragmatic understanding of American politics. NRLC recognizes that sweeping policy changes are the exception rather than the rule, and it takes every opportunity to chip away at legalized abortion. A former president explained that this approach was the most practical: "It is better to save some lives than no lives."[18] Wanda Franz, president of the organization from 1991 to 2011, echoed this sentiment:

> We have seized every available opportunity to save as many lives and make the maximum progress possible each day and each year without compromising our ultimate goal. Legislatively, we support full, legal protection for unborn children. We also support more limited legislation, which can be passed more quickly, to begin saving lives immediately.[19]

[13] Interview with a reporter at *The New York Times*.
[14] Interview with an executive producer of *NBC Nightly News*.
[15] Interview with a journalist at *Human Events*.
[16] Interview with an editor at *National Review*.
[17] Letter, Ronald Reagan, January 7, 1986, GCRTL, Folder: 1986–1988.
[18] Interview with an NRLC founder and former president.
[19] Unknown. "A Winning Pro-Life Strategy Better to Save Some Lives Now than None at All, Ever." *NRTL News* online, July 2001.

In 1992, *Fortune* magazine named NRLC the most publicly recognized and politically effective pro-life organization in America; an honor it earned again in 1998.

NRLC carefully situated itself in the pro-life movement. It dealt with Dilemma 1 by engaging external media outlets at a measured pace. NRLC targeted and built a reputation among a sympathetic audience before trying to sell itself to mainstream journalists. This strategy was aided by NRLC's public image, which moved the organization away from religious rhetoric and focused on scientific and medical facts that supported the pro-life position. This mainstream image, buttressed by its credentialed leaders, helped the organization build a diverse membership, political legitimacy, and a strong reputation in the media field. These were hard-fought advantages that NRLC wanted to keep. Of course, this is often easier said than done. The remainder of the chapter outlines the media dilemmas NRLC faced and the tradeoffs they made in response to allies both inside and outside the political system.

CONTENDING WITH THE MODERATE MIDDLE

The political opportunity created by the Reagan presidency also produced intra-movement turmoil. Pro-lifers could not agree on whether a Constitutional Amendment should allow the abortion procedure in order to save the life of the mother. Organizations supporting an abortion exception, including NRLC, argued the clause was politically necessary. If pro-lifers wanted politicians and the citizenry to support an amendment, they needed to recognize those instances in which abortion was medically necessary. A contingent of groups disagreed, positing that support for an exception allowed politics to trump morality. One organization that refused to support the exception was the American Life League (ALL), which was created after two of the NRLC founding members, Judie and Paul Brown, left the group in protest of its support for legal abortion in some situations (rape, incest, and to save the life of the mother). The goal of ALL, which identifies itself as a Catholic organization, is to imbue the abortion issue with a vision of morality that includes only one acceptable solution – to end all abortions immediately, "without exception, without apology." Political pragmatism is not part of ALL's organizational worldview, where pro-lifers are called to "fight in God's battle" and to "be faithful not victorious."[20] Compromise on abortion legislation, in short, was not an option. ALL criticized the Human Life Amendment (HLA) and introduced its own – one designed to deal with the "deficits" of the HLA. The Paramount Amendment erased the exception, proclaiming, "The paramount right to life is vested in each

[20] Brown, Judie. "Letter from the President." *Celebrate Life!* online, January 1989.

human being from the moment of fertilization without regard to age, health, or condition of dependency."[21]

ALL's vocal opposition to the HLA created a dilemma for NRLC (Dilemma 3). Leaders were convinced that an amendment would not pass without an exception, and that the Paramount Amendment was a losing issue that served only to divide pro-life energies and resources. However, rather than simply denounce ALL's efforts, NRLC tried to build consensus within the movement. It did so by working with moderate groups to draft legislation that would reduce political support for abortion and ease the passage of the HLA. For instance, NRLC worked with Senator Helms (R-NC), National Pro Life PAC, the Moral Majority, the Committee to Elect a Pro-Life Congress, the Christian Action Council, the National Committee for a HLA, and several pro-life scholars and attorneys to draft the Abortion Funding Prescription Act of 1981, which was designed to prohibit public funding for abortion and abortion research.[22] Additionally, NRLC formed a committee comprised of the "major" pro-life groups (such as the Moral Majority) and sponsored a series of conferences designed to end the "polarization" over the wording of the HLA.[23]

The conferences were a media and a political tactic designed to present the movement as unified and pressure dissenting groups to fall in line with mainstream proposals (Dilemma 3). Building consensus around the HLA was particularly important because pro-choicers publicly exploited these divisions to highlight the "extremes" of the pro-life movement.[24] The process was slow. In January 1981, more than a year after negotiations begun, the committee reported that members were unable to form a consensus and, instead, tried "to narrow the disagreements within the movement and to define those disagreements as clearly as possible."[25] For the next several months, the *NRTL News* featured articles by movement leaders and scholars outlining the kind of amendment most likely to pass and withstand legal scrutiny, and tracked the progress of the committee.[26] Finally, on October 13, 1981 the committee reached a consensus. NRLC announced:

> Bridging years of division in a single stroke, the NRLC Board of Directors now stands united behind the working of a single Human Life Amendment. Appropriately, the Board reached its historic agreement on Respect Life Sunday, Oct. 4, 1981. Met with tears of joy and happiness, the wording of the Committee's new HLA solved what formerly appeared to be an irreconcilable difference over a fundamental question: how to allow for just those

[21] "The Human Life Amendment: FAQs" on the ALL website. http://www.all.org/article/print/id/MjM4Ng=

[22] Memo, John Wilke to Board and State Offices, February 16, 1981, GCRTL, Folder: 1980–1981.

[23] Willke, John. "Human Life Amendment Committee – Good News." *NRTL News*, September 1980.

[24] Willke, John. "HLA – Progress Toward Unity!" *NRTL News*, February 1981.

[25] The report was reprinted in the *NRTL News* January 1981.

[26] Edwards, Kathy. "HLA Seminar to Instruct on HLA Preparation." *NRTL News*, August 1981.

abortions truly needed to prevent the death of the mother without at the same time making her right to life superior to that of her unborn child.[27]

The new amendment was called the NRLC Unity Human Life Amendment. The pro-life movement, NRLC argued, had found "symmetry" between mother and child, which later became one of the central messages of its media campaign entitled, "Love them Both."[28]

ALL refused to support the Unity HLA or any other NRLC proposal. Instead, it attacked NRLC's methods, urged pro-lifers to terminate their NRLC memberships, and join ALL (Dilemma 2). For instance, as the Supreme Court considered the *Webster v. Reproductive Health Services* case in 1989, NRLC crafted model state legislation that it could immediately introduce in state legislatures if the decision went their way. After the favorable decision was issued, NRLC flooded state legislatures with proposed restrictions on abortion[29] and launched the "Abortion Stops a Beating Heart" media campaign, which was designed to shift public debate away from women's rights.[30] ALL criticized NRLC's strategy, arguing that NRLC had compromised the movement's goals. An ALL board member circulated a statement, which was later printed in the ALL newsletter (1990), calling NRLC's post-*Webster* strategy a compromise on human life:

> Compromise on a matter of principle does not reflect wisdom, but weakness, and our enemies know the odor of weakness and will exploit it to the full ... I call upon the National Right to Life Committee to publicly renounce the model bills they are alleged to have sponsored and admit they were mistaken ... I call upon everyone in the Right to Life movement to ask for this renunciation by National Right to Life."[31]

ALL echoed these criticisms in editorials, advertising, and in fundraising material targeting pro-life supporters.

These attacks continued throughout the 1990s. ALL was particularly unimpressed with NRLC's successful campaign against partial-birth abortion. The debate on this type of abortion was a watershed for the pro-life movement. Although pro-lifers knew of the procedure in the early 1990s, it was commonly referred to as "brain suction abortion" – a phrase that had little resonance beyond the movement. That changed in 1995 when the legislative director of the National Right to Life Committee coined the term "partial-birth" abortion. The phrase, which elicited strong negative emotional reactions from focus group participants, became the cornerstone of NRLC's attack on legal abortion. NRLC launched a national media campaign, which included paying for 9 million inserts in *USA Today*, and initiated state legislation in Ohio banning the

[27] Unknown. "Symmetry of Protection for Mother and Child." *NRTL News*, October 1981.

[28] Interview with NRLC founder and former president.

[29] Memo, Darla St. Martin to NRL directors and state officers, July 6, 1989, GCRTL, Folder: 1989.

[30] See issues of the *NRTL News*, 1990, 1991, and 1992.

[31] ALL lodged similar attacks in *Celebrate Life!* in 1989, 1990, and 1992.

procedure. Within months, debate over the partial-birth abortion procedure dominated abortion discourse.[32]

NRLC heralded its success, noting that the movement had finally shifted attention from women to unborn babies. This, a NRLC board member explained, was an important accomplishment because "When the debate is about women, we lose. When the debate is about babies, we win."[33] Judie Brown rejected NRLC's alleged victory, noting "There is no such thing as 'partial-birth' abortion." The debate, she argued, was an effort by NRLC to "generate headlines."[34] Jerry Horn, the senior vice president of ALL, echoed the sentiment, adding:

> We have grave concerns about the bill's "life of the mother" exception. We question why a loophole large enough to drive a truck through is included when doctors have testified that partial-birth abortions are never "necessary" to save a mother's life. Moreover, we question any legislation that treats one person's rights to life as superior to that of another. Frankly, why should we be involved in efforts to pass a measure that will probably not save the life of even one baby?[35]

ALL leaders urged pro-lifers to reject the issue and embrace the only "acceptable" political strategy[36] – "a constitutional amendment that protects all human beings from fertilization on[wards]."[37]

NRLC initially decided to temper its response to ALL and did not directly respond to the organization. NRLC took this approach in large part because leaders worried that attacking other pro-life groups might undermine its legitimacy. Shortly after the formation of ALL, Charles Donovan, the Administrative Assistant of NRLC's legislative office, advised:

> The pro-life movement is clearly at a turning point of immanent significance in its development. The movement now is being sorely tested, not from without but from within. It is my conviction that NRLC has no crisis in leadership but a crisis in "follow"-ship and in fellowship. Because it can neither invent nor patent its ideas the pro-life movement can be led by anyone who sincerely maintains a sense of both the magnitude of our ends and the disproportion of our means as human being to accomplish those ends. Our tone must be conciliatory, even when outspoken; our approach must be gentle, especially because it is unyielding."[38]

32 Interviews with a former NRLC president and a current board member.

33 Interview with NRLC board member.

34 Unknown. "Right to Life Act Is Next Logical Step for Pro-Life Movement." *PR Newswire*, May 20, 1997.

35 Horn, Jerry. "The Problem with the Partial Birth Abortion Bill." *The Washington Times*, January 28, 1996.

36 Unknown. "Courts Will Offer No Protection for the Preborn." *PR Newswire*, March 23, 1998.

37 Unknown. "American Life League Issues Wake-Up Call to Pro-Life America." *PR Newswire*, September 18, 1998.

38 Memo, Charles Donovan to Carolyn Gerster, January 30, 1979. GCRTL, Folder: 1977–1979.

However, as ALL became more virulent in its attacks, NRLC decided to respond to the organization directly (Dilemma 2). In its newsletter and mailings to supporters, NRLC leaders questioned the motives and credibility of Judie Brown and ALL. In an eight-page memo dated July 8, 1988, from the legislative director to NRLC chapters, the board of directors, and "selected pro-life contacts," Douglas Johnson noted that Brown's recent attacks on politicians and the NRLC are "perfectly characteristic of her past behavior." Johnson continued:

Mrs. Brown's tales of woe generally deal with some situation in which one or more pro-life congressmen or lobbyists failed to see the wisdom of some course of action recommended by Mrs. Brown. Each such event is written up by Mrs. Brown as another betrayal! – recounted by Mrs. Brown in overheated rhetoric with lots of exclamation marks! – heavily tinged with self righteousness and near-paranoia. In these accounts pro-life congressional leaders or lobbyists who don't follow Mrs. Brown's lead are defeatists, moral cowards, afraid to take risks and so on. In Mrs. Brown's eyes, only Judie Brown and her staff stand steadfast in defense of innocent babies.[39]

Johnson questioned the motives and ethics of the ALL leadership and Judie Brown. He recounts the numerous way in which ALL has "impeded pro-life efforts in Congress" by opposing good legislation at critical moments and using unethical tactics, such as fabricating statements from the NRLC and forging Senator Gordon Humphrey's signature on a fundraising document, to advance their own narrow and radical agenda. He went on to say that Judie Brown:

Generally seems to be more interested in "making a statement" than in "making a difference." One way which Mrs. Brown has of "making a statement" is to oppose pro-life amendments which are less than perfect in her eyes. As a result, most of the important pro-life measures which have actually been enacted into law during the past seven years, have been enacted without support from A.L.L. – and in some cases, over the *active opposition* of A.L.L. It requires harder work and harder thinking to accomplish something worthwhile in the real world of legislatures and government agencies than to issue grand pronouncements and denouncements in the manner of Judie Brown [emphasis in original].[40]

Throughout the 1990s, NRLC continued to question the legitimacy of ALL as an effective organization. Leaders criticized ALL's "extreme" and "unrealistic" all–or-nothing approach to the abortion issue.[41] In 1997, NRLC published an article in the *NRTL News* responding to "deceptive and derogatory statements" made by ALL in a recent fundraising letter. The article chronicles the history of attacks made by ALL against NRLC, concluding that ALL actively opposes all bills that do not immediately stop all abortions, "even though a lesser bill might

[39] Memo, Douglas Johnson to board of directors and state offices, July 8, 1988, GCRTL, Folder: 1986–1988.

[40] Memo, Douglas Johnson to board of directors and state offices, July 8, 1988, GCRTL.

[41] See issues of the *NRTL News* in 1989 and 1990.

save many lives."[42] NRLC also questioned the ability of ALL to accomplish its promise to pass a constitutional amendment that would end all abortions. One NRLC president warned, "A personality with a mailing list does not make an effective pro-life organization."[43] In an interview, another former NRLC president agreed, noting, "She [Judie Brown] was totally unrealistic. The way I phrased it, I said she will certainly save her soul, but she is not saving many babies."

DEALING WITH DIRECT ACTION GROUPS

ALL was not the only difficult ally with which NRLC had to contend. The favorable political environment of the 1980s not only spurred the dramatic growth of NRLC but led to the formation of a range of pro-life groups, including the Family Research Council, the Army of God, the Pro-Life Action Network, and the Christian Coalition. One of its most visible allies was Operation Rescue (OR), a religious group that used civil disobedience to close clinics. OR burst onto the political scene in 1988 at the Democratic National Convention in Atlanta, where activists attempted to "rescue" unborn babies from abortion at a local clinic and were arrested. While the rescue did not immediately get media attention amid the numerous other protests, journalists eventually noticed that more than one hundred jailed OR activists, who referred to themselves as "martyrs" to a corrupt system, chose to remain in jail rather than reveal their identities to the authorities. This tactic not only posed a big problem for the local judicial system, but led to a flurry of media coverage that presented OR as an organized and growing part of the pro-life movement (Risen and Thomas 1998).

Many mainstream groups were critical of OR's tactics and made clear distinctions between themselves and what they considered the radical flank of the movement (Dilemma 2). Bill Price, president of Texans United for Life, distanced himself from the organization, noting, "This is a holy war to them. To me, it is not. They are religious fanatics."[44] NRLC leaders, however, did not denounce OR. This was in part because NRLC could not publicly criticize OR without condemning its own membership. Many of its constituents and leaders were members of the group and participated in its campaigns (Blanchard 1995; Risen and Thomas 1998). Likewise, NRLC found that the emergence of OR had benefits – it drew new members and money into the organization at a time when NRLC needed funds. In a 1986 letter to sustaining members, Willke outlined the financial outlook of the organization:

> I am once again pleading for your continued support of NRLC just as I have done in my letters to you in the past. Frankly, I feel like I am begging sometimes, and it is painful for

[42] Parker, Don. "American Life League's Attacks on Pro-Lifers Draw Criticisms." *NRTL News*, February 1997.

[43] Franz, Wanda. "From the President's Desk." *NRTL News*, March 1992.

[44] McNamara, Bob. July 15, 1993. "Operation Rescue is Controversial." *CBS News*.

me to keep asking those who have done so much to keep doing more. But at this moment, *NRLC is facing a potentially dangerous financial emergency*. By September 19th, the NRLC must raise approximately $265,000 just to keep our doors open and to avoid cutting back on any crucial baby-saving programs . . . At the same time, *NRLC must raise an additional $295,000* to carry us through the November election contest which could be a real turning point for the right-to-life movement. *Of course, since this grand total of $560,000 represents the largest amount which NRLC has ever had to raise in a ten week period, your friendship is needed now more than ever* [emphasis in original].[45]

OR lessened the financial hardship by garnering attention for the movement, which translated into more members and money for a range of groups, including NRLC (Risen and Thomas 1998).

NRLC also found it difficult to criticize OR publicly because it approved of the organization's goal – to prevent abortions. A NRLC board member explained that Willke (the NRLC president for over a decade) was supportive of OR but would not publicly sanction the group's activities because sponsorship could undermine NRLC's political legitimacy:

NRLC's lack of participation with them reflected legal concerns. It boiled down to this: our general counsel said "if you participate in illegal activity, you put the future and welfare of your organization in jeopardy." We drew a distinct line between the two. Dr. Willke wasn't personally opposed to Operation Rescue. He saw the value in what they were doing. But for the sake of continuing what NRLC was doing, they put that wall of separation to protect the organization. It was a legitimate concern.[46]

Willke also worried that NRLC would be mired in lawsuits if it were involved in legal direct action. He explained:

In my city recently, Planned Parenthood sued Cincinnati Right to Life and several other groups and individuals. It was a clear harassment suit because the picketing was legal. Moreover . . . the judge dismissed Cincinnati Right to Life from the suit because it was not involved in the organizing of this legal picketing. Planned Parenthood tried desperately to keep the Right to Life organization involved, "for the media value," its lawyer said . . . Public witness and picketing has and will continue to play a part in this effort. It is important. Do remember, however, that all the pickets in the world will only save a small percentage of babies, and as important as this is, if the picketers aren't there the next day, the killing will be right back up to what is was. When, and if, however, the law changes, *all* the babies will again be protected, and the change in law will only come through the RTL groups. Therefore, we must not let these crucial organizations be knee-capped by lawsuits. That is why such public, non-violent, legal picketing must be organizationally and legally completely separate from your local Right to Life office [emphasis in original].[47]

These concerns meant that NRLC worked with OR informally and outside of the media spotlight. OR leaders and members attended and spoke at the NRLC

[45] Letter, John Willke, August 14, 1986, GCRTL, Folder: 1986–1988.
[46] Interview with an NRLC board member.
[47] Willke, John. "A Place for Public Witness?" *NRTL News*, May 1986.

annual conventions, where NRLC leadership tacitly supported direct action and included OR on political planning (Blanchard 1995; Risen and Thomas 1998).

Cooperation with OR involved tradeoffs. NRLC derived political benefits from the "radical flank effect" (Haines 1988). While OR's tactics generated media attention, it was not popular among pro-life politicians, who were quick to distance themselves from illegal activities. President George H. W. Bush, for instance, publicly supported peaceful and legal protests. Because OR often violated state and local laws, Bush refused to meet with OR leaders after he was elected. In short, the relatively radical tactics of OR increased the political legitimacy of NRLC and improved its access to political processes. During the early 1990s, NRLC had great success introducing legislation to further restrict abortion at the state level. In a fact sheet outlining the legislative progress of the NRLC since the *Webster* decision, Nancy Meyers notes:

> Nearly every state in session in 1990 will consider pro-life proposals. Already, fourteen states have voted on specific abortion legislation on one or both floors .... Of 28 votes on *pro-life* bills ... 21 have passed. Four states have voted *on pro-abortion* bills ... *Thus, of the total 32 clear-cut abortion related votes since* Webster, *23 (71 percent) have been pro-life victories* [emphasis in original].[48]

Cooperation, however, had a public relations price. OR quickly bumped NRLC out of the media spotlight. Randall Terry, founder and leader of OR, regarded getting media attention as important as OR's campaigns to disrupt clinics because coverage allowed him to spread his message. During a CNN interview, Terry explained:

> My mission is to get Christians to act like Christians so that the God haters that we see outside are afraid [of] us, because they recognize that it's either going to be us and God's principles that are leading this country, or it's going to be them and the principles of wickedness running the country.[49]

Pro-choice organizations fell in the latter category and were labeled the "enemies of God ... that are bent on destroying the family, that make a mockery of public decency."[50]

Terry's fundamentalist message made for great press (see Figure 3.2). Part of the appeal from a journalistic standpoint was the spectacle of OR's tactics. OR activists stormed into clinic lobbies, chained themselves to furniture, or sabotaged the facility and, then, were dragged out of clinics in handcuffs by police.[51] Journalists gobbled up the story, especially after pro-choicers mobilized to defend clinics from OR's antics. Even as the battles outside clinics waned,

[48] Factsheet, April 2, 1990, GCRTL, Folder: 1990.

[49] Unknown. "Operation Rescue Pickets a Local Church in Buffalo." *CNN*, April 26, 1992.

[50] McNamara, Eileen. "New Activist Tactics for a No-Choice Message." *The Boston Globe*, April 16, 1989.

[51] Crier, Catherine. "Tactics and Ethics an Issue in the Abortion Controversy." *CNN*, April 21, 1992.

Terry's adeptness at crafting inflammatory sound bites generated a great deal of media attention for OR. After the murder of Dr. David Gunn, an abortion provider, by Michael Griffin, a pro-life extremist, Terry told an NPR reporter:

> The illegal activities and the madness, really, of Michael Griffin, cannot be blamed on Operation Rescue. We abhor what he did. We condemn it. And we grieve for this man's family ... [However,] we will not – and, I repeat – we will not passively coexist with child killers without confronting them. Now, we demand of our people that they are involved in non-violent tactics. But we can't control every single person on the face of the earth. This Michael Griffin had no history with Operation Rescue whatsoever. We wish he hadn't done what he did. But I'll say this, Linda. David Gunn was a mass murderer.[52]

He was not the only OR activist to label Gunn a "mass murderer." Another OR activist added, "This was a murder of a mass murderer and just as, you know, we didn't mourn Hitler's death ... I don't believe it was appropriate to mourn Dr. Gunn's death."[53]

Much to NRLC's dismay, the outlandish proclamations and dramatic displays outside clinics made Terry the new spokesperson for the movement (Risen and Thomas 1998) and allowed OR to weigh in on legitimate political issues. When the *Webster* decision was handed down, Terry situated himself on the steps of the Supreme Court and was among the first to be interviewed. Terry called the ruling, "'a faltering step in the right direction ... The writing is on the wall – *Roe* is going to go down."[54] Terry added, "We're calling on thousands of pro-life Americans to peacefully blockade these killing centers with their bodies to prevent children from dying, and we will launch an equal force against state legislatures to chip away at *Roe*."[55] The statement by Willke was more subdued: "We are smiling. We are thumbs up all the way!"[56] It became so difficult for NRLC to get media attention that Willke asked Chris Smith (R-NJ) to intervene on his behalf. Smith called Terry and asked him to forego television appearances for the evening so that Willke could get some airtime (Risen and Thomas 1998, 294).

OR also reinforced stereotypes about who constituted and controlled the pro-life movement; a point pro-choicers often made in their public statements. An NRLC board member explained:

> The problem I have with Operation Rescue is that while they were well-meaning, they played into the hands of the biased media and the pro-abortion movement ... You have got Randall Terry with his megaphone spewing whatever and fitting that awful stereotype

52 Wertheimer, Linda. "Randall Terry Labels Slain Doctor 'Mass Murderer.'" *NPR: All Things Considered*, March 11, 1993.

53 Unknown. "Activism." *Abortion Report*, February 7, 1997.

54 Anderson, David. "Women's Groups Angered, Abortion Opponents Encouraged." *United Press International*, July 3, 1989.

55 Unknown. "Abortion Opponents Set Strategy for Coming Battles." *The New York Times*, July 5, 1989.

56 Bronner, Ethan. "Split Supreme Court Allows States to Restrict and Regulate Abortions." *The Boston Globe*, July 4, 1989.

of the white, male Bible-banger. They were used against the cause for unborn children. It was frustrating for me to see that they didn't get that.[57]

This was a point upon which the two groups vehemently disagreed. Terry viewed media as a tool for galvanizing Evangelicals, which meant there was little concern for the public face of the movement. NRLC, which spent a decade combating the stereotype, saw Terry's persona as regressive. An NRLC board member explained:

There was a lot of discussion [about media] that went on. It didn't go anywhere. It was water off the duck's back. These people [OR activists] felt so passionately about what they were doing, most of them were religiously motivated and to disagree with them was "get thee behind me" type Satan stuff. They would have no part in that.[58]

Again, NRLC did not publicly criticize OR. In a rare public statement, Willke deflected questions about OR by stating, "I don't have any comment about that kind of action. We do not become involved in anything outside the law."[59] In reality, silence was the most powerful strategy the organization could employ. It enabled the organization to cultivate its political advantages while allowing audiences to deduce NRLC's position on OR for themselves. Carol Maxwell (2002) argues that NRLC's silence implied censure for OR's tactics. For some audiences, NRLC's silence was a denouncement of OR's illegal activities and extreme rhetoric. However, given the behind-the-scenes cooperation between the groups, silence could just as easily have signaled NRLC's support for OR's ability to prevent abortions at the clinic level.

Additionally, silence stymied the opposition. While pro-choicers frequently attacked OR and its extremism, it could not link OR's activism to NRLC. In a confidential July 29, 1986, memo detailing the recent NRLC Convention, PPFA's vice president for communications detailed the division of labor in the pro-life movement. He categorized the pro-life groups as falling into three categories: "religious pedagogues," who use "noxious" doctrine to provide moral arguments for the "storm troopers," who carry out direct action and provide a hospitable media environment for the "front man," the NRLC president, who sells the goals of the pro-life movement to a broader public.[60] Publicly, pro-choicers accused NRLC of inciting illegal and violent tactics through its inflammatory rhetoric. NRLC, however, denied supporting extra-institutional means for ending abortion. In January 1985, Willke noted:

We see such violence as being exactly opposite to what our movement is all about. We are people of peace. The total thrust of our movement is to stop violence, the violence of the ruthless killings of tiny preborn babies, a continuing slaughter that is taking the life of

57 Interview with an NRLC board member.

58 Interview with an NRLC board member.

59 Kurtz, Howard. "Operation Rescue: Aggressively Antiabortion." *The Washington Post*, March 6, 1989.

60 Memo, Douglas Gould to the affiliate executive directors and state public affairs coordinators, July 29, 1986, Sophia Smith Collection, Smith University. Accession 93S–9, Box 1.

almost every third baby conceived in America ... But they charge that our "inflammatory rhetoric" incites people to do this. That charge is both clever and false. It is clever in that through it, they hope to silence our voices, voices that are being increasingly effective in telling the world of their ghastly activities and the damage done to women."[61]

NRLC's decision to remain silent and absorb the bad press created by OR made it impossible for pro-choicers to link the organizations publicly.

Despite the political advantages of cooperation, NRLC leaders wanted to counter the public image of OR and, to the greatest extent possible, recast the movement as a mainstream effort to secure the civil liberties of the unborn (Dilemma 2). This was easier said than done, particularly because there were limits to the kinds of tactics NRLC could employ without undermining its intent and public image. Sponsoring a nationwide rally seemed the best way to attract attention to mainstream organizations. It was a giant gamble. If the event failed to generate media attention, the organization could find itself in deep debt with little to show for it. In 1990, NRLC took a chance and organized a "Rally for Life" in Washington, D.C. The purpose of the event was to attract pro-lifers from across the country for a march that would revitalize existing supporters, mobilize new supporters, and provide extensive media coverage for the movement. The event was not nearly as successful as NRLC had hoped. Despite high attendance and a speech by Vice President Dan Quayle, the march received limited coverage and most of it involved disputes over the number of attendees. The United States Park Police estimated that 200,000 participated in the march, a figure that incensed Willke, who argued that aerial photos clearly indicated at least 700,000 in attendance. Moreover, the event failed to generate meaningful monetary support and pushed the organization into the red. In a letter to supporters, Willke reported:

Since April, NRLC has been operating on almost a day-to-day basis. First of all, our historic Rally for Life – which brought more Americans to Washington, D.C., than any single event since the Vietnam era – put NRLC over $400,000 in debt. But it galvanized pro-life forces – especially at the grassroots level – to a degree we never dreamed possible. Yet the $400,000 debt was an expenditure we could ill afford.[62]

NRLC's efforts paid off in the long run. Within a few years, OR was devastated by pro-choice lawsuits and NRLC re-emerged as the spokesperson for the movement. A former president of NRLC, reflecting on OR's tactics and Terry's public persona, noted:

We didn't agree with a lot of what Randall Terry did. And, we told him so! [Laughter]. He is his own person, and he did what he wanted to do ... [even though I tried to convince him that] we were not going to win the public's heart if we are either too violent or too radical ... There is an example of a movement that did not succeed and it has sort of died away, hasn't it?

[61] Willke, John. "Opposing Clinic Violence." *NRTL News*, January 1985.

[62] Letter, John Willke to NRLC Supporter, October 22, 1990, GCRTL, Folder: 1990; Accounting Statement, Amaire Natividad to John C. Willke, October 19, 1990, GCRTL, Folder: 1990.

THE PROBLEM OF THE REALLY RADICAL FRINGE

NRLC did not work with all of its radical allies. In fact, NRLC leaders categorically renounced groups that advocated or used violence against clinic property and personnel as a means to end abortion (Dilemma 3). The kidnapping of a reproductive health care physician and his wife in 1982 and an increased number of clinic bombings garnered a great deal of negative media attention for the pro-life movement throughout the mid- and late 1980s, which posed a serious threat to the political and public legitimacy of moderate pro-life groups. This threat was exacerbated by activists such as Joseph Scheidler, author of *99 Ways to Close the Abortion Clinics*, who refused to renounce violence as a legitimate tactic. In response to attacks on clinics, Scheidler suggested that "bombs may be planted by pro-abortion groups to arouse sympathy. Why not – they can afford it. The insurance company will pick up the tab."[63] Pro-choicers were furious with the assault on clinics and accused pro-life extremists of going to any length to impose their version of morality and femininity on all Americans. Several groups, including NOW and PPFA, called upon the Department of Justice to investigate clinic violence as domestic terrorism. The pro-choice response, coupled with the tacit approval of the use of violence by some pro-life leaders, threatened to discredit the entire pro-life movement. A former NRLC president described the public backlash as "One clinic burnt down and the entire movement is tarred and feathered by this happening!" It was critical for NRLC to publicly denounce violence as a legitimate tactic for ending abortion.

The use of renunciation was clear in the case of Paul Hill long before he killed Britton and his bodyguards. NRLC vigorously disagreed with Hill's position on violence, insisting that the movement was peaceful. In a "letter to a potential arsonist" the NRLC president wrote, "Your violence hurts our cause. It turns people off, people who otherwise might listen to our story, consider it, join us ... We are a civil rights movement. We exist to return equal protection under the law to all Americans, no matter how tiny or helpless."[64] Hill's rhetoric and methods garnered him media coverage and, surprisingly, an audience with President Reagan. When Reagan met with pro-life leaders on the *Roe v. Wade* anniversary in 1986, Hill asked the president to pardon those individuals who used violence to end the murder of unborn children. Although Reagan did not respond to the request, Hill left the White House and informed the press that Reagan announced he would consider this option. The NRLC president tried to counter this interpretation, but to no avail. The media ran with the story, and later that day, *Larry King Live* cancelled its interview with NRLC, announcing that the show would feature Hill and discuss this issue of clinic violence.

Renouncing groups that advocated violence and chastising mainstream media venues for covering these extremists was the only strategy NRLC could

[63] McCarthy, Colman. "Abortion Crossfire." *The Washington Post*, July 15, 1984.
[64] Willke, J. C. "Letter to a Potential Arsonist." *NRTL News*, February 1986.

employ without affecting its public image. This was especially true because pro-choice organizations such as NOW organized large-scale counterdemonstrations to defend clinics from both OR and the more extreme elements of the pro-life movement (Barasko 2004). The resulting clashes between the two movements played out on the evening news and resulted in precisely the kind of stereotypical portrayals of pro-lifers that NRLC sought to avoid. NRLC did the only thing it could do, which was to continue to denounce the most radical elements of movement. It launched an "unending" media campaign to reach every national reporter who covered "the statements of deranged individuals who advocate killing abortionists, asking them to please refrain from holding up these people as leaders, so to speak, whose messages might be followed by unstable people."[65]

CONCLUSION

Although Reagan's victory signaled that a friend of the pro-life movement was moving into the White House, pro-lifers were not of one mind on how to take advantage of the political opportunity. Many organizations rallied around different Constitutional amendments, focusing intramovement debate on whether or not pro-lifers should support an abortion exception. Dissention within the movement increased once it became clear that Reagan had no intention of championing legislation that would overturn *Roe*. Unable to agree on a single course of action, pro-lifers advocated for reform both inside and outside the political system in ways that were consistent with their organizational identities. In short, the organizationally diverse pro-life movement found tactical and ideological divisions a sizable obstacle in their efforts to bring about change.

Conflict among like-minded groups during moments of political opportunity is not uncommon. As illustrated above, intramovement conflict can become so absorbing that groups miss an opportunity to effect more sweeping policy changes. More importantly, intramovement conflict rarely occurs behind closed doors. Divisions among organizations quickly become apparent to supporters and are often broadcast to a larger public via mass media. As groups call on adherents to back their political strategies and renounce those of their allies, intramovement divisions can deepen and make it vulnerable to public attack by opponents. Intramovement conflict, in short, does not just create political challenges but also media dilemmas with which a group must contend.

As the leader of the pro-life movement, NRLC found itself caught in the middle of intramovement strife. It is clear that different allies created different media dilemmas for NRLC (its strategic choices are summarized in Table 4.1). Moderate groups that opposed an abortion exception created a sizeable media dilemma (and a big political problem) because they championed a losing

[65] *NRTL News*, February 1991. Also see the *NRTL News* in 1995 and 1996 and NRLC Press releases.

TABLE 4.1. *Summary of NRLC's strategic choices*

Organizational Identity	Secular
Framing the Abortion Issue	Scientific framework
Public Image	Mainstream organization led by respected professionals
Reputation in the Media Field	Strong
Dilemma 1: Access External Media?	
Perception of Mainstream Outlets	Saw mainstream as hostile to their message, but necessary to be effective.
	Initially, targeted sympathetic media. Its efforts to get in mainstream venues grew with its financial resources.
Example	No, Operation Rescue mobilized people and money as well as increased organizational access to politicians
Dilemma 2: Respond to Negative Attention?	
Examples	Yes, to renounce the violence of pro-life extremists
	No and Yes, ignore and then refute American Life League claims
Dilemma 3: Weigh in on Losing Issues?	
Example	Yes, to create consensus among mainstream groups (tried to turn a losing issue into a winning one)
Tradeoffs	
	Bad press for money, members, and support
	Bad press for political access
	Political progress for movement consensus

position during a moment ripe with the possibility for change (Dilemma 3). Because change would be out of reach if pro-lifers could not agree on a political position, it made sense for NRLC to try to build consensus among the moderate pro-life core. NRLC's consensus-building efforts, however, also played an important public relations role. Focusing on consensus enabled NRLC to publicly sidestep a losing issue without providing ammunition to their opponents – or their disgruntled allies. NRLC's willingness to use its status to build consensus among moderate groups cast the movement as a united front that had collectively found a way to protect both the lives of both the unborn child and, when needed, the mother. The image of a pro-life movement that "loved them both" undercut the arguments championed by its opponents.

NRLC's consensus-building strategy did not placate all of its allies, however. ALL accused NRLC of "selling out" and launched a number of public relations attacks on the group (Dilemma 3). While these attacks outlined real differences between the organizations in terms of their political goals, ALL hoped to build its political credibility and clout at NRLC's expense. Strategically speaking, this was a good move at the right time. Reputable organizations are hesitant to sling mud at an influential – or aggressive – ally. As a result, a successful attack can chip away at an organization's credibility and yield additional members and money for the assailing group. Given its history with the Browns and its status as a leader in the pro-life movement, NRLC had to be careful in its response to this dilemma. In fact, NRLC initially did not respond to the negative attention generated by ALL's attacks for fear that it would cast the organization as petty and damage its reputation with politicians and the public. The cost of remaining silent eventually became too much for the organization to bear and NRLC retaliated by discrediting ALL's leadership and tactics and questioning its political clout.

There are costs associated with picking fights with your friends. Intramovement sniping provides fuel for opponents, who will publicize the extremes in a movement for their own political purposes. Likewise, in-fighting takes time, energy, and resources away from organizational goals. ALL's public relations attack spanned several years and required NRLC leaders to constantly monitor, discuss, and craft a response to the group's claims. The tradeoff (a slow, costly response over a quick and decisive one), however, paid off in the long run. NRLC maintained its public image as a moderate, pro-life leader throughout its conflict with ALL.

Radical allies such as OR also created a media dilemma for NRLC (Dilemma 2). OR's fiery, fundamentalist rhetoric made the group a media darling and pushed NRLC out of the media spotlight. Rather than publicly respond to the tactics and rhetoric of OR, NRLC silently absorbed the bad press. There were several reasons for this strategic choice. First, even if NRLC had wanted to, it could not denounce OR without criticizing its own leadership and membership. Silence was the most reasonable response because it could be read as either a sign of support or a refutation of OR and its tactics by its members and the public. Second, NRLC discovered that OR's dramatic protests brought new members – and more money – to the organization. These funds came during a moment when NRLC was struggling financially and helped breathe new life into its legislative efforts. Third, because pro-life politicians were eager to distance themselves from the dramatic, and sometimes illegal, tactics of OR, NRLC found that it had more political clout. NRLC's broad membership base, moderate rhetoric, and practical approach to political change made it a favorite with politicians looking to appease their pro-life constituents and get re-elected.

There does come a point where the costs associated with silence outweigh its benefits. If an ally adopts extreme tactics, the movement will not only be "tarred and feathered" in mass media but politicians may also decide to withdraw their support from the movement and stall legislation. Radical flank effects, in short, are not always beneficial, nor are the negative consequences always confined to the mass media field. When allies move from feisty tactics to violence, the ability of a group to forward its goals may diminish rapidly. This is why NRLC chose not to ignore extremists who used violence to shut down clinics. NRLC quickly renounced violent tactics and tried to respond to the onslaught of negative media attention.

Finally, silence made it possible for NRLC to work with OR without risking its public image or reputation. NRLC opposed OR's illegal tactics, but was generally supportive of the group's decision to take the battle to clinics. While NRLC did not give OR money, it shared information with the group and, to some extent, worked in tandem with OR in order to launch pro-life challenges on multiple fronts simultaneously. This strategic choice clearly had benefits. At least until NRLC decided it wanted to reclaim some of the media spotlight for itself, cooperation mitigated competition between the two groups and helped each pursue its distinct political goals – OR got media attention and NRLC got political access. Because the groups did not talk about – or talk to – one another in public, the groups could challenge pro-choicers in multiple venues simultaneously, effectively spreading their opponents' resources to the breaking point. When pro-choice organizations cried foul, NRLC denied supporting or working with OR, and pro-choicers were hard pressed to prove otherwise.

Despite some setbacks, NRLC's strategic choices paid off over time. Not only did ALL's strength and position wane in the late 1990s, but OR virtually disappeared after pro-choicers successfully sued Terry, and President Clinton, elected in 1993, took decisive action to protect clinics. By the late 1990s, NRLC had reemerged as the undisputed leader of the pro-life movement.

5

Reputation, political change, and the National Organization for Women

Not all movement actors have the same experiences in the mass media field. While one group may have a relatively easy time accessing mainstream journalists and getting its ideas in the news, another organization may struggle to attract the media spotlight. These different experiences are a function of an organization's *reputation* in the media field. The more an organization's identity aligns with the norms and practices of an outlet, the stronger its reputation will be. A strong reputation has benefits. A group with a strong reputation has an easier time directly accessing mainstream (and other) news venues and also receives more and better quality coverage (Rohlinger and Brown 2013).

Reputation is stable, but not static. While journalists assess an organization's reputation based on its identity, they also determine the reputation of one organization by comparing it to its allies. As seen in the previous chapter, organizations may experience brief periods of reputational decline as their allies grab center stage using tactics and spouting rhetoric that are too juicy for most journalists to ignore. While these declines may vex an organization, the weakening of its reputation may be temporary. Journalists need credible sources of information and, ultimately, will return to those organizations that understand and can fulfill this function. Reputation, in short, can shift with intramovement dynamics and the broader political environment.

The ability of a group to bounce back from a reputational dip depends on at least three factors. First, whether a group specializes in one or more issues shapes its ability to reestablish its reputation in the media field. Social movement scholars typically regard specialization as a function of competition among groups that share a general goal. The more groups there are in a movement, the more pressure there will be for organizations to differentiate themselves from their like-minded competitors (Rohlinger and Quadagno 2009; Soule and King 2008). While some organizations will distinguish themselves by focusing on a single policy area, others will do so by working on behalf of an aggrieved population and advocating for change in multiple institutional settings simultaneously. Only the former is likely to reap reputational benefits in the media field. It is far easier for a group to (re)establish and maintain its credibility on one issue (Rohlinger 2007).

Second, the number of professional organizations championing mainstream positions determines a group's ability to strengthen its reputation in the media field after a decline. Journalists assess a group's reputation comparatively. If a journalist needs a quote for a story and there is only one mainstream group mobilizing around the issue of interest, this organization will find it fairly easy to (re)establish its reputation in the media field. Reestablishing a reputation in a movement crowded with professional organizations is more difficult. In these movements, journalists have a range of organizations from which they may solicit sound bites, and the decline of one organization has little impact on their ability to put together the news. Consequently, once a group loses reputational ground to one of its similarly situated allies, it may be hard pressed to reestablish itself with journalists.

Finally, an organization will find it difficult to reestablish its reputation if some aspect of its identity comes under scrutiny or is criticized in the broader culture. Actors routinely single out opponents and attack their ideology, motivations, and campaigns. If these claims gain traction in the broader culture, journalists may not only pick up the rhetoric but also reevaluate the reputations of organizations representing this newly stigmatized ideology. In short, factors external (e.g., movement composition) and internal (e.g., organizational identity) to a movement organization affect its reputation in the media field and whether reputational declines become permanent.

Shifts in reputation influence how an organization responds to media dilemmas. For example, how a group chooses to engage external media will change as its reputation weakens. Instead of relying primarily on "earned," or free, media coverage, an organization may focus more of its resources on direct media that it can control and use to counter negative media attention (Dilemmas 1 and 2). Additionally, when it does want earned media attention, it may target its efforts more carefully. Trying to get decent coverage on a middle-of-the-road cable news channel may be relatively easier than getting a quote in *The New York Times* because the former has a much larger news space to fill than the latter. Likewise, an organization with a weak reputation is more inclined to speak out on losing issues than a group with a strong one (Dilemma 3). A group with a strong reputation can often leverage itself and its ideas in several institutional fields simultaneously (Rohlinger and Brown 2013), which makes it easier for an organization to distance itself from or remain silent on losing issues. This is not true of a group with a relatively weak reputation, which is likely to grab media opportunities when they arise, even if it might reflect it or its issue poorly.

This chapter examines the declining organizational reputation of the National Organization for Women (NOW) and analyzes how its weakening reputation altered the group's response to media dilemmas. During the 1980s, NOW's reputation weakened relative to other groups organizing around the abortion issue. Given the organization's focus on the Equal Rights Amendment (ERA) campaign, NOW came across as a newcomer to abortion politics. Worse, the organization decided to engage its opponents outside clinics, which made NOW activists seem as radical as the pro-lifers with whom they faced off – just as an attack on feminism was reaching a frenetic pitch. With its weakened reputation in the media field, NOW had to find new ways to respond to media dilemmas and use mass media to forward its goals. I begin the chapter by situating NOW in the pro-choice movement and detail how NOW leaders crafted a mainstream public image for the group. This public image was not always consistent with the group's organizational identity as a "revolutionary" women's organization. In order to keep organizational in-fighting in check, NOW leaders employed a strategy of "principled pragmatism," which prioritized short-term outcomes over long-term organizational maintenance. While this strategy helped the organization weather the storm of its ERA defeat, it contributed to its weakening reputation in the media field and forced the group to rethink how it used mass media to bring about political change.

THE PROBLEMS OF PRINCIPLED PRAGMATISM

NOW was founded on June 30, 1966 by more than two dozen seasoned activists, academics, attorneys, and media professionals attending the Third National Conference of the Commission on the Status of Women. Frustrated by their inability to use the commission as a way to encourage full enforcement of Title VII of the Civil Rights Act, which prohibited intentional discrimination as well as practices that could lead to discrimination, and the reluctance of the Equal Employment Opportunity Commission to investigate gender-based discrimination claims, attendees created an organization that would advocate for women's equality and remain "unhampered by official connection with the government" (Barasko 2004, 22). The group's mission statement, which was written on a napkin by NOW's first president, Betty Friedan, at the conference read, "The purpose of NOW is to take action to bring women into full participation in the mainstream of American society now, exercising all the privileges and responsibilities thereof in a truly equal partnership with men" (Barasko 2004, 23).

Organizationally, NOW was modeled after the National Association for the Advancement of Colored People (NAACP). NOW has a formalized organizational structure, meaning it is hierarchically organized with a national office in Washington, D.C., nine regional divisions, state-level organizations, and 600 local chapters. The national convention is the "supreme governing body" of the organization. At the conventions, delegates, who are appointed by the chapter members, vote on proposals and determine the organizational priorities and policies. Once the organization establishes a position on an issue, the board of directors, which is composed of forty-two members from each of NOW's nine regions, interprets and implements the policy (Haney 1985).

Unlike the NAACP, NOW did not intend to keep its activism confined to institutional politics. NOW positioned itself as a "revolutionary" organization interested in engaging the government to further women's equality by working both inside and outside political institutions. NOW's Statement of Purpose asserted that:

> The time has come to move beyond the abstract argument, discussion and symposia over the state and special nature of women which has raged in America in recent years; the time has come to confront, with concrete action, the conditions that now prevent women from enjoying the equality of opportunity and freedom which is their right, as individual Americans, and as human beings (Barasko 2004, 27).

The revolutionary changes envisioned by NOW would require the organization to bring public attention to gender inequalities through demonstrations and boycotts and get women in positions of power so that they could effect political and institutional change (Dilemma 1).

Given that a handful of its founders were journalists, it is not surprising that the NOW leadership recognized the ability of mainstream media coverage to help or hurt women's issues (Barker-Plummer 2002; Turner 1980). NOW established media attention as an organizational goal and dedicated human and financial resources to this end. NOW set up a communications department to manage media requests, hold press conferences to announce its activities and campaigns, create a news service to provide information to journalists, build an "issue beat" with female reporters, and produce information for media dissemination (Barasko 2004). Additionally, in December of 1968, NOW implemented its "guidelines on public relations," which prohibited NOW spokeswomen from commenting on issues that were controversial or on which the organization had not taken an official position (Costain 1992, 48). Organizational policy also stipulated that only elected officials could speak on behalf of NOW, unless granted special permission by the board of directors. In short, establishing media attention as a goal early in its history allowed NOW to position itself as an important player on women's issues even when the organization was not particularly active on Capitol Hill.

NOW has been unable to maintain a strong reputation, particularly with mainstream media outlets, over the years. NOW's reputation has weakened over time, in part because of the tension between its organizational identity and public image. NOW identifies itself as a "revolutionary" feminist organization that is designed to push important women's issues from the margins to the mainstream of society, while simultaneously trying to sell itself as a "mainstream" women's public policy organization to journalists and the broader public.[1] It is important to note that this tension is a direct result of the

[1] NOW's use of the term "revolutionary" should not be confused with the more radical variants of feminism. NOW does not advocate separatism or replacing the existing system of politics. Instead, it seeks to revolutionize the existing system by increasing women's roles in politics and eradicating gender discrimination from institutional life.

organization's choices during the 1980s. There was a highly publicized battle over the NOW presidency in 1985 in which Eleanor Smeal, a trained advocate of street activism, wrested control of the organization from Judy Goldsmith, who preferred to use institutional avenues such as lobbying to forward organizational goals. In her victory speech, Smeal proclaimed that it was time for NOW to get back into the streets and promised constituents, "You'll see this movement explode in size."[2] Patricia Ireland carried this tradition into the 1990s, pledging that she would "not allow NOW to become another Washington lobbying group making humble courtesy calls on Capitol Hill and begging men for our rights."[3]

While NOW's organizational identity (a "revolutionary" feminist organization) and public image (a mainstream public policy organization) are by no means mutually exclusive, its use of confrontational tactics and fierce rhetoric often draws media fire for being "militant" rather than mainstream. NOW leaders do not apologize for being strident in their tactics or rhetoric and, in fact, see it as necessary to create social and cultural change. Patricia Ireland, NOW president from 1991 to 2001, noted:

> We [NOW] lead public opinion, we do not follow it. That's who we are. Sure, it has its down side. Taking a leadership position makes people uncomfortable. But my ultimate value isn't comfort. My ultimate value is progress for women.[4]

NOW's rhetoric and actions, in short, deviate from the "mainstream" image it presents and, over time, this has eroded its reputation in outlets across the mass media field.

The tension between NOW's organizational identity and public image also created intraorganizational conflict regarding the best way to move forward a feminist agenda (Reger 2002a; Reger 2002b; Staggenborg 1991). NOW primarily mitigated organizational tension by employing a strategy of "principled pragmatism," which allowed it to engage in public and political action simultaneously but also undercut the reputation of the organization in mainstream outlets. NOW leaders tried to capitalize on the news of the day and generate controversy around previously uncontested events. In the mass media field, this meant interpreting events through a feminist perspective and illuminating practices that were oppressive to women. In the political arena, this meant creating and coordinating actions to bring additional attention to an issue and pressure to bear on those positioned to enact change.[5] For example, in 1994 NOW used media coverage of Nicole Brown-Simpson's murder to discuss issues of domestic violence. In 1998, NOW brought the issue of domestic violence into mainstream

[2] Klemesrud, Judy. "Woman in the News." *The New York Times*, July 22, 1985.

[3] Gross, Jane. "Does She Speak for Today's Women?" *The New York Times*, March 1, 1992.

[4] Gross, Jane. "Does She Speak for Today's Women?" *The New York Times*, March 1, 1992.

[5] This term was coined by a NOW activist, Eleanor Humes Haney (1985), and used to describe NOW's political strategy.

discourse again by vigorously protesting the reinstatement of Mike Tyson's boxing license and citing his history of violence against women for their actions. Principled pragmatism couples the "news of the day" with confrontational rhetoric or protest, which satisfies NOW's members, who expect action from the organization.

While principled pragmatism helps NOW manage organizational tension, it has done little to help maintain the group's reputation with journalists. Principled pragmatism focuses on short-term outcomes (getting media coverage and mobilizing members to bring about situational change) rather than how to sustain an organizational mission and achieve goals over time. As a result, journalists working in mainstream and liberal news outlets alike do not look to NOW when putting together their stories on abortion. It is important to note that the perception that NOW is not a good source of information is exacerbated by two factors. First, the pro-choice movement is rife with professional groups, which means journalists have a fairly broad range of organizations from whom they can get information and quotes. As previously discussed, in such a movement it is far easier to diminish an organizational reputation than to rebuild it. Second, NOW is not as specialized as other groups in the movement (e.g., NARAL Pro Choice America). NOW represents multiple issues (e.g., abortion, discrimination, and sexual harassment) while many of its allies mobilize around abortion alone. Thus, while media professionals recognized that NOW mobilized around "women's issues," they did not regard it as an authority on abortion.

A journalist at *The New York Times* said that NOW doesn't come to mind when she is thinking about who to include in abortion coverage because although "they care a lot about abortion ... on any given day, they are not as enmeshed in what's happening on the Hill for example, as some of the other groups I mentioned before [NARAL and Planned Parenthood]."[6] Another *New York Times* journalist agreed: "I know where they are coming from but, I don't find them on the front lines with litigation or data compiling or things that would get my attention."[7] An executive producer at NBC Nightly News credited NOW's weak reputation to their shotgun approach to media and women's issues. He offered an analogy:

> If I want to talk about car safety or if I want to talk about using seat belts or cell phone distraction, I'm not going to call AAA, I am going to call the National Highway Traffic Safety Administration or I am going to call Ralph Nader's Center for Auto Safety because that's all they do. Because AAA handles maps, guidebooks, and it's true that they are concerned about driving and autos, and they are concerned about safety, and they do a lot of stuff, but that's not their specialty.[8]

[6] Interview with a journalist at *The New York Times*.
[7] Interview with a journalist at *The New York Times*.
[8] Interview with an executive producer at *NBC Nightly News*.

A writer from the progressive magazine, *The Nation*, gave a less flattering assessment of NOW. She quipped, "I know more about abortion than they do."[9] While NOW may find ways to fit itself into the news cycle, media professionals working in moderated venues simply do not regard NOW as a credible expert on all of the issues it tries to represent.

The tension between organizational identity and public image is not the only reason for NOW's reputational decline. NOW's visibility on women's issues was circumscribed in the 1990s by its decision to engage pro-lifers outside abortion clinics. As discussed below, NOW saw its campaign against groups such as OR as an opportunity to rebuild its membership and coffers after its failure to pass the Equal Rights Amendment (ERA). The dramatic images of activists facing off outside abortion clinics fueled a media feeding-frenzy from which NOW initially benefited. However, its decision to launch a campaign (and then a court battle) to end clinic violence had long-term consequences for the organization. When the political climate changed, NOW found that it lacked the resources to take on new issues and had difficulty in making itself and its campaigns newsworthy. This, coupled with the backlash against feminism (Dilemma 3), further eroded NOW's reputation with mainstream journalists and forced the group to rethink how it used media to reach a broader public.

SHIFTING THE FOCUS FROM ERA TO ABORTION

The legalization of abortion was among NOW's early goals. NOW formally supported the repeal of existing abortion laws in 1967 at its second annual conference. That said, the legalization of abortion was not the primary focus of NOW in its early years; the passage of an ERA was, and NOW campaigned vigorously on its behalf (Barasko 2004; Staggenborg 1991).[10] The emergence of conservative women's organizations, such as Eagle Forum and Concerned Women for America, that opposed the ERA proved to be a challenge for NOW and, by 1978, NOW's president, Eleanor Smeal, declared an ERA "state of emergency." Two years later, NOW members supported a "total ERA mobilization," which expanded the size, diversity, and range of the campaign. This commitment was not inconsequential. NOW dedicated one quarter of its entire budget to the ERA campaign in 1980 and 1981 (Barasko 2004, 71–73). However, as the deadline for ratification approached, it became clear that the ERA was not going to pass and that NOW would have to identify a new political path (Dilemma 3). NOW leaders focused on electoral politics and sought to "feminize" power by increasing the number of women holding elected office,

[9] Interview with a writer at *The Nation*.

[10] The ERA was designed to give women "equal justice under the law." The amendment passed in 1972 and was sent to the states for ratification. It failed to pass during the seven-year time limit, and Congress extended the ratification date to June 30, 1982. The ERA fell three states short of the constitutional requirement.

backing politicians who supported women's rights, and removing opponents from office. This organizational shift was clear in Smeal's 1982 news conference, where she told reporters:

> We will not again seriously pursue the ERA until we've made a major dent in changing the composition of Congress as well as the state legislatures to include a significantly larger proportion of women and of men who are genuinely feminists ... We are announcing today that the Equal Rights Amendment Countdown Campaign, coordinated by the National Organization for Women, has ended. However, the fight for equality for women will go on, stronger than ever, until justice is ours.[11]

The emphasis on electoral politics did not excite many of NOW's constituents and the organization lost 90,000 members between 1982 and 1985 (Barasko 2004, 90). To make matters worse, by 1985 NOW was on the brink of financial disaster with nearly US$ 1 million of debt.[12] These organizational realities dramatically diminished the political options available to NOW. The organization could not take on new projects and needed to find an issue that would energize its waning membership and attract new constituents. The abortion issue was ideal. Reagan's hostility to legal abortion and the rising tide of violence at abortion clinics provided a good opportunity for NOW to recommit itself to reproductive freedom and to link the violence in the streets to the "violent" legislation imposed upon women by the Reagan administration.

This was not a difficult transition for the organization to make. NOW began criticizing Reagan and his "woman problem" almost immediately after his election. One NOW activist opined in the April 1981 newsletter that:

> Ronald Reagan has a woman problem. No, not a problem with any woman in particular, but with a significant group of American women, working women to be specific ... These doubts were generated initially by Reagan's position on what have been called "women's issues," particularly the Equal Rights Amendment. Reagan is opposed to the adoption of the ERA and he is also strongly antiabortion.[13]

This woman problem caused Reagan to prioritize the rights of fetuses above women and pack his administration with "antiabortion fanatics." Reagan placed pro-lifers in prominent positions in his administration, including Marjorie Mecklenburg, who served as a president of a pro-life organization, to run the Title X family planning program; C. Everett Koop, who served as a board member for two pro-life groups and narrated a controversial film titled, "Whatever Happened to the Human Race?," to Surgeon General; and Donald Devine, who ran the Life Amendment PAC, to head the U.S. Office of Personnel Management. By 1982, NOW primarily focused on Reagan's opposition to abortion, accusing him of:

[11] Shepard, Robert. "Untitled." *United Press International*, June 24, 1982.

[12] Financial documents, Accession 99-M70-99-M148, Box 15, Folder: Financial Reports 1985, Radcliffe Institute for Advanced Study (RIAS).

[13] Unknown. "Reagan's Woman Problem." *National NOW Times*, April 1981.

Orchestrating the assault on all fronts from the White House – by his appointment of well known anti-abortion and anti-birth control leaders to top positions in the Department of Health and Human Services; by his administration's regulations and proposals that make it more difficult to get an abortion and to use preferred methods of birth control; and by his endorsement of a constitutional amendment that would prohibit abortion and certain forms of birth control.[14]

At the same time, violence at clinics and against clinic personnel was on the rise. NOW responded by linking Reagan's rhetoric on abortion to the increased violence at abortion clinics and used the publication of Reagan's book, *Abortion and the Conscience of the Nation*, as the foundation for their argument. In an analysis of the book a *National NOW Times* writer reports:

Within his 20-page section of the book, Reagan compares abortion to slavery four times, refers to it as a "holocaust" twice, compares it with murder six times, and twice links abortion to infanticide. In the second sentence, Reagan refers to our "nationwide policy of abortion-on-demand through all nine months of pregnancy," and later asks, "How many Americans are aware that abortion techniques are allowed today, in all 50 states, that burn the skin of a baby with salt solution in an agonizing death that can last for hours?"

In the same article, NOW President Judy Goldsmith argues, "Reagan's book goes beyond offensive. To simultaneously ignore the recent wave of terrorism at abortion clinics and to publish an emotional, misleading, callous diatribe against women who exercise their constitutionally protected rights is unconscionable."[15] Moreover, NOW argued that Reagan's book fueled extremism. Goldsmith told reporters on several occasions that Reagan needed to "cease his irresponsible and inflammatory anti-abortion, anti-woman rhetoric,"[16] adding, "If Reagan and the anti-abortion extremists persist in calling American women murderers, they must accept responsibility for the violence that is occurring."[17] This line of argument was buttressed by Reagan's silence on the issue and the refusal by the Department of Justice to intervene and curb clinic violence.

The threat to legal, accessible abortion provided NOW a way to reengage progressive women and highlight the ability of the organization to confront these challenges (Dilemma 1). NOW linked the Reagan administration with the violence on the streets and initiated grassroots campaigns to "fight back" against harassment and the Right more generally.[18] In the March/April 1984 issue of the *National NOW Times*, a reporter described the campaign:

[14] Wells-Schooley, Jane. "Reagan Leads Republican Assault on Abortion, Birth Control." *National NOW Times*, August 1982.

[15] Unknown. "Reagan Book Compares Abortion to Holocaust." *National NOW Times*, May/June 1984.

[16] Unknown. "Reagan's Rhetoric Fuels Anti-Abortion Clinic Terrorists." *National NOW Times*, March/April 1984.

[17] Unknown. "Clinic Terrorism Continues." *National NOW Times*, May/June 1984.

[18] Campaign materials, Box 92-M8-92-M96, Carton 5, Folder: Legislative Action, RIAS.

Activists are organizing escort services for clinic patients, meeting with law enforcement officials to ensure clinic protection, holding counter demonstrations and exposing the tactics of the anti-abortionists.[19]

Likewise, NOW began identifying their opponents on the Right, which they labeled a "new breed of anti-abortion fanatics."[20] One opponent was Joseph Scheidler, leader of the Pro Life Action Network, who promised to shut down clinics using "any means necessary."[21] This strategy worked in the short term, garnering NOW media attention and growing its coffers enough to pull the organization from the brink of financial disaster in 1985.[22] This strategy was not without consequence, however. Once an organization picks up a cause, it needs to follow through, which can be very resource-consuming and can even prevent a group from taking up other issues. This is a lesson NOW learned the hard way.

In 1986, the recently elected NOW president, Eleanor Smeal, convinced the Delaware Women's Health Organization and the Pensacola Ladies Center to file suit in a federal district court against Joesph Scheidler and other pro-life activists. The suit was brought under federal antitrust laws and charged the defendants with a "nationwide criminal conspiracy to close women's health clinics." This legal strategy was successful and, in 1988, NOW expanded the case to include Randall Terry and OR. In 1989, NOW altered its suit again, adding charges of extortion and violation of the Racketeering Influence and Corrupt Organizations (RICO) laws. The case was dismissed in 1991 and it took NOW two years to get the case before the Supreme Court. In 1994, after eight years of legal wrangling, the Supreme Court ruled in favor of NOW and permitted the trial to go forward. NOW expanded the complaint to include the perpetrators of clinic violence (such as Paul Hill) and, in 1997, a judge certified NOW as representative of all women and designated the complaint as a class action law suit. Twelve years after filing the suit, the case finally went to trial and NOW won.[23] The jury agreed that the co-defendants were racketeers under RICO and awarded US$ 54,471.28 to Summit Women's Health Organization Inc. and US$ 31,455.64 to Delaware Women's Health Organization Inc. (which tripled under RICO to a total of US$ 257,780.76).[24] Additionally, the judge issued the first nationwide injunction, prohibiting the co-defendants from interfering with clinic services and women's right to obtain them. The nationwide injunction and application of RICO to pro-life threats were eventually overturned by the

19 Unknown. "Reagan's Rhetoric Fuels Anti-Abortion Clinic Terrorists." *National NOW Times*, March/April 1984.

20 Unknown. "Joseph Scheidler: One of the 'New' Breed of Anti-Abortion Fanatics. *National NOW Times*, March/April 1984.

21 National Organization for Women Foundation website.

22 Box 99-M70, Carton 39, Folder: Untitled, RISA; Box 92-M8-92-M96, Carton 5, Folder: DOJ, RIAS.

23 National Organization for Women Foundation website.

24 Lash, Steve. "Supreme Court Corrects 7th Circuit – Twice." *Chicago Daily Law Bulletin*, July 3, 2006.

Supreme Court, which ruled that noneconomic violence was not covered by antitrust laws.

The twenty-year battle exacted costs on the organization. First, it meant that NOW had to constantly mobilize around abortion rights in order to raise support and money for its legal activities. Between 1986 and 1992, NOW organized five national events and campaigns featuring the abortion issue: The National March for Women's Lives on March 16, 1986; the March for Women's Equality/Women's Lives on April 9, 1989; the Freedom Campaign for Women's Lives on November 12, 1989, which included a reproductive caravan that traveled through the United States as well as a reproductive freedom ride in June 1990, where ten women rode their bikes 4,000 miles across the United States; and the We Won't Go Back! March for Women's Lives April 5, 1992. Additionally, in August 1992, NOW President Patricia Ireland and Feminist Majority founder Eleanor Smeal staged an illegal speak-out in front of the White House that resulted in several arrests and media attention.

Second, the focus on clinic violence (as well as the expenditure of resources) restricted the organization's ability to effectively mobilize at the state level and win political battles. This was clear in NOW's failed attempts to thwart the passage of restrictive abortion legislation in several states. Between 1978 and 1986, NOW was defeated in twenty-one of twenty-two statewide anti-abortion referenda.[25] Public relations firms hired to analyze the effectiveness of the organization's campaigns attributed NOW's losses to a reactive "put-out-the-fire" strategy. For instance, C. Montgomery Johnson Associates, one public relations firm offering NOW a retrospective on its campaigns, argued that the organization should have won several state referenda but didn't because the campaign lacked organization, a clear message, and a "pro-active" media strategy.[26]

Third, the focus on clinic violence made it more difficult for the organization to negotiate a changing political environment at the national level. In the early 1990s, policy-making on abortion turned to parental involvement laws. While most American citizens supported some limits on abortion, particularly those involving minors, NOW argued that such restrictions would lead to illegal back-alley abortions and death, particularly because 20 percent of young women get pregnant before the age of eighteen and one in four of these have an abortion.[27] NOW used the case of Becky Bell, who died at the age of seventeen from complications related to an illegal abortion, as an example of the problems caused by parental involvement laws. Becky, NOW argued, was like many young women from good families. She could not bear the thought of disappointing or hurting her parents and, because the state required parental consent, turned to an illegal,

[25] Various Documents, Box 99-M11, Carton 1, Folder: NOW History & General Information 1987–1993, RIAS.

[26] Box 7, Operation Rescue; Box 48; Box 65, Folder: Abortion Funding; Box 67, Folder: State Strategies, RIAS.

[27] Box 99-M11, Carton 1, Folder: NOW Issue Papers, ca 1992–97, RIAS.

back-alley abortion.[28] NOW also launched a "Caravan for Young Women's Lives" in which activists traveled across the country training high school- and college-aged women to organize their peers and confront elected officials regarding abortion restrictions.[29] While these activities were consistent with NOW's efforts to end violence against women, they did not resonate well beyond its membership. As I will discuss in Chapter 6, even like-minded groups such as Planned Parenthood labeled NOW's position as extreme.

NOW's ability to adapt to a changing political environment did not improve after Bill Clinton, a pro-choice ally, took office in 1993. In fact, many pro-choice supporters believed that Clinton's presence in the White House ended the threat to abortion rights, which led to a dramatic decline in support for groups mobilizing around the issue (Warner 1993). Because NOW continued to have so many resources tied up in the legal proceedings against pro-life activists, it could not abandon or significantly reframe its position on the abortion issue. Instead, NOW had to try to broaden its conceptualization of violence against women to fit contemporary events (e.g., the Nicole-Brown Simpson murder and the reinstatement of Mike Tyson discussed earlier in the chapter) and politics. For example, at its 1995 "Rally for Women's Lives," NOW tried to extend its ideas to include the Republican majority in Congress and Newt Gingrich's Contract with America. Ireland argued that the purpose of the rally was to draw "national attention to the links between physical attacks on women, terrorist attacks at clinics, and political and economic attacks in Congress."[30] NOW's action vice president, Rosemary Dempsey, elaborated:

> There is a clear connection between violence against women in all its forms and the oppression of women ... Violence is used as a strategy to keep women in their place – whether it is the harassment that young women face in the schools, the experience and threat of rape that restricts our mobility or the murders and beatings of women by intimate partners that is condoned by the judicial system.[31]

NOW continued to make these links throughout the mid-1990s and worked to buttress its arguments that extremism was alive and well. Some of these efforts focused on keeping violence at clinics and their efforts to end it in the media spotlight (Dilemma 1).[32] In 1995, when Paul Hill received the death penalty for murdering Dr. Bayard Britton and NOW activist Jim Barrett, Ireland noted:

[28] Unknown. "The Tragedy of Parental Involvement Laws." *National NOW Times*, January/February 1990.

[29] Unknown. "NOW Launches Caravan For Young Women's Lives." *National NOW News*, Fall 1990; Thomson, Kristin. "Caravan Gets Out Young Vote." *National NOW News*, Nov/Dec 1990.

[30] Minor, Diane. "Massive NOW Rally 'Only the Beginning.'" *National NOW Times*, May/June 1995.

[31] Corbin, Beth. "Stop Violence Against Women NOW." *National NOW Times*, March 1995.

[32] Because clinic blockades and violence were largely a legal issue by the mid-1990s, there were not additional political actions for which NOW could advocate.

> The most effective way to protect society from the Paul Hills of the world is for the government to investigate and prosecute anti-abortion racketeers as vigorously as they do other organized crime and mob violence ... Until we stop the entire network of anti-abortion terrorists who are threatening our lives, none of us will feel safe.[33]

Likewise, NOW explicitly drew out the religious motivations used to defend extremism. NOW Executive Vice President Kim Gandy noted that John Salvi, who murdered two clinic workers in Massachusetts in 1996, justified his actions by citing his Christian faith and belief that God sanctioned the killing of killers. This Gandy equated with religious terrorism:

> The murders John Salvi committed are not unlike those perpetrated by terrorists around the world – who frequently call on religion to justify their heinous crimes ... We won't give in to terrorism – physical or legislative – and we'll carry our abortion rights work into the November elections and beyond.[34]

NOW's efforts yielded limited media success (Dilemma 1). Recall that Figure 3.5 shows a precipitous decline in NOW's coverage on the abortion issue after 1994. While NOW did get some coverage, leaders often found themselves engaging in debates with the very extremists they opposed. This is an important point. Organizations that have a strong reputation with media professionals also have the ability to decline media opportunities that they perceive as potentially harmful to the group and/or cause. Organizations with weak or declining reputations cannot afford to pick and choose the media opportunities they exploit, which can have public relations consequences. These groups find their organizations are not always cast in a positive light and are even criticized by media professionals.

This problem was exacerbated for NOW, which was forced to contend with an explicit rejection of feminism (Dilemma 3). The backlash against feminism, which moved from the fringes of the evangelical community in the 1970s to the White House by the mid-1980s (Faludi 1991), was embraced by many mainstream media professionals, who proclaimed the "death" of feminism as a new generation identified as "feminine not feminist."[35] NOW was caught in the crossfire of the backlash. For instance, in 1990, Al Neuharth, founder of *USA Today*, declared NOW passé as a result of its support for marginal issues, its "them vs. us" strategies and out-of-touch leadership. NOW, he argued, "helped [women] win a number of important battles. It grew in membership and stature, peaking in 1982. But after it lost the ERA war, the slide began." He concluded that the NOW leaders prefer "publicity-seeking marches to meaningful meetings with government or business leaders," making them irrelevant in the contemporary women's movement.[36]

[33] Velte, Kyle. "Anti-Abortion Terrorist Guilty of Murder." *National NOW Times*, January 1995.
[34] Phillips, Brooke. "Salvi Guilty But Clinics Still Under Fire." *National NOW Times* online, May 1996.
[35] Wallis, Claudia. "Onward, Women!" *Time*, December 1989.
[36] Neuharth, Al. "Why NOW is Passe with Women of Today." *USA Today*, June 22, 1990.

In 1997, a CBS commentator agreed with a critique of NOW's campaign against the Promise Keepers, an evangelical group dedicated to helping men commit to and follow the teachings of Jesus Christ:

Basically NOW thinks Promisekeepers [sic] wants to keep women padlocked to the stove or something, but think about it. Don't most women want their men to be promise keepers, not promise breakers? ... Feminists might find themselves more relevant today if they actually start working with groups like Promisekeepers instead of attacking them. Instead, feminists seem narrowly focused on an agenda of abortion and gay rights, issues that most ordinary women aren't affected by in their daily lives. Unless groups like NOW put their own political agenda in the back seat in the interest of women in the front seat, they're going to continue to see their influence and their credibility deteriorate.[37]

NOW was even publicly criticized by one of its founders, Betty Friedan. Friedan publicly opposed the group's narrow agenda in 1992, arguing that NOW had "become stuck in the quicksand of its early platform and failed to address problems of a new generation of women who are juggling jobs, husbands and children."[38] Some of the media professionals I interviewed (a decade later) still parroted this position, viewing NOW as "out of touch" with contemporary women and, consequently, not a credible source of information on issues such as abortion. An executive producer at NBC Nightly News explained:

I truly don't mean this as a judgmental thing but I'm just speaking as a journalist ... There are a number of women who think that NOW is a little tainted and maybe they wandered away from what they started out to do. A lot of people think feminism needs to change, that they [NOW] are not professional. They [NOW] wouldn't be the place I would go to [for information].[39]

In sum, NOW's reputation with outlets across moderated media declined as a result of its organizational choices and a shift in the broader political environment. NOW engaged in the abortion battle in the 1980s because it needed a new cause after the defeat of the ERA and saw the abortion issue as one that would re-energize its membership and help manage the tension between its organizational identity and public image. While this strategy captured headlines in the short term, NOW quickly found itself mired in a two-decade-long court battle and publicly cast opposite the extremists they opposed. This resource-intensive battle not only made it difficult for NOW to take on new issues, but also circumscribed its ability to challenge a changing political environment that was critical of feminism generally and NOW specifically. NOW, however, continued to try to spread its feminist message. It simply changed how it did so.

[37] Unknown. "NOW Influence Seen As Waning." *The Bulletin's Frontrunner*, July 14, 1997. Also see Coleman, Sandy. "NOW Sees 1998 as Good for Women in Politics." *The Boston Globe*, November 2, 1997.

[38] Gross, Jane. "Does She Speak for Today's Women?" *The New York Times*, March 1, 1992.

[39] Interview with an executive producer at *NBC Nightly News*.

REASSERTING NOW'S PUBLIC IMAGE

While NOW could not easily change the political environment in which it operated, it could try to improve how it was represented in mainstream media (Dilemma 2). The organization largely did so by calling mainstream media professionals to task for "unfair" and "biased" reporting as well as increasingly focusing its resources on direct media efforts. NOW began by identifying the parties responsible for the organization's reputational decline, namely conservatives and the Religious Right, who had successful fabricated a backlash against feminism and NOW. The central goal of the backlash, NOW argued, was to stigmatize feminism, which created a "terrible public relations battle" for the organization. The backlash put NOW on the defensive and forced the group to battle its new (and externally derived) public image as an organization composed of "femi-nazis," "man haters," and "bra burners."

NOW noted that mainstream outlets, which were predominantly owned by conservatives, had intentionally contributed to the smear campaign against feminism. A long-time activist and executive director of a state NOW chapter explained:

> We have had a conglomeration of media [and] it's affected the quality of the media. I've been doing press for twenty years and in the mid 1980s I started to see a rapid decline in our ability to get our stories out. I think [this is] because of commercialism and right wing bias. There are six major media companies and they are definitely right wing.[40]

Similarly, in a 1998 *National NOW Times* article discussing media coverage critical of NOW's response to the Monica Lewinsky scandal, Laura Flanders opined:

> Media pundits are on the anti-feminist warpath. Again. This time, feminists are under attack for their response to Monica Lewinsky. Casting all women's rights advocates as "Clintonites," Maureen Dowd invented a grisly pact that she suggested they had made with the President [Clinton]: "Ms. Lewinsky must die so that women of America can have better child care." ... Laura Ingraham's colleagues at the Independent Women's Forum dubbed NOW the National Organization of Womanizers. On Fox News, Jennifer Grossman of the Cato Institute berated feminists for two contradictory things: on the one hand, for promoting, "victim feminism" and, on the other, for downplaying the president's abuse of an immature "girl." ... It would do us all good for newspaper columnists to use their platforms to launch a serious discussion about the complicated relationships between power and age, and sex. But that's not what the anti-affirmative action, anti-ERA feminists are howling for – they're out for their own political gain.[41]

NOW made an effort to document and respond to misrepresentations of the organization and feminism more generally. For example, NOW took *Time* magazine to task for a 1998 cover story that proclaimed feminism was dead, which

[40] Interview with an executive director of a state NOW chapter.

[41] Flanders, Laura. "The Media Strike Again." *National NOW Times* online, March 1998.

NOW called "mainstream media's latest attempt to shut down (and shut up) the women's rights movement." NOW flooded the outlet with approximately 1,300 pro-feminist letters and hundreds of feminists canceled their subscriptions to the magazine.[42] Additionally, NOW offered *Time* some friendly advice on how to better cover the feminist movement, which included:

1. **Do some research.** If you're going to do an article on feminism, it's a good idea to talk to feminists. *Time* never called the most recognizable feminist organization – the National Organization for Women – or the organization with the subject in its name – the Feminist Majority ...
2. **Show some depth.** One of the strongest criticisms the magazine makes is that feminism has gone Hollywood – "Today it's a whole lot of stylish fluff." (page 56) The tone and substance of *Time*'s coverage of feminism suffer from much the same problem. There's rarely substantive discussion of women's rights or any mention of tangible gains won or battles fought by the feminist movement ...
3. **Show some consistency.** In the cover story entitled "Is Feminism Dead," *Time* reports that "A hefty 50% of those from ages 18 to 34 told the pollster ... that they share 'feminist' values." Yet the entire article implies that the movement lacks support ...[43]

The group created new campaigns that stressed the "mainstreamness" of the organization and its goals to journalists and the larger public (Dilemma 2).[44] In 1999, NOW launched a "Feminist Image Campaign" designed to challenge stereotypes about feminism and reinvigorate the movement. The campaign, which consisted of two television and fifteen print advertisements, provided diverse images of women, including construction workers, CEOs, mothers, daughters, wives, and partners. Ireland suggested that:

> The success of these commercials will help advance feminist issues and candidates, and bring new members into our organization, but that's only the tip of the iceberg ... It will also shape the way women in the movement are viewed by the public. For many years, advertising has been used to sell, degrade and demean women. Now we're using advertising to do just the opposite – to uplift and honor women.[45]

Likewise, NOW stressed that it was a grassroots organization and, therefore, both democratically structured and representative of women from all ages and walks of life. In a letter to NOW members, Ireland notes:

[42] Weinstein, Mira. "NOW Takes On *Time* Magazine." *National NOW Times* online, Fall 1998.
[43] Unknown. "NOW Issues Friendly Advice for *Time* Magazine." *National NOW Times* online, Fall 1998.
[44] Ireland, Patricia. "The State of NOW." *Ms. Magazine*, 1992.
[45] Condon, Hillary. "Feminist Image Campaign." *National NOW Times* online, Fall 1999.

NOW has a very conscious commitment to grassroots democracy in our organization. The national officers are elected and national policy is set by delegates representing chapters at the National Conference. The number of delegates each chapter has is determined by its size. Voting delegates to the National Conference also include state coordinators and national board members who are elected at state and regional conferences at which every NOW member can vote ... This democratic structure helps NOW keep our policies and actions tied to, and reflections of the dominant beliefs of our members. By putting real power in the hands of our chapters' delegates, as they vote in conference, and in our elected officers and board members, we keep our tie to the grassroots people who spawned NOW and distinguish NOW from the many Washington-based lobby groups who have no grassroots. The process may at times be vexing; democracy can indeed be a cumbersome process. However, it ensures that those of you who have joined NOW will have a real voice in the direction of your National Organization for Women.[46]

NOW also changed how it targeted journalists. It relied less on e-mails and more on building relationships with journalists – as it did in its early years. In an interview, the press secretary for NOW noted that a good personal relationship with a journalist "pulls a different weight for us and it shows in the media packages and articles."[47]

Finally, NOW spent more time and energy developing its own materials and outlets so that it could target potential supporters directly (Dilemma 1). In 1999, NOW created its first brochure for "Spanish-speaking activists and prospective members" titled "Juntas Podemos Cambiar El Mundo," or "Together We Can Change the World." The brochure highlighted "NOW's accomplishments, real-life situations that women experience, quotes from feminist activists, a call to get involved and a membership application."[48] NOW also became more reliant on its website (which it developed in 1996) as a way to speak directly to the public without the "filtering" of "pundit commentary."[49] The organization increasingly saw media opportunities not as a way to get good coverage, but as a way to introduce the audience to NOW and to entice the audience to visit their website. Because journalists often include websites in the online versions of their stories, even critical coverage could stimulate interest in a campaign and foot traffic to a website. Discussing its campaign against the Promise Keepers, NOW's Internet and LAN Manager noted:

Over 35,000 visitors looked at our Promise Keepers page, not including users on services such as American Online or CompuServe, who look at local copies of the NOW pages, leaving their visits unrecorded. Sometimes those visitors were referred to our page from the web pages of well-known media sources. Over 4,100 visitors came to NOW from the CNN site, 1,400 came from the MSNBC site, and 800 came from the *Washington Post* web

[46] Ireland, Patricia. "The Future is NOW." *National NOW Times* online, May 1995.
[47] Interview with a press secretary for NOW.
[48] Unknown. "NOW Seeks to Attract More Spanish-Speaking Members with New Publication." *National NOW Times* online, Winter 1999.
[49] Stapleton-Gray, Sarah. "CyberNOW." *National NOW Times* online, January 1998.

site. Even the online magazine Slate, while critical of NOW's position on the Promise Keepers, referred their readers to our web page so that they could – and 500 did – read our materials. Thousands more reached our page from the popular Yahoo site's Promise Keepers page.[50]

In short, although NOW ascribed blame for its declining reputation to conservatives and the Religious Right, it made efforts to improve its public image and to find other ways to reach audiences. NOW relied less on moderated news media coverage and invested its resources in direct media projects such as advertising campaigns, pamphlets, and websites. At the same time, however, the organization articulated suspicion regarding mainstream media and their motivations as they related to covering the feminist movement and women's issues. While its efforts to build relationships with media professionals likely helped the organization get better coverage in some instances, it also set a new tone for how the organization viewed mainstream media – as antagonistic to the organization and its goals – and narrowed the range of media professionals with which it would work.

CONCLUSION

Organizational reputation matters. A group with a strong reputation among moderated outlets has more and better media opportunities than an organization with a weak one has. An organization's reputation, however, is not set in stone; it can change over time and change is not always for the better. At least three related factors can diminish (or potentially improve) an organization's reputation. First, the composition of the social movement can affect the ability of an organization to improve its reputation. When a movement is crowded with professional, mainstream organizations, a group that falls out of favor may find it difficult to reestablish itself with media professionals, who evaluate a group relative to its allies. From its inception, NOW regarded mainstream media as critical to its goals and tried to coordinate its messages across its chapters. This strategy worked well until the 1980s, when NOW had to refocus its efforts in the wake of its failed ERA campaign. NOW tried to reestablish itself as a player in abortion politics, but received a lukewarm reception from media professionals, who did not regard the organization as entrenched in (and knowledgeable of) the issue.

Second, a group's decisions regarding campaigns and tactics can affect its reputation. If an organization with a strong reputation stays on the tactical straight and narrow, it will be well positioned to maintain its credibility with media professionals and get favorable media attention. A group that strays from institutional politics to more confrontational tactics, however, is likely to see a decline in its reputation. This was true for NOW, which engaged the more

[50] Stapleton-Gray, Sarah. "CyberNOW." *National NOW Times* online, January 1998.

radical branches of the pro-life movement on the streets when its allies did not.[51] NOW had excellent reasons for engaging its enemies outside clinics. After the ERA loss and the lackluster support for its emphasis on electoral politics, NOW was hemorrhaging members and deeply in debt. The direct action campaign fit with its strategy of principled pragmatism and promised to reinvigorate the organization with money and members. While the gamble paid off in the short term, NOW found itself featured in coverage with its radical enemies. Even after the protracted battle moved to the courtroom, NOW was unable to untangle its activities or image from this larger battle and unable to make up its reputational ground.

Finally, the broader political climate can make it difficult for an organization to reestablish its reputation. Culture is not static and, consequently, ideas that were previously embraced may be challenged. This was true of feminism. The backlash against feminism dramatically altered the environment in which NOW operated. As "feminism" became a dirty word, organizations such as NOW were deemed to have little relevance and its leaders were seen as disaffected militants with no army to lead. In this climate, NOW's campaign against violence and verbal battles with extremists fed stereotypes about feminists and the organizations representing them. When NOW was finally in a position to fight back, it was more cynical about the prospects of using mainstream media to forward its goals and make feminist issues "part of public opinion." While NOW did not give up on the mainstream entirely, it decided that using direct media would be a useful course of action.

When an organization's reputation in the media field changes, its responses to media dilemmas change as well (the strategic choices are summarized in Table 5.1). First, it changes how a group engages mass media (Dilemma 1). Options that are available to an organization may disappear as its reputation declines. Early in its career, NOW successfully relied on mainstream media to disseminate its ideas to a broader audience. However, as mainstream media professionals became "hostile" to feminism, NOW targeted its efforts and relied more heavily on direct media efforts. Second, a reputational decline affects how a group responds to negative media attention (Dilemma 2). As I discuss in the next chapter, groups with a strong reputation are sometimes inclined to ignore negative coverage in order to protect their public image. However, most organizations are not in this position and find ways to respond to negative attention. This was true of NOW, which directly responded to negative coverage of the organization and women's movement. NOW, however, did not just systematize its response to coverage, but also changed how it regarded mainstream media attention. Instead of treating coverage as an end goal, it increasingly saw mainstream media attention as a way to get an audience to visit its website and learn more about NOW's issues and campaigns.

51 Groups such as Planned Parenthood eventually engaged in clinic defense, but it was not until the late 1990s and was an explicit attempt to get young women to support the organization.

TABLE 5.1. *Summary of NOW's strategic choices*

Organizational Identity	Feminist
Framing the Abortion Issue	Liberal feminist framework
Public Image	Mainstream, feminist organization
Reputation in the Media Field	Starts strong, but weakens over time
Dilemma 1: Access External Media?	
Perception of Mainstream Outlets	Initially saw mainstream as a tool to help them forward their political goals. Over time, increasingly saw mainstream media as a tool of conservatives that uncritically attacked feminists and feminism.
Example	Yes, radical pro-lifers, including Operation Rescue, provided an opportunity for NOW to reinvigorate the organization during a time of financial crisis.
Dilemma 2: Respond to Negative Attention?	
Example	Yes, to criticize media's attack on feminism and feminists.
Dilemma 3: Weigh in on Losing Issues?	
Examples	Yes, to get media attention. Yes, to encourage the broader public to visit its website and learn more about the organization.
Tradeoffs	
	Status as a mainstream group for organizational survival Bad press for a chance to reach a broader audience Resources for a chance to reach new member through direct media

Finally, reputational decline shapes how a group responds to losing issues (Dilemma 3). As I illustrate in the next chapter, organizations with a strong reputation can remain silent on losing issues and decline media opportunities that they fear will depict them in a negative light. An organization with a weaker reputation cannot afford to employ either approach. Likewise, a group with a relatively weak reputation may find that it is inextricably entwined with losing ideas, in which case there is little that can be done other than try to keep framing the issue in ways that will capture attention and, hopefully, generate support. NOW struggled with losing issues. For example, despite their popularity with the general public, NOW spoke out against parental involvement laws and found itself lambasted in the media (and by its allies).

With the twenty-year court case behind them and no clear victory, NOW is poised to reinvent the organization again. While the organization clearly continues to push controversial issues such as same-sex marriage, it has also adopted causes that appeal to a broad swath of the American public. Paid parental leave and accessible childcare are good examples. Although both have long been on the radar of NOW, they only recently have been brought to the forefront of the organization's activities. In part, this move is an attempt to create new images of feminism for the twenty-first century. Feminism continues to raise the hackles of some, and focusing on fundamental family struggles can counter claims that NOW is out of touch with the mainstream. While arguably these struggles are more pressing to women, who are disproportionately left with childcare responsibilities, affordable childcare, paid family leave, and flexible work, provide an set of issues around which NOW can mobilize and combat stereotypes regarding feminism and the organization's feminist agenda. This will not be easy. NOW has a new set of savvy competitors, such as Momsrising.org, which does not have to contend with the baggage of the feminist label and has the ear of the Democratic White House. Nonetheless, there are fewer competitors around these issues and, consequently, NOW has a fighting chance.

6

Branding and the success of Planned Parenthood Federation of America

Not all movement actors have the same advantages with moderated media. Organizational dynamics affect reputation and how a group navigates the media field. A well-funded, well-staffed organization can write a letter to the editor, craft and post an op-ed, contact mainstream journalists and writers working in sympathetic outlets, and create an advertising campaign at the same time. Likewise, groups with substantial financial resources can afford to invest in market research to refine movement messages as well as purchase professional campaign materials and advice. This is not a small advantage. While most groups rely primarily on "earned" coverage, activists recognize the value of speaking directly to an audience without distortion or distraction, particularly when they want to reframe a debate. It was not a coincidence that NRLC used direct media to launch its campaign to end partial-birth abortion. Paid advertising allowed NRLC to introduce a new way to think about the abortion procedure without the interference of its opponents.

Financially flush organizations can also spend more time and money framing themselves in ways that resonate with the general public. A well-to-do organization can finely tune a public image so that it appeals to a broad cross section of the citizenry and, then, use its mainstream appeal to build its credibility with journalists. I am not suggesting that there is a particular financial threshold that organizations must cross in order to be effective in the mass media field. As seen in the NRLC case, an organization can set itself apart from its allies on a relatively small budget if it draws on culturally resonant values and institutional credibility. I am arguing that a resource-rich organization can craft a brand for the group that can be leveraged across institutional fields and issues.

A brand establishes a connection between an organization and its target audience (Aaker 1991). Successful brands not only have a distinctive name and symbol, but also form an emotional bond and a lasting commitment with targets (Smith 2009). One way in which corporations can create brands that appeal to the heart is by exhibiting characteristics that are desirable to the target audience. For example, the Department of Public Health in Wisconsin launched an anti-smoking campaign for teenagers using the theme "Be Free." The successful campaign played on teen rebellion by positioning cigarette companies as another form of adult domination. By not smoking, teens were exercising their independence from authoritative controls (Aaker 1991). Brand is different from public image because it elicits emotions in and creates experiences for individuals that extend beyond the use of a product (Smith 2009) – or, in this case, movement organization.

Organizations that successfully generate "distinctive patterns of associations and meanings that make the brand more attractive" (Feldwick 2009: 140) build "brand equity," which can make the difference between life and death in a crowded marketplace (Blackett 2009; Brymer 2009). Corporations that build brand equity share three key characteristics. First, the companies regard branding as a long-term investment. Second, corporations make a substantive commitment to maintaining a brand. This extends beyond the sizable financial investment necessary to refine and promote the brand. Successful companies "embody the brand" (Brymer 2009, 74), or make brand position, purpose, and values central to their decision-making. Finally, corporations actively promote their brand and ensure that all of their public relations efforts reinforce their identity (Feldwick 2009). Public relations, in short, is more than making statements and issuing press releases. It is a strategic attempt to shape how the public perceives a company (Bowker 2009).

Although brands are typically associated with the corporate world, they increasingly are important in a "social movement society" (Meyer and Tarrow 1997) where activist groups vie for attention. Organizations that have the time, money, and wherewithal to craft and maintain a brand may reap big advantages. With brand equity comes a boost in reputation (Blackett 2009), which, like corporations, movement groups can leverage in their efforts to change debates. A group with a successful brand, for instance, can deflect controversy and shape political processes largely outside the view of the public.

Branding has at least two related benefits for a movement organization. First, it gives a group a reputational boost in the mass media field, which leads to more and better media opportunities. Recall in the previous chapter I argued that the strength of an organization's reputation is, in part, a function of how a group ranks relative to its allies. A brand can help an organization stand apart from its allies and elicit emotions and connections that transcend issue politics. An organization may highlight its tradition, place in history, or commitment to a general cause as a way of distinguishing itself from its allies and building brand equity. A generally positive association of a group in broader culture influences journalistic evaluations of an organization and boosts the group's reputation, sometimes positioning it as a superior source of information relative to its allies.

Having a brand does not mean a group is always effective at getting media attention, let alone capturing the hearts and minds of the broader public.

Organizational identity tempers how a group can sell itself to the broader public and constrains the effectiveness of its brand. This is one reason why a group such as People for the Ethical Treatment of Animals (PETA), an animal rights organization, is met with public resistance – it uses extrainstitutional means to transform how humans regard animals (not as food). Organizational identity also explains why PETA relies so heavily on celebrity endorsements, which can evoke positive associations and help an organization build its brand equity (Till 1998) in its efforts to promote itself and its cause. Not all brands are created equal, but organizations that can brand themselves effectively will be well positioned to influence public debate and policy.

Second, an effective brand can change how a group frames its issues. While a group's choice of frames is constrained by its identity, brands are flexible insofar as they embody "indelible impressions" (Blackett 2009) that an organization can elicit for its own purposes. More importantly, an organization can elicit these impressions in different ways. An activist group can use its brand to deflect criticism and even avoid unpleasant debates by focusing attention on emotions and ideas rather than the issue at hand. Of course, a movement group, like a corporation, will feel compelled to protect its brand. An organization with a brand primarily will champion carefully crafted ideas that test well in market research so that it can maintain its brand equity. If the debate becomes too rancorous, an organization may try to ignore its allies and opponents and reframe a debate in a way that is more palatable to a mainstream audience or opt out of the debate altogether.

While having the ability to cash in brand equity makes getting and using media coverage easier (Dilemma 1), it does not mean an organization is immune to organizational strife, a changing political environment, or media dilemmas. As seen in Chapter 4, an organization cannot control what its allies do or say and sometimes finds itself struggling to clean up a public relations mess not of its own making. Similarly, having a successful brand will offer a group limited protection from opponents, who will likely make concerted efforts to tarnish its brand (Dilemma 2), or elite opponents and allies, who may set a political course that a movement organization does not wish to follow (Dilemma 3). Branding does not make media dilemmas disappear. It simply changes the organizational calculus regarding how to respond. Protecting the brand will top the organization's to-do list and influence how it responds to media dilemmas.

This chapter examines how Planned Parenthood Federation of America (PPFA) crafted a brand that it could use to navigate a changing political environment and public debate on abortion. Unlike the other groups included in the study, PPFA's practices and funding levels are affected by legislation. In an effort to effectively shape a range of reproductive policy issues (including issues of funding), PPFA crafted a brand that avoids laying a claim to any one reproductive issue and focuses on family planning more generally. The family planning brand is a successful one insofar as it gives the organization flexibility in terms of when and how it publicly weighs in on the abortion debate. I illustrate the strategic utility of this brand through an examination of the debate over parental involvement laws. However, using a brand alone to navigate the media arena has limitations; a lesson that PPFA learned after Bill Clinton, a pro-choice supporter, was elected to office. While Clinton upheld his campaign promises insofar as he rescinded existing restrictions and supported pro-choice legislation, passing universal health care legislation was his political priority. Consequently, legal abortion was reframed in terms of accessibility and whether a universal health care system would include access to the abortion procedure. Although all pro-choice organizations struggled to find a foothold in this new, less hostile, political world, the shift in the debate rocked PPFA to its organizational core. If universal health care passed, how (and what) clinics were funded would change dramatically; if PPFA wanted to survive, it too would have to change. There was no internal consensus regarding how the organization would fit in this new environment. Internal disputes became public as some affiliates and the national leadership battled over the public face and fate of PPFA.

THE PPFA BRAND AND THE ABORTION ISSUE

PPFA was founded in 1942 after a long and contentious battle within the birth control movement. Margaret Sanger, a prominent leader in the movement, helped merge two competing birth control organizations, The Birth Control Clinic Research Bureau and the American Birth Control League, after a decade of internal strife. The newly formed Birth Control Federation of America was quickly renamed Planned Parenthood of America after one of its leaders, Kenneth Rose, successfully campaigned for the change. He argued that birth control was too much of a "fighting word" and advocated that the organization adopt a less controversial name, a position that was overwhelming supported by its membership (Chesler 1992). Given its history, it is not surprising that PPFA has interests beyond the abortion issue. PPFA focuses on reproductive issues broadly and, according to its mission statement, "believes in the fundamental right of each individual, throughout the world, to manage his or her fertility, regardless of the individual's income, marital status, race, ethnicity, sexual orientation, age, national origin, or residence … [PPFA believes that] reproductive self-determination must be voluntary and preserve the individual's right to privacy" (www.ppfa.org).

PPFA has two organizational foci. First, it provides services through its affiliates, which are located throughout the United States. Second, it advocates for public policy that recognizes and protects women's reproductive decision-making. PPFA has a fairly complicated organizational structure. It is controlled by a board of directors and consists of regional assembles, state-level public affair offices, and a number of committees that report to the national board. PPFA affiliates are separately incorporated and governed by their own board of directors, meaning that while national PPFA supports its affiliates, it does not dictate policy, positions, or actions to local leadership. PPFA also has a developed communication department, which consists of media relations, communications, and media production. Essentially, PPFA has a well-oiled media machine that is staffed with professionals who contact media and field questions, generate publicity for the organization, monitor the coverage the group receives, and develop media campaigns and materials.

As a provider of reproductive services and a political organization, PPFA is uniquely situated in the abortion debate. Because PPFA is directly affected by policy shifts on reproductive issues the organization is well positioned to provide journalists a distinct perspective on reproductive rights – one that involves political activism, medical research, and clinical experience.[1] This unique position is something that PPFA tries to use to its advantage, particularly when it is involved in controversial issues such as abortion. This was not always the case. Before 1980, PPFA focused on advancing its political goals, paying little attention to its public image or to the role of mass media in organizational success. PPFA discovered that smaller and less politically active pro-choice groups were attracting members and generating income via media attention. In a 1981 letter, the vice president of communications informed PPFA affiliates that the organization needed a "universal" public image soon "because continued support no longer depends on group size alone; it depends on group visibility! In fact, many groups today, much smaller than Planned Parenthood, are receiving as much if not more support simply because they appear stronger and better organized."[2] Organizational leaders quickly decided that PPFA needed a "brand" that could be used to cultivate its membership and public support (Dilemma 1).

Developing PPFA's brand as a family planning organization was an obvious choice for two reasons. First, it connected the organization to a legacy of change as it relates to family planning and reproductive health care policy – a successful strategy that allows organizations to "return to their roots" and recapture lost sources of brand equity (Feldwick 2009; Keller 1999). Margaret Sanger championed the family planning framework in the early 1900s. She believed that if women were to be on a more "equal footing" with men, they needed to be able to control when (and how many) children they would bear (Lader 1955; Sanger 1938). However, information regarding family planning was difficult for women to obtain because the Comstock Law of 1873 made it a crime to distribute contraceptive information and devices via mail and doctors generally would only discuss abstinence with their patients. In a campaign spanning nearly five decades, Sanger challenged laws limiting women's access to contraception and revolutionized family planning in the United States (Chesler 1992; Lader 1955). Developing a brand around family planning enabled PPFA to highlight an important historical figure, Sanger, and its long record of political involvement and success in reproductive policy.

[1] The organization has a long history of funding research on reproductive issues.

[2] Letter, November 1981, Sophia Smith Collection (SSC), Smith College Archives. Accession 90S-33, Box 4.

Second, the family planning brand was politically effective. The family planning framework allowed PPFA to advocate on behalf of a range of reproductive issues without letting any single cause define the organization. This flexibility made it easier for PPFA to advocate on behalf of a variety of issues – even controversial ones – as elites (and their agendas) changed. For instance, Alan Guttmacher, PPFA's president from 1962 to 1973, used the "family planning" framework to fit population control and legalized abortion into President Lyndon B. Johnson's War on Poverty. Johnson, who was promoting his "Great Society," embraced the family planning framework because it allowed him to publicly discuss poverty without focusing on the inequalities at its root or mentioning population control, which had the potential to alienate Roman Catholic and African-American voters (Critchlow 1999). In testimony given to the Senate, Guttmacher argued that legal abortion was an essential component of family planning because contraceptive devices are not 100 percent effective. He pointed out that illegal abortion had become a "pandemic disease of the first magnitude" among poor women and suggested that if politicians wanted to diminish poverty, safe and legal abortions were necessary to do so.[3]

Family planning also had political cache during Richard Nixon's administration. The best-selling book *Population Bomb* (1968), which warned that overpopulation would lead to mass starvation and political upheaval, mobilized a zero population growth movement in the United States. Nixon legitimized movement concerns calling population growth "one of the most serious challenges to human destiny in the last third of this century" (Hoff 2010, 25) and made solving the "population growth problem" a priority. Family planning, Nixon argued, was one way for the government to curb overpopulation, control welfare dependency, and minimize urbanization and environmental pollution (Critchlow 1999). PPFA viewed this as an opportunity to advocate on behalf of legal abortion. PPFA leaders suggested that legal abortion was a critical tool in the war on poverty because it (along with access to contraceptive devices) would increase the odds of a family being able to adequately care for that child. Likewise, PPFA argued that legal abortion would eliminate the numerous social and health problems created by unsafe back-alley abortions (Ziegler 2009).

Developing its brand represented a strategic effort to maximize PPFA's flexibility in the political and media fields in terms of when and how it weighed in on controversial issues (Dilemmas 2 and 3). Leaders believed that if the public regarded PPFA as a "long respected, responsible service organization," it would have unrivaled credibility and more influence over how politicians and media professionals framed the abortion debate. For example, in a memo to affiliates describing the group's first "Images and Issues Campaign,"Faye Wattleton, PPFA's president, explained:

[3] Unknown. "Washington News." *Journal of the American Medical Association* online, August 23, 1965.

In developing that image, we pave the way for public acceptance for our positions on the more hard-hitting reproductive freedom issues. We create a climate of credibility so that when we speak out on rights to legal abortion or on rights to sexuality education or on the need to maintain adequate levels of government funding for family planning, we will be listened to.[4]

In order to construct this brand, organizational leaders moved away from advertising, or simply getting coverage for the organization, to "social marketing," which defines target audiences and "packages" PPFA relative to these "targets."[5] PPFA makes distinctions among the formats available to carry organizational messages – newsletters, paid advertisements, public service announcements, and "earned" media coverage on television and in the newspaper – and uses each to target a specific audience.[6] As a result, the messages on abortion vary according to the target. In organizational newsletters, PPFA's support for unregulated legal abortion is much clearer than it is in advertisements placed in *The New York Times* because leaders assume its members support legalized abortion. Creating a brand for the organization allowed PPFA to market itself broadly while, at the same time, tailoring messages that would appeal to different kinds of targets.

The initial goal of PPFA was to get media attention for the organization so that it could "sell" the brand to journalists and the public (Dilemma 1). At the center of PPFA's media strategy was Faye Wattleton, the organization's president from 1978 to 1992. Wattleton, who spent her early career working as a nurse, capitalized on her medical expertise and her status as the first African-American and youngest female head of the organization to attract media attention to the organization (Wattleton 1996). This was a successful tactic indeed. Journalists responded to her powerful presence, and PPFA quickly learned that Wattleton's public appearances had a "snowballing effect," bringing more media attention to the group.[7] By 1982, just a year after it embraced a social marketing approach, PPFA expanded its media department and trained new spokespeople to keep up with the influx of media requests.

Since the late 1980s, PPFA has had little difficulty getting its ideas in mainstream media. PPFA considers "earned" coverage the "bread and butter" of its media strategy and has little difficulty "spinning" coverage in ways that made the abortion issue more palatable to a mainstream audience.[8] The senior press officer attributes the organization's success to its highly coordinated media efforts. She notes:

We [PPFA] do a non-stop flow of earned media activity, which includes announcing what the affiliates are doing, what services and programs they are adding as well as what

[4] Memo, Faye Wattleton, President, November 18, 1981, SSC, Accession 90S-33, Box 4.

[5] Gould, Douglas. "National Marketing Strategy Planned." *The Insider*, 1987. Katherine Dexter McCormick Library (KDML).

[6] Various documents, SSC, Accession 91S-23, Box 1; Accession 93S-7, 94S-27.

[7] PPFA's coffers also swelled during Wattleton's tenure, growing from 90 to 384 million dollars.

[8] Interview with a PPFA Senior Press Officer; SSC, mailings, reports, memos, public service announcements, Accession 90S-33, Box 1.

position we are taking at the federal level on issues. Where ever you look, we are putting information out in the form of press releases, public service announcement campaigns, . . . and [making] personal contacts [with journalists].[9]

The success of the PPFA brand is evident in the organization's strong reputation in the mass media field. Media professionals (even those working in conservative outlets) always cited PPFA as an established authority on the abortion issue and looked to PPFA for an assessment on reproductive issues. A reporter at *The New York Times* noted:

They are the people who know the issues; they have followed it for a very long time. They have very focused lobbying [and] they follow the legislative aspect, they follow the legal aspect [and they follow] political campaigns when it's presidential season.[10]

An executive producer at NBC agreed:

Planned Parenthood would rise to the top [of the list of credible sources on the abortion issue]. Those would be the kind of folks [that we contact for information and quotes] because . . . they do a lot of distribution of literature and that kind of thing and they are also involved in clinics . . . They are plugged into the issue.[11]

Getting media attention and shaping the debate, in short, is not a problem for PPFA.

Its success has not gone unnoticed by opponents. NRLC tried to duplicate aspects of PPFA's strategy for its own purposes.[12] In 1985, NRLC hired Kay James, a young, attractive, African-American woman, specifically to combat the "pro-abortion" rhetoric of Wattleton. While the tactic worked insofar as it challenged stereotypes regarding the gender and racial makeup of the movement, pro-choice leaders, including Wattleton, refused to debate James on several occasions. For instance, Wattleton, who pulled out of a debate at the last minute on *The Today Show* in 1986, told the program coordinator that James "was not on her level – that she would only debate heads of organizations." The NRLC public relations director offered a different interpretation of Wattleton's move:

Faye Wattleton has gotten a lot of mileage out of portraying the Pro-Life Movement as comprised of nothing but white males. To go one-on-one with Mrs. James, who, like Wattleton, is an articulate black spokesperson would only serve to tear down the misleading stereotypes and force Wattleton to debate the issue – abortion.[13]

[9] Interview with a senior press officer at PPFA.
[10] Interview with a reporter at *The New York Times*.
[11] Interview with an executive producer at *NBC Nightly News*.
[12] A spy at the 1986 NRLC convention noted that the NRLC leadership expressed great admiration for PPFA's structure and successes (Memo, Douglas Gould, July 29, 1986, SSC, Accession 93S-9, Box 1).
[13] Andrusko, Dave. "Pro-Abortionists Take Pains to Avoid Debating Kay James." *NRTL News*, June 2, 1988. A spy at the 1986 NRLC convention reported that James asked the "ever present Planned Parenthood spy" to remind Wattleton that she would debate her any time, any place.

Wattleton's withdrawal from the debate should not simply be understood in didactic terms. It is just as likely that PPFA decided that having Wattleton debate James on one issue – abortion – might negatively affect its family planning brand.[14] Given the time and money the organization invested in promoting its brand, it is unlikely that leaders would engage in any media appearances that might put their efforts at risk.

Indeed, the brand quickly became one of the most important tools available in the organization's arsenal. PPFA found that its brand gave it political and media clout *and* allowed the group to support controversial issues without being defined by them. However, it was costly to maintain. PPFA found it had to keep the pulse of the "mainstream" so that the organization did not advocate positions that appear out of step with public opinion. Beginning in the mid-1980s, the organization began conducting an annual poll to determine the public's current attitudes on a wide range of reproductive issues and assess how it should situate itself in political debates. In a memo to the PPFA board of directors and affiliate leaders, Douglas Gould, the vice president of communications, noted that "This information will be essential to our planning a strategy for the careful protection of Planned Parenthood's image and the successful advancing of its position in a variety of issues."[15]

PPFA's decision to craft a brand for the organization is significant for two other reasons as well. First, PPFA's desire to protect its brand influenced whether and how it publicly weighed in on political debates over abortion (Dilemma 1). PPFA often worked behind the scenes to get good coverage for the issue rather than itself. After the *Casey* ruling, PPFA directed CBS to a story that ultimately aired as a feature piece about the "overground railroad," which transported women seeking abortions from one state to another, and ABC to a "friendly" doctor, who discussed the medical implications of the Supreme Court ruling.[16] Second, it made brand maintenance a critical function of the group. Because brands must be infused with meaning on a regular basis, PPFA had to find ways to reinforce its family planning image. Revisiting the past (Keller 1999) – in this case reminding the public of Sanger's role in the family planning movement – became the primary way PPFA maintained its brand. Leaders, for example, crafted a campaign that celebrated PPFA's "Tradition of Choice for 75 Years." The purpose of the campaign was to underscore the "PPFA story," highlight the group's role as a leader in the family planning movement, and increase public support for the organization by reinforcing the brand. In order to do so, PPFA targeted ten major media markets and crafted "media-genic" events that emphasized the

James went on to accuse Wattleton of avoiding such a debate (Memo, Douglas Gould, July 29, 1986, SSC, Accession 93S-9, Box 1).

[14] I did not find any references to this event in the PPFA archives.

[15] Letter, Douglas Gould, August 30, 1985, SSC, Accession 89S-57, Box 5.

[16] Memos and mailings, SSC, Accession 96S-26 Box 6, 1981, 1991–1996.

organization's history.[17] Additionally, PPFA paid for six op-ed pieces to circulate in national print outlets and created several public service announcements that featured celebrities discussing their experiences with PPFA as well as the organization's positive contributions to communities across the country.[18]

Maintaining a brand is not easy to do. A group's brand can become a target of opponents, who seek to replace positive associations with ones that are less flattering (Dilemma 2). PPFA has periodically faced these challenges. The most sustained effort has been by American Life League, which helped found Stop Planned Parenthood (STOPP) in 1994. According to the group's website, "The purpose of STOPP is simple. We intend to cause such discontent with Planned Parenthood's programs that it will have no choice but to close its doors and leave town!"[19] STOPP primarily accuses Sanger and PPFA leaders of promoting a "humanist" agenda. Consequently, it fights the organization by spreading the word of God. According to STOPP's website:

> The basis for fighting Planned Parenthood follows the realization that Planned Parenthood supports ideas, philosophies and actions that are completely opposed to the Ten Commandments given to us by God. If people would live their lives according to those Commandments, Planned Parenthood could not exist. Thus, a large part of our work is to spread the word of God in our communities.[20]

Given the religious nature of their arguments and actions, these criticisms rarely surface in mainstream media. PPFA, however, is aware of their opponent's criticism and is careful to downplay some of Sanger's more controversial strategic choices (e.g., her vocal support of eugenics). The point here is that concerns over brand equity drove PPFA's decision-making and influenced how it responded to media dilemmas.

REFRAMING THE DEBATE OF PARENTAL RIGHTS

The battle over abortion was not just political, but also a fight over how the issue would be framed for a broader public. As previously discussed, pro-choicers initially had the discursive advantage because the *Roe* and *Doe* decisions framed abortion in terms of women's rights. Pro-life groups, however, have found ways to frame abortion restrictions within this dominant discourse (e.g., discussing the rights of taxpayers) while steadily chipping away at the availability of the procedure. The emphasis on government monies and what procedures taxpayers should (and should not) be required to pay for posed a challenge for PPFA in the 1980s because, as a government-funded entity, it was affected directly by Reagan's pro-life policies. The "squeal rule," "gag rule" and "Mexico City Policy," for instance, all directly affected the funding and

[17] Summary of Strategy and Objectives, SSC, Accession 91S-19, Box 1.
[18] Advertising Campaign, SSC, Accession 91S-19, Box 1.
[19] American Life League's STOPP website.
[20] STOPP website.

operations of PPFA.[21] Its clinics also were affected by state laws regulating abortion. As the previous chapters makes clear, pro-lifers challenged the idea that a woman always had a right to privacy when it came to making medical choices. Pro-life groups introduced a number of parental involvement laws, reasoning that parents had a right to be involved in a minor's decision to have an abortion. This argument had political legs and a great deal of public support. The focus on parental rights put pro-choicers in an awkward position rhetorically. Groups either had to defend all women's right to a legal abortion regardless of age or circumstance or find a way to skirt the parental involvement issue; and there was no consensus within the movement regarding how opposition to parental involvement laws should be framed (Dilemma 3).

NOW opposed the restrictions in no uncertain terms and maintained that all women had a right to obtain an abortion without exception. PPFA activists also disagreed with these restrictions, believing that these laws would push teens into riskier late-term procedures. The arguments made by PPFA leaders were no less passionate than those by NOW, just less public. In an impassioned memo to the affiliate board presidents and executive directors, Kenneth C. Edelin, M.D., supported breaking parental consent and notification laws. He wrote:

> *We must not yield in our unequivocal defense of the right of minors to confidential family planning and abortion services.* Some among us, having measured onerous restrictions against the tenets that guide our actions, may well choose another path – that of following unyieldingly our efforts to ensure unrestricted access to confidential services, even in violation of untenable laws. The PPFA board strongly supports and commends those whose actions, motivated by conscience in concert with our policies, follow this route. As part of its examination of this issue, the board hopes to find ways in which this moral support will be translated into more tangible assistance [emphasis is original].[22]

This rhetoric was only circulated internally because PPFA recognized that parental involvement laws had broad support and were a "losing issue" that could damage the organization's brand and legitimacy.

Externally, PPFA focused on the fact that the government was intruding on individual decision-making. In a confidential memo dated November 1989, Doug Gould, the vice president of communications, outlined the arguments that activists should use in the debates over minors and abortion access:

[21] The "squeal rule" required Title X-funded clinics to notify parents when teens were issued prescription contraceptives. PPFA and other family planning organizations successfully challenged the rule, and it was overturned in 1982. The "Mexico City Policy" denied funds to overseas groups, including PPFA and its sister organization International Planned Parenthood Federation (IPPF), that used any of their funding for abortion services, counseling, or referrals. PPFA and IPPF refused to comply with the restrictions and lost their funding from the U.S. government, which they challenged in court throughout the 1980s. The "gag rule," which prohibited personnel working in Title X-funded clinics from discussing abortion with clients, was implemented by the Department of Health and Human Services in Fall 1987. PPFA challenged the rule in court, but it was ultimately upheld by the Supreme Court in the 1991 *Rust v. Sullivan* decision.

[22] Memo, Kenneth C. Edelin, September 14, 1990, SSC, Accession 91S-19, Box 1.

The minors cases present us with a much trickier communications challenge ... We must reframe it ... Our confidential Harris poll sent to you in September of 1988 shows that there are messages that enlist public support. Use these exact words when talking about minors cases: [1] If teenagers feel that they can't talk to their parents, another adult should be able to give them help or advice (94%). [2] The government should not interfere with a private issue like teenage abortion (61%) ... [3] The real issue has nothing to do with teens – it has to do with chipping away at American families' rights to make these most private choices about abortion without government interference.[23]

PPFA brought to the forefront the "government interference" argument after the Supreme Court ruled that parental involvement laws did not constitute an undue burden on a woman's right to an abortion. The 1989 *Webster* decision, PPFA argued, proved that the government was willing to meddle in individual decision-making and leaders were sure that this argument would generate support for the organization. Gould advised:

Fortunately, the *Webster* decision last summer allows us to focus on whether abortion will remain a woman's private decision or whether the government will interfere. Planned Parenthood spokespersons must adopt a constant refrain when answering questions about clinic standards and teen access: but the real issue is whether politicians will decide when and whether women will have a child or whether women, in consultation with their physicians, can make this decision without government interference.[24]

This frame provided PPFA a way to oppose parental involvement laws without discussing parental rights directly. PPFA highlighted the consequences of government interference in an advertising campaign featuring an Indiana couple, Karen and Bill Bell. The centerpiece of the campaign was an emotional documentary outlining the high costs of government interference on happy families with responsible kids. The film presented the circumstances of Becky's death and indicted Indiana law, which required Becky to either tell her parents she was pregnant or go to court for permission to have an abortion.[25]

The government interference frame also helped PPFA contend with its allies and opponents in the moderated media (Dilemma 2). PPFA used its brand equity and its opposition to government intervention to distance itself from pro-choice groups that were adopting "extreme" rhetoric in the debate over parental involvement. NOW, for example, argued that parental consent and notification laws lead to illegal back-alley abortions and death.[26] In an analysis of the laws, one NOW activist noted that the problem with parental involvement laws was "Girls dying from illegal or self-induced abortion – because they couldn't, or wouldn't, tell their parent(s) they were pregnant."[27] This rhetoric was not inconsequential.

[23] Mailings, reports, and memos, SSC, Accession 90S-33, Box 1.

[24] Memo, Douglas Gould, November 7, 1989, SSC, Accession 90S-33, Box 1.

[25] Memo, Janel Radtke, September 28, 1990, SSC, Accession 91S-19, Box 1.

[26] Papers, 1992–97, RISA, Accession 99-M111, Box 1.

[27] Unknown. "The Tragedy of Parental Involvement Laws." *National NOW Times*, January/February 1990.

Pro-lifers highlighted these arguments to illustrate just how "out of touch" pro-choice organizations were with the American public. Pro-lifers argued that the movement was composed of activists bent on winning a cause rather than working in the best interest of women. In a memo from Gould to PPFA affiliates, he noted:

> The emergence of extremist groups on our side, and calls by political pundits for a "compromise" on the abortion issue, demand that PPFA position itself as centrist. We must be seen first as a health care provider with massive grassroots support, not a political organization. We speak for the millions of clients we serve and the public must understand that we are working for: access to safe legal abortion before viability and through pregnancy when a woman's life or health is endangered.

The focus on government interference allowed PPFA to deflect pro-life criticism and argue that it represented a "compromise" position on abortion that protected women's rights, kept the government out of individual's lives, and buttressed PPFA's brand.[28]

The debate over parental involvement laws was important for another reason as well. Research by consultants indicated that PPFA needed to actively shape public debate over the abortion issue in order to mobilize a broader public and stave off political losses. A confidential report conducted by Hamilton & Staff surmised that effective communication on abortion was a "necessary defensive measure against the anti-choice forces." The report concluded that if PPFA was going to prevail in the abortion war it needed to win over the "mushy middle," or those citizens who either did not consider abortion to be an important issue or supported some restrictions to the abortion procedure.[29] The debate over parental involvement provided PPFA an opportunity to use its brand equity to engage the mushy middle directly as well as introduce a frame that emphasized the importance of individual rights and questioned government intrusion in private medical decisions. Likewise, the government interference frame represented a strategic attempt by PPFA to contend with a losing issue, allies anxious to fight for women's right to abortion without exception, and opponents eager to further diminish support for abortion by highlighting extremism in the pro-choice movement.

ELITE AGENDAS AND ORGANIZATIONAL CONFLICT

An effective brand is not a panacea. The environment around an issue can change quickly and leave a group reeling. This was true for PPFA in the 1990s after Bill Clinton took office. Clinton championed the pro-choice cause on the campaign trail. Once elected, he rescinded several pro-life policies, lifted the ban

[28] Memo, Douglas Gould, July 17, 1989, SSC, Accession 90S-33, Box 1.

[29] A Ten-Year Strategic Plan for Securing Abortion Rights, October 1990, SSC, Accession 91S-19, Box 1.

on fetal tissue for medical research, allowed the importation of emergency contraception, signed the Freedom of Access to Abortion Clinics (FACE) legislation into law, and approved privately funded abortions in overseas military hospitals. While these actions were achievements for the pro-choice movement, they also signaled to supporters that the crisis to abortion rights finally had ended. Financial contributions to pro-choice organizations dropped dramatically. PPFA experienced an 18 percent decline in donations after Clinton's election and laid off 20 percent of its national staff (Warner 1993).

The pro-choice movement faced another problem as well. The passage of universal health care legislation, which would provide health care coverage for all Americans and slow medical care cost inflation, was at the top of Clinton's agenda. While access to abortion was part of the plan, it provided a different framework for understanding legal abortion – one that took women's right to an abortion for granted and treated abortion as a legitimate health care procedure. The inclusion of abortion in Clinton's Health Security Plan represented a victory for pro-choicers because it assumed women's rights to an abortion before viability. However, it presented a new challenge because it redefined the contours of the debate. The entrenchment of abortion policy in a health care framework required pro-choice groups to either stay the political course and fight pro-lifers on familiar turf or adopt new understandings of the abortion issue. While staying the rhetorical course may have been desirable, it was not an option for PPFA, whose operations would be directly affected if the Health Security Plan passed.

Pro-lifers quickly mobilized in opposition to health care reform, arguing that Clinton's plan would grow an already bloated government and intrude on individual decision-making insofar as it would require people to pay for a procedure with which they did not agree. Ralph Reed, the executive director of the Christian Coalition, contended that "The Clinton plan is really a Trojan horse for a not-so-hidden agenda to expand government bureaucracy, pay for abortions with tax dollars, and promote a radical social agenda."[30] Concerned Women for America made similar claims, warning that the plan would result in government-subsidized abortion, further government intrusion into the economy and individual decision-making, and erode the current care received by Americans. A staff writer for the *Family Voice* opined:

> We must ask ourselves if we are ready to hand over such a large portion of our economy to government for control. Before deciding, we must realize that sacrifices will be made. Doctors will be forced to change their methods of practice. Care and compassion may be the first to go as doctors rush patients through to compensate for lost income . . . Doctors and hospitals will make medical decisions based on cost control – not good medicine . . .

[30] Reed, Ralph. 1994. "What Do Religious Conservatives Really Want?" in *Disciples and Democracy: Religious Conservatives and the Future of American Politics*, edited by M. Cromartie. Washington, D.C.: Ethics and Public Policy Center. Page 29.

We could end up with a system heavy on bureaucracy and taxes, light on choice – and devoid of freedom."[31]

NRLC also voiced opposition to the plan. The organization's president, Wanda Franz, warned:

Children would grow up finding out that their siblings were killed and that they themselves could have been killed, too, because the government's health plan offered their mothers abortion as an "option." Mothers would find themselves under pressure to abort their children because the bureaucrats administrating it will be under pressure to save money by avoiding more costly services for birth.[32]

PPFA responded by focusing on the importance of making abortion and other reproductive health services accessible under Clinton's health care plan. This decision was the result of two factors. First, consultants advised that PPFA could survive the Clinton era if it moved away from abortion and emphasized its "unique expertise in reproductive health and prevention."[33] Second, there was a change in leadership. After serving as PPFA president for fourteen years, Wattleton left the organization to host a daytime television talk show.[34] Her replacement was Pamela Maraldo, who was hired in early 1993.

Initially, Maraldo, the former chief executive of the National League for Nursing, seemed the ideal choice to help navigate PPFA through the new era of managed care.[35] Maraldo argued that if PPFA was going to thrive in this new environment, it would need to fundamentally alter its organizational structure and change its service focus. Rather than simply provide reproductive health services, PPFA would need to become a primary care health organization. Maraldo quickly created a task force to study the health care system and assess how PPFA could ensure the "financial health" of the organization in a competitive health care market. Many PPFA affiliates and activists quickly followed Maraldo's lead and began to beat the drum for health care reform and focus on women's health more generally. Some PPFA activists even publicly expressed relief that they were finally able to come out of the shadows after years of being "branded and defined by the abortion battle" and reclaim their public image as a provider of quality health care services.[36] Mary Rauh, a PPFA board member, noted that change was critical because PPFA was approaching "the threshold of an era. The question is will there be a place in the reformed

[31] Wallace, Marian. "Reform or Ruin? National Health Care." *Family Voice*, January 1994.

[32] Franz, Wanda. "The REAL Health Care Crisis Created by the Clinton Health Proposal." *National Right to Life News*, February 1994.

[33] Planned Parenthood Presentation of Findings from a Nationwide Study of 900 Adults, 1993, KDML.

[34] Lewin, Tamar. "Planned Parenthood Chief Resigns to Be TV Host." *The New York Times*, January 9, 1992.

[35] Lewin, Tamar. "Parenthood Plus: A Special Report." *The New York Times*, August 7, 1995.

[36] Unknown. "Texas: Planned Parenthood Redefining Its Role, Image." *Abortion Report*, August 18, 1993.

health-care system for a niche provider, a reproductive health provider? It looks very risky to depend on that for our future ... We might get frozen out of the system."[37]

Support for reform, at least as envisioned by Maraldo, was not universal. When the task force released its sixty-eight-page report, dissent over the proposed restructuring emerged and became a media spectacle (Dilemma 2). The Associated Press obtained a confidential letter in which leaders from affiliates in New York, Chicago, and Los Angeles slammed Maraldo's reinvention plan, exclaiming that "never has a document seemed so out of touch with our mission ... The word abortion is mentioned only eight times [in the plan] and never in the discussion of our future." Bill Sheppard, executive director of Planned Parenthood Health Services of Southwestern Oregon, added, "Our concern is that Planned Parenthood continue to focus on its historic mission of reproductive health ... We think it would be a mistake for primary care to become a primary focus of Planned Parenthood."[38]

The internal dissent had three sources. First, PPFA allies, such as NOW and former PPFA president Faye Wattleton, publicly criticized this strategy and accused the organization of compromising women's rights and lives by "mainstreaming" the abortion issue (Warner 1993). Maraldo rejected this accusation:

> The mission of Planned Parenthood will be to secure reproductive health, equality, and self-determination for all individuals. These are unequivocally feminist ideals; moreover, they are quintessentially "mainstream." We have no need to repackage Planned Parenthood. We have represented mainstream public opinion for many decades; it's our presidents who were outside the mainstream. Our principles remain uncompromised, but our tactics must adapt to a very different political climate. Our political reality today consists of a pro-choice majority that is battle-weary and too prone to complacency; congressional leaders who were elected on pro-choice promises but have turned their backs on key issues; and a religious far Right that has lost its friends in the White House and is resorting to increasingly violent measures. After 12 years defending the *right* to abortion, we must shift our focus to ensuring *access* to abortion ... This vision brooks no compromise and no retreat from Planned Parenthood's 77-year-old mission [emphasis in original].[39]

Maraldo added that the focus on "centrism" was necessary for organizational survival (Maraldo 1994; Warner 1993). When Maraldo accepted the presidency, PPFA was US$ 4.5 million in debt.[40]

Second, the abortion issue continued to be a lightning rod for pro-life activism inside and outside the political system. By the time PPFA leaders released the reinvention plan, Clinton's Health Security plan was dead and Republicans had

[37] Unknown. "Untitled." *Abortion Report*, March 3, 1995.

[38] Price, Joyce. "Planned Parenthood Considers Primary Care." *The Washington Times*, March 3, 1995.

[39] Maraldo, Pamela. "Letter to the Editor." *Ms.*, May 1994.

[40] Unknown. "Ex-chief: Planned Parenthood Resists Change." *United Press International*, August 6, 1995.

taken a majority in the Congress. By 1995, the Congress was considering measures to criminalize partial-birth abortion, end abortions in the military, deny Medicaid-financed abortions to rape and incest victims, and remove requirements that doctors be trained to perform abortions. Violence against abortion providers and clinics surged in the 1990s. Extremists murdered three abortion providers, two escorts, and one police officer between 1993 and 1998, and took steps to disseminate their message of violence to a broader audience. In 1995, the American Coalition of Life Activists distributed "wanted" style posters, which listed the names, addresses, and phone numbers of twelve abortion providers labeled the "Deadly Dozen" and offered a US$ 5,000 reward for "information leading to arrest, conviction and revocation of license to practice medicine."[41] In January 1997, Neal Horsley created the Nuremberg Files website that compiled information on providers and high-profile abortion supporters and noted which individuals were active, which had been injured, and which had been killed by pro-lifers.[42]

The renewed importance of the abortion issue during the Clinton era and criticism from other pro-choice organizations were not the only source of affiliate dissention. In fact, Maraldo and other national leaders took steps to address these concerns by establishing PPFA's first clinic defense program and suing the American Coalition of Life Activist for violating the Freedom of Access to Clinic Entrances. The reinvention plan curtailed affiliate autonomy by homogenizing them in terms of the kinds of services offered at clinics, raising the ire of directors. Alexander Sanger, the executive director of Planned Parenthood of New York City, criticized the plan, arguing that it undermined the core mission of the organization:

> The question about our future should not be, "How do we fit into the new health care system?" but rather, "In the new health care system, what will our clients still need from us?" The goal is not to keep ourselves in business, but to make sure every woman has access to reproductive health care by filling needs others aren't meeting.[43]

Maraldo resigned in July 1995 after she failed to muster a vote of confidence from the PPFA board.[44] In an interview, Maraldo attributed the failure of the reinvention plan and her resignation to an organizational tradition that revered affiliate autonomy:

> I was an advocate of seeing many more common denominators among the affiliates in terms of how they price their services and in terms of the kind of services that were provided ... In their almost eighty-year history, affiliates have been extremely autonomous, and there is a desire to hold dear that autonomy.

She added:

41 "ACLU Foundation of Oregon Amicus Curiae." ACLU website.

42 The Ninth Circuit Court of Appeals Decision determined the website format constituted a true threat to those listed.

43 Lewin, Tamar. "Parenthood Plus: A Special Report." *The New York Times*, August 7, 1995.

44 Lewin, Tamar. "Planned Parenthood President Resigns." *The New York Times*, July 22, 1995.

I think my programs and my initiative will go forward. I came in and created a framework for change, but by nature it's a volatile situation, and now my piece is done.[45]

Her assessment was correct. Gloria Feldt, who took over the presidency in 1996, spent the next several years trying to balance the need for organizational reinvention in a complicated and competitive managed care system with affiliate autonomy.

Despite the internal conflict, Maraldo's repositioning of PPFA in the abortion debate had its advantages. It allowed the organization to attract additional federal funds, which helped put PPFA back in the black during Maraldo's tenure.[46] Additionally, it enabled PPFA to largely avoid the rancorous debate over the Partial Birth Abortion (PBA) Ban Act. PPFA opposed the ban and knew that the partial-birth abortion debate could open a "floodgate of legislation" undermining abortion rights. That said, PPFA understood that the focus on late-term abortions was a losing issue (Dilemma 3). The organization's market research found that arguments opposing the ban as a violation of abortion rights – and the argument that the ban was one step in a broader agenda to make abortion illegal – were not only ineffective but damaging to the cause and the organization's brand. Thus, PPFA remained relatively silent on the issue.

When PPFA leadership did discuss PBA publically, it focused on the fact that the procedure was only used in cases where fetal defects were incompatible with life outside the womb – one of the few frames that resonated with the broader public.[47] In her testimony to the Senate Judiciary Committee in 1997, Feldt did not attack the legislation but challenged the terminology being used in the debate:

To speak to the truth about women's lives, we must start by discussing the term "partial-birth abortion." Use of this vague and medically inaccurate term – accompanied by diagrams of fully formed, healthy fetuses being aborted, has utterly corrupted public discussion of this issue . . . It is inaccurate to equate so-called "partial-birth abortion" with "intact D&E" [dilation and evacuation], one of the abortion procedures that would be eliminated by this legislation. But outlawing intact D&E or any of the procedures affected by this ban will not eliminate the circumstances that call for them. It will eliminate safe health care options for women . . . This is an important distinction to make. Many times, the "when" has been confused with the "why" or the "how" an abortion is performed.[48]

It is important to note that the presence of an ally in the White House enabled PPFA to take this position and avoid the more controversial aspects of the PBA debate. Clinton renounced the partial-birth abortion ban and vetoed the

45 Unknown. "Ex-chief: Planned Parenthood Resists Change." *United Press International*, August 6, 1995.

46 Price, Joyce. "Planned Parenthood Suffers Year of Losing Clinics, Clients; But with Friends in High Places, Group Sees Funding Rise." *The Washington Times*, January 14, 1997.

47 PPFA's Summit for Goals for Campaign, 1996, SSC, Accession 96S-26, Box 6.

48 Testimony Senate Judiciary Committee, Gloria Feldt, March 11, 1997, Federal Document Clearing House Congressional Testimony.

legislation in 1996 and 1997. This changed with the election of George W. Bush, a staunch pro-life supporter who overturned Clinton's pro-choice measures and signed the Federal Abortion Ban, which eliminated the partial-birth abortion procedure, into law. PPFA acted quickly, issuing public statements and filing injunctions in three cities across the country.

CONCLUSION

Crafting an organizational brand that focuses on general rather than specific issues has political and media advantages. It strengthens a group's reputation, which enables an activist group to work behind the scenes and shape legislation and media coverage. As seen in the debate over parental involvement laws, a brand makes it easier for an organization to deflect criticisms of a movement and pitch arguments that appeal to the mainstream (Dilemmas 2 and 3). Because PPFA sold itself as a family planning organization, it could frame debates over parental involvement as an issue of government intrusion in medical decision-making instead of directly addressing the issue of whether minors had a right to an abortion. This line of argument allowed PPFA to transcend squabbles over fetal and women's rights and appeal directly to a segment of the audience who were unwilling to cede private decisions to government regulation. While its efforts to stop parental involvement legislation were unsuccessful, PPFA effectively navigated the debate insofar as it was considered a mainstream voice on an otherwise contentious issue.

Having a brand changes how an organization responds to media dilemmas (Table 6.1 summarizes PPFA's strategic choices). Maintaining brand equity is central to organizational decision-making, which alters how a group approaches mass media (Dilemma 1). PPFA drew on both organizational outlets and earned media attention extensively; what varied were the ideas disseminated in each. PPFA constructed two sets of messages – one set aimed at the converted and another targeting those it sought to convert – in the debate over parental involvement laws. Privately, PPFA opposed parental notification and consent laws and fought their passage. Publicly, PPFA tried to steer the debate away from parental rights to the government's intrusion on individual rights. Again, while this line of argument did not win the day, it reassured constituents that PPFA was working on this and other reproductive issues. In short, the dilemma for PPFA was not which of the outlets it should rely on to forward its cause, but what kind of messages should be disseminated in different venues and whether these messages were consistent with the brand.

The kinds of negative attention PPFA dealt with varied from that NRLC and NOW faced (Dilemma 2). PPFA had little difficulty distancing itself from rancorous debate and found that it primarily had to contend with coverage of intra-organizational strife. There was not much PPFA could do regarding the coverage of its internal battle beyond assure journalists, its constituents, and the public that the organization was stronger as a result of the process. Arguably,

TABLE 6.1. *Summary of PPFA's strategic choices*

Organizational Identity	Reproductive health and rights
Framing the Abortion Issue	Family planning framework
Public Image	Mainstream, reproductive health organization
Reputation in the Media Field	Strong
Dilemma 1: Access External Media?	
Perception of Mainstream Outlets	PPFA did not target mainstream outlets until the 1980s, at which point it began to develop its family planning brand.
Examples	Yes, but target different messages to different audiences. No, if the organization can influence the debate behind the scenes or if an elite will carry the water on an issue (e.g., partial-birth abortion).
Dilemma 2: Respond to Negative Attention?	
Example	No, ignoring groups such as STOPP makes their criticisms a "non story."
Dilemma 3: Weigh in on Losing Issues?	
Example	Yes, to try to reframe the debate such as the discussion over parental notification and consent laws.
Tradeoffs	
	Resources for an effective brand The ability to speak freely in media about the abortion issue for a brand The ability to speak freely in media about the abortion issue for political clout

self-examination helps organizations endure. Finally, PPFA generally found it easier to deal with losing issues because it could distance itself from an issue, its allies, and opponents (Dilemma 3). All groups encounter debates that they are likely to lose. The trick is for an organization to minimize the extent to which a debate casts the group in a negative light. This is not always easy to do. Groups that are extreme in word and deed can easily dominate public discourse and "tar and feather" organizations that are unable to distance themselves from their provocative allies. Recall that NRLC had to devise strategies to contend with allies and this was done occasionally at the expense of the group's public image. Similarly, NOW found itself scurrying for media attention and engaging in debates with the extremes of the pro-life movement. While PPFA expressed concern over extreme rhetoric in the movement, it did not try to cajole its allies to accept a different position nor did it engage in coverage that would cast the brand in a negative light. Instead, it simply avoided the abortion issue altogether and circulated ideas to counteract the messages of other pro-choice groups. Organizations with an effective brand, in short, find it easier to avoid public rancor because they can deflect public attention to other issues, campaigns, and partnerships with which they are involved.

Organizations with a brand still make tradeoffs. Brands require a great deal of resources to maintain and affect how an organization weighs in on a debate publicly. This is clear in the debate over parental involvement where the passionate private discourse did not match the mainstream message. Likewise, brands cannot immunize an organization against a changing political environment. Just as PPFA struggled to find its footing after Clinton took office, it is likely to face such difficult moments again. The intraorganizational battle in the 1990s well prepared the organization for Obamacare in 2012. However, the battle lines have been drawn again around abortion access and whether federal or state governments should fund PPFA clinics that provide abortion services. Politicians championing the Tea Party platform took seats in federal and state government in 2010 and, shortly thereafter, made clear their intentions to see how far they could push the "undue burden" clause. In 2011 and 2012, state legislators began defunding PPFA. At the time of this writing, the state affiliates affected by these new laws were challenging them in the court system. Clearly, PPFA will not be able to distance itself from the abortion issue in this climate and will have to find ways to maintain its brand in a contentious debate.

7

Concerned Women for America and sympathetic media

Moderated media consist of outlets that are more or less sympathetic to a movement. I conceptualize the media field as composed of three different categories of outlets over which activists have more or less control. In each of the previous cases, the organization has relied heavily on earned media attention in mainstream venues and supplemented their efforts with direct media and coverage in sympathetic outlets. So far, sympathetic outlets have not played a critical role in media strategy. Based on these cases alone, it would seem that sympathetic media are a good way to keep in touch with supporters but have little consequence for effecting political change. In this chapter, I show that if an organization is interested in building its clout with politicians on only one side of the ideological aisle, it can make a lasting impression by minimizing the resources it puts into its mainstream media efforts.

Ignoring mainstream outlets, while still using mass media to forward organizational goals, is possible for three related reasons. First, institutional fields overlap, which means the happenings in one field can influence another. This is particularly true of the political and mass media fields, where politicians make determinations about media content and ownership and journalists try to uncover the inner workings of the political world. The relationship among actors in these different fields is not necessarily adversarial. Media professionals employed by ideologically-driven news venues may rely heavily on (or even work closely with) like-minded politicians when putting together their stories, just as politicians may look to sympathetic outlets for cues on how to interpret an opponent or an event (Jamieson and Cappella 2010). Objectivity, in short, is not a universal norm and media professionals working in ideologically driven outlets may be more interested in influencing (rather than reporting on) politics.

This is true of conservative outlets at the extremes of the mass media field. Rush Limbaugh, FOX News, and the opinion-makers at the *Wall Street Journal* have consolidated their considerable resources in order to capitalize on the overlap between the media and political fields, and created an "echo chamber" that amplifies the positions and actions of the Republican leadership (Jamieson and Cappella 2010). Outlet owners and media personalities alike use media platforms to advance a political agenda (Warf 2007). Organizations too may benefit from this overlap. Groups that can fit their ideas with the vision offered by conservative powerhouses may find that they get plenty of play and that mainstream media do not need to be part of their strategic calculus.

Second, an organization can create media formats that enable it to talk directly to a sympathetic audience. I am not referring to websites, advertising, or the public service announcements that activist groups routinely produce and disseminate to news venues in case journalists have space to fill, but full-length programs featuring movement personalities and organizational leaders. While these efforts may have a lot of start-up costs, it is a strategy that can pay off in the contemporary media environment. After all, advertisers, who pay for media content, are interested in target – rather than mass – marketing, and media owners and producers promise to deliver desirable audiences. In the 1980s and early 1990s, the bulk of the distinctions marketers and media producers grappled with fell into one of five categories: income, gender, age, race, and ethnicity. Advertising agencies fractured these categories and cobbled together hundreds of new ones in their efforts to find desirable targets. Media owners and producers responded by creating content to attract these target demographics and advertiser support (Turow 1997). This is no less true of conservative media, which provide a steady stream of content to three markets: "secular conservatives," "the far right," and the "theocratic right" (Berlet 1998). Savvy organizations can capitalize on the hyper-segmentation of media markets by creating content that simultaneously allows them to speak to sympathetic audiences directly and attracts advertiser support.

Some groups will find this easier to do than others. Some organizations will be priced out of such elaborate ventures. Others may simply lack the star power necessary to sell a show to even sympathetic outlets. Having a celebrity involved in programming is particularly important in a hyper-segmented media market. Lifestyle programming, whether it is the Food Network or the Christian Television Network, needs celebrity hosts who can sell both products and a demographically tailored version of the American Dream (Gamson 1994; Sternheimer 2011). Star power is not limited to popular culture or merely based on box office and book sales. Celebrity can be constructed or, in some instances, claimed (Gamson 1994). Activists and politicians can claim to represent a group or cause, and, then, quite visibly do so (Gitlin 1980; Street 2004). Likewise, in a hyper-segmented media market an individual needs only to be recognized by and appeal to a niche audience in order to assume the "celebrity" title and the cultural power that comes with it (Marshall 1997). Organizations that have a recognizable figure – or celebrity – at the helm will be well positioned to leverage themselves in the contemporary media marketplace.

Finally, the overlapping institutional fields and the ability of groups to create content that appeals to a desired demographic allow an organization to accomplish basic media goals without targeting mainstream outlets. A group can create and leverage its programs across different mediums (e.g., radio, television, concerts, and the Internet) in ways that allow it to build its membership and quickly mobilize sympathetic audiences to action; both of which can help establish the political legitimacy of an organization. Employing a media strategy that largely relies on sympathetic media has consequences. Because the media system is hyper-segmented, an organization may find that it has a strong reputation with a relatively small number of outlets and a weak reputation with virtually every other moderated outlet. This can pose a problem for a group that decides to extend its media efforts beyond sympathetic audiences because – as an unknown – it will lack credibility with media professionals. This hill may be particularly steep if a group's allies have embraced a more traditional route and successfully wooed journalists from a range of outlets, including mainstream media. An organization may find its ideas marginalized or excluded altogether if its more reputable allies want to give statements.

How a group deals with the first media dilemma – whether or not to engage mass media – does not have to involve mainstream media, but its decision to avoid these news venues shapes its response to other dilemmas. A media strategy that emphasizes paid advertising and self-produced content requires substantial resources. A group that regularly produces a radio or television program will spend a fair amount of time creating, placing, and promoting their content. As such, even if a group knows that it is getting bad press in mainstream media, it may not be willing to allocate (or have) the personnel necessary to respond. Similarly, a group with this strategy is likely to find that its best mainstream media opportunities are around issues where it will inevitably be cast as the villain or the extremist. As seen in previous chapters, a group with a strong reputation in the media field may be able to avoid rancorous debates. A group that wants mainstream media attention but has a weak reputation, however, will be more inclined to jump into the debate because it has far fewer media opportunities.

A narrowly focused media strategy involves a tradeoff: political clout for media notoriety. In this chapter, I explore the consequences of this tradeoff for Concerned Women for America (CWA), which primarily used paid advertising and self-produced content disseminated in sympathetic media to maintain control over how the organization and its issues were represented to the public. This strategy has advantages and disadvantages. On the one hand, CWA found that this strategy enabled it to reach its media goals – to grow its grassroots structure and mobilize constituents around its issues – and build its political clout with Republicans inside and outside the White House. On the other hand, CWA found itself on the receiving end of negative coverage that lambasted the organization for its opposition to gay rights. Over time, CWA reframed its position in the debate and focused public attention on its right to express an alternative perspective in a democratic society. This experience was transformative insofar as CWA began to view mainstream outlets as a means to advance its political goals and made efforts to use mainstream news venues for this end.

THE STRATEGIC BENEFITS OF CONSERVATIVE, CHRISTIAN MEDIA

Beverly LaHaye, the wife of the well-known Christian fundamentalist Tim LaHaye, came up with the inspiration for CWA after she heard Betty Friedan interviewed on television. LaHaye was offended that Friedan, whose values she regarded as anti-God, anti-family, and otherwise humanistic, championed herself and NOW as the spokesperson for the majority of women. According to LaHaye, the interview left her convinced that "Friedan's plan represented not a march to liberation, but rather a misguided attempt to dismantle the bedrock of American culture: the family."[1] LaHaye decided to create an organization that would represent the values and political visions of Christian women and highlight the diversity of the women's movement. In a public statement, LaHaye sent a "message" to politicians, media, and the American public:

> The feminists do not represent all women of America. The women of this country are every bit as pluralistic as the men. It is the height of absurdity to suggest that all women are in lockstep march led by Betty Friedan and Gloria Steinem. This suggestion is not only absurd, but, ultimately, it is also nothing more than recycled sexism to suggest that "all women" follow the liberal ideology touted by the feminists. To suggest that feminists speak for all women insults me as much as the suggestion that all women should be homemakers offends the feminists ... We think it is time for all women to be heard. Let America understand that we will not be represented by a voice with which we do not agree.[2]

The initial goals of the group were to distribute information exposing the feminist agenda to the Christian community and establish a prayer network among Christian women. LaHaye and eight of her friends organized sixty coffee klatches over a four-month period and held an anti-feminist rally in San Diego, CA. Before long, news of LaHaye's efforts spread and requests for information on feminism and CWA's efforts to stem NOW's agenda flooded in from other states. LaHaye quickly incorporated the organization and CWA was officially born.[3]

The fledgling organization grew by leaps and bounds throughout the 1980s. In March 1979, CWA had twenty-four members. Within a year, it had 655 members and, by 1992, CWA claimed a membership of 600,000.[4] The tremendous growth of the group in a relatively short amount of time required LaHaye to reenvision the organizational structure and political potential of CWA. Initially, LaHaye imagined CWA as being composed of prayer chapters that would provide

[1] Arnold, Lori. "Beverly LaHaye Marks Three Decades of Promoting Traditional Values Through CWA." *Christian Examiner* 27(12), December 2009.

[2] Unknown. "CWA Arrival on Capitol Hill Blacked Out by Most Major Media." *Concerned Women for America (CWFA) Newsletter*, November 1983.

[3] Bush, Rosaline. "Reflections on 50 Golden Years." *Family Voice (FV)*. July 1997.

[4] Unknown. "CWA Press Conference." *CWFA Newsletter*, June/July 1980.

a grassroots base for local mobilization.[5] As the membership ballooned, LaHaye realized that CWA could rival NOW on the national political scene. LaHaye adopted a national, hierarchical structure capable of coordinating chapter activities and diffusing information among a rapidly growing membership.[6] These changes happened quickly. In 1980, CWA began looking for "Organizational Chairmen" to coordinate the prayer chapter activities in each of the fifty states. In 1983, LaHaye formed a National Advisory Council, created a national field director position, and sounded a call for Christian women with leadership skills to apply for regional representative positions – all efforts to help LaHaye coordinate the organization's campaigns across the country. At the same time, CWA opened an office in Washington, D.C., for its general legal counsel, Michael Farris, who was charged with providing a "presence" for the organization on Capitol Hill. The following year, the organization established a "535" lobbying program and began training grassroots activists to represent CWA and its issues.[7] The transformation was complete in 1985 when CWA officially moved its headquarters from San Diego, CA, to Washington, D.C.

While this formalized, hierarchical structure helped cement CWA's status as a legitimate political player, the organization was very slow to use mainstream media outlets to advance its political agenda (Dilemma 1). This is in large part because CWA leaders regarded mainstream media as biased against conservative issues. In one of the group's early newsletters, for example, a CWA activist opined, "the [mainstream] media is controlled – it is not free. It is only free for humanist liberals to get their message to the American people leading them to vote for liberal socialist-type politicians and programs."[8] CWA cited its early, and negative, experiences with mainstream news as evidence for this claim. A CWA activist reported that the mainstream media intentionally "blacked out" the organization's arrival to Washington, D.C.:

> September 27 [1983] was a momentous occasion for CWA. And it may well be a memorable one in the history of family and women's issues. The American public, however, will never be informed of it by the media . . . Although 30 or more representatives from various media came during the day with cameras, microphones, recorders and note pads, *very little coverage* was seen or heard. In fact, in most areas it was totally blacked out. The pro-family and anti-feminist movements are not the silent majority; the media has made them the SILENCED MAJORITY. Among the secular press, the only known reports appeared in *USA Today* and *Washington Times*. (The notoriously liberal *Washington Post* sent a reporter who requested a private interview with Beverly LaHaye,

[5] Peters, Shirley. Untitled. *CWFA Newsletter*, January 1980.

[6] Unknown. "CWA Opens Office in Washington, D.C." *CWFA Newsletter*, September 1983.

[7] Unknown. "Reps Sought for CWA State Chapters." *CWFA Newsletter*, June/July 1980; LaHaye, Beverly. "A Word from Beverly." *CWFA Newsletter*, December/January 1983; LaHaye, Beverly. "CWA Forms National Advisory Council." *CWFA Newsletter*, September 1983; Unknown. "Positions Available for CWA Regional Representatives." *CWFA Newsletter*, September 1983.

[8] LaHaye, Tim. "What Happened Nov. 4?" *CWFA Newletter*, December 1980.

and after two hours of challenging her position on women's issues, rather than conducting a fair interview, the reporter and/or the *Post* chose to ignore the whole story!) [emphasis in original].[9]

Leaders often noted that mainstream media's coverage of the abortion issue, and violence at abortion clinics, perfectly illustrated liberal bias. In an article outlining the liberal media's deliberate efforts to conflate extremism and religion, a CWA activist argued that mainstream outlets purposefully cast Christians as mentally unstable:

Liberal columnists who dominate the journalistic world have had a heyday linking evangelical Christians to all the whackos who have captured the nightly news spotlight . . . Another top news story that many in the press used to stereotype Christian America was the shooting of Dr. David Gunn, the Florida abortionist. Journalists were all too eager to paint *all* pro-life Christians as psychotic fanatics. Many reporters jumped at the opportunity to only quote the pro-life groups who would not condemn the murder, ignoring groups who criticized the actions of Michael Griffin, the man who was arrested for the murder [emphasis in original].[10]

Another CWA writer agreed with this assessment, adding that liberal journalists have worked to cast the entire pro-life movement in a negative light:

Liberal reporters would have the public believe that every pro-lifer has the potential for burning abortion clinics and shooting abortionists. By deliberately concentrating on a lunatic fringe element in our society – the Paul Hills and John Salvis – the media has painted a negative picture of the whole movement. The 'mug shot,' sketched by the media and endorsed by Planned Parenthood and other pro-abortion advocates, describes an average pro-lifer as uneducated, easily lead, violent, unbalanced and insensitive to women and the baby after its birth. Although this picture is distorted, the power of the media has prevailed.[11]

The perception that mainstream news is biased against conservatives persisted throughout the 1980 to 2000 time period, although spokespeople used less inflamed rhetoric to explain CWA's reluctance to target these venues. A former communications director for the organization, who continued to work on legislative issues for CWA, explained that mainstream journalists travel in narrow "social circles" and are less knowledgeable about conservative issues. This causes journalists to exclude or misrepresent conservative positions in media coverage.

Looking back at Figure 3.2, one could argue that CWA has a legitimate complaint. The organization rarely received media attention on the abortion issue. Likewise, when mainstream journalists were asked what organizations they considered good sources of information on the abortion issue, CWA was

9 Unknown. "CWA Arrival on Capitol Hill Blacked Out by Most Major Media." *CWFA Newsletter*, November 1983.

10 Hutchins, Trudy. "A Politically Correct Target." *FV*, July 1993.

11 Unknown. "Whatever Happened on the Way to the Clinic?" *FV*, August 1995.

never mentioned. Mainstream media professionals said that abortion did not seem to be a major focus of the organization. CWA did not get much media attention in secular conservative outlets either. The organization was mentioned or quoted in only three stories (1.1%) focused on abortion. Moreover, the journalists and editors I spoke with noted that the credibility of the organization was "spotty" at best. Media bias does not explain the relative absence of CWA from media coverage. More importantly, it is a poor indicator of the organization's media goals and strategy during this time period.

CWA primarily wanted to use mass media to grow its grassroots structure and mobilize sympathizers around organizational issues (Dilemma 1). In order to do so, the organization focused on controlling how the group and its messages were represented to the public. CWA regarded conservative Christian venues as ideal for selling the group and its ideas to a broader audience. Targeting sympathetic outlets made sense for two reasons. First, conservative Christian media grew in availability and strength throughout the 1980s and 1990s. In 1983, the National Religious Broadcasters already claimed more than 900 radio station members and Christian television broadcasts had an estimated viewership of between thirteen and sixty-one million (Diamond 1995). Second, LaHaye was a celebrity among conservative Christians, which made it relatively easier for her to get her ideas featured in Christian channels. For nearly two decades, she traveled the world with her husband, Tim, offering seminars on family life. By the early 1980s, the couple was delivering its message to millions through television and radio programs featuring their pro-family teachings.[12] Beverly LaHaye, however, was a conservative, Christian powerhouse in her own right. In 1976, she published her first book titled the *Spirit Controlled Woman*, which sold more than 810, 000 copies, and in the 1980s LaHaye was selected as one of the ten most admired non-congressional women in the U.S. for five years running.[13] LaHaye had an established following, which made it easier for her to cultivate opportunities in conservative, Christian outlets and craft programming that highlighted the organization and its pro-family message.

CWA has done a remarkable job leveraging conservative, Christian outlets to spread its pro-family message. Radio, in particular, has been a boon for CWA. While radio generally has a smaller audience than other media outlets, the number of conservative and Christian programs over the last twenty years has increased exponentially and provided a forum for conservative, Christian issues and organizations (Fetner and Sanders 2012). As the press secretary for CWA noted, "conservative issues do well on radio. It's an area where

[12] Beverly traveled to more than forty-six countries with her husband offering more than 1,000 seminars. In October 1981, Tim and Beverly LaHaye hosted a thirty-minute TV show that aired once a week in primetime. In 1982, they began a radio program, which broadcast in twelve states throughout the country.

[13] In 2005, LaHaye was named one of the most influential evangelicals in the United States by *Time*.

conservative ideas are strong [because] ... you do not have to go through liberal media."[14] In 1990, LaHaye began hosting a daily (*Beverly LaHaye Live*) and weekly (*This Week with Beverly LaHaye*) program. By 1994, LaHaye's programs were on ninety major stations across the United States with an estimated listening audience of 650,000.[15] That same year, CWA began its own radio station and produced programs for public access and Christian television outlets. During the same time period, CWA joined the National Empowerment Television Network (NET), which was designed by Paul Weyrich to "counterbalance the liberal airwaves with a conservative perspective."[16] CWA aired a weekly program, "Concerned Women for America – Putting Families First!" on the network. Three years later (in 1996), it introduced another broadcast program titled "American Family Show," which provided weekly commentary on Capitol Hill and news updates by prominent CWA activists.[17] CWA also used Christian music tours to spread the pro-family message and build its membership. In 1997, the organization sponsored concert tours for two female artists, Kim Hill and Kathy Troccoli, who also served as spokeswomen for CWA. Troccoli's "Love and Mercy" concert tour visited twenty-four cities in two months. Troccoli, who was a two-time Grammy nominee and was nominated for the Dove Award thirteen times as well as had five hits in the top 10 and eleven no. 1 Christian radio hits, began each show by discussing CWA's important work and introducing grassroots organizers, who handed out information to concert goers.[18]

This strategy allowed CWA to achieve its media goals. Because CWA produced its own formats and programming, it had complete control over the message and organizational representation. This level of creative control is very different from mainstream news outlets, where groups often can do little more than express an opinion on an event. CWA produced content that cast the organization as an important player in American politics, outlined the issue and campaign of the day, and invited the audience to join the organization. According to CWA's press secretary, these programs enabled CWA to continuously reach and mobilize new constituents:

> You tend to think it's the same people listening every day [to the radio programs], but the phone calls tell us [something] different. There are a huge number of people responding [to CWA programming] and saying, "I've flipped to the station for the first time. I didn't know CWA was out there and I want to get involved." I think we get most of our activists from radio. It seems to have a [mobilizing] effect on people. I think this is because you get to talk about something for longer than you do on TV or in the paper. I think all of it

[14] Interview with a press secretary at CWA.
[15] LaHaye, Beverly. "From the President's Desk." *FV*, February 1994.
[16] Halbig, Jacqueline. "National Empowerment Television." *FV*, February 1994.
[17] LaHaye, Beverly. "From the President's Desk." *FV*, February 1994.
[18] Bush, Rosaline. "The Fire Again!" *FV*. Page 26; Bush, Rosaline. September 1997. "In His Hands." *FV*, March 1997.

makes an impression on people and as you build that impression there's going to be some final [breaking] point and people get involved.[19]

There is other evidence that CWA effectively used its self-produced programs to mobilize individuals into political action. In 1995, CWA alerted its audience that AIDS education was mandatory in the federal workplace. The story generated audience outrage that was picked up by conservative outlets, including the *Washington Times* and talk radio stations from around the country. After receiving hundreds of calls from angry Christians, the White House rescinded the mandatory training. Likewise, in 2003, CWA used its station and programming to generate support for Justice Roy Moore, a state judge who sought to display the Ten Commandments in an Alabama Judicial Building. Its intensive radio campaign culminated in a rally "to stand for the public acknowledgement of God and to oppose judicial tyranny" on the steps of the Supreme Court building.[20]

The focus on Christian and conservative outlets as a primary means to communicate with and mobilize a constituency ultimately grew CWA's political influence in the Republican Party. CWA built a political reputation early in its career, primarily as a result of LaHaye's status in Christian circles. Ronald Reagan, who recognized LaHaye as an influential Christian leader, sought her endorsement during his presidential campaign. Once elected, Reagan maintained his links with Christian organizations and regularly invited prominent leaders to the White House. LaHaye was among those invited. With a burgeoning organization behind her as well as growing political concern over the "gender gap" between men and women on policy issues and voting behavior, LaHaye was soon regarded as one of the most powerful women in American politics. In 1982, for instance, CWA was invited to a press conference in the White House Rose Garden, where Reagan announced his intention to restore voluntary prayer in schools. When the bill was defeated two years later, Reagan invited LaHaye to the Oval Office where she and her husband presented him four leather-bound volumes of letters from American families asking the president to uphold children's right to pray. Additionally, Reagan spoke at CWA's 1987 national convention.[21] This is not a trivial matter. NRLC, a powerful organization in its own right, was unable to convince Reagan to appear personally at its annual convention. CWA, in short, had a level of political legitimacy unrivaled by other organizations.

Its political clout did not end with the Reagan administration. CWA had a good relationship with George H. W. Bush and excellent rapport with George W. Bush while they were in office. A former president of NRLC, commenting on CWA's access to politicians and political processes, noted that "they [CWA] have had the ear of more than one Republican president."[22] CWA's convention

[19] Interview with a press secretary at CWA.
[20] CWA website.
[21] Reagan was first scheduled to appear at CWA's second annual convention in 1985, but cancelled.
[22] Interview with a former president and founder of NRLC.

has become a destination for politicians looking to mobilize a conservative, Christian base. Jack Kemp, Newt Gingrich, Pat Robertson, Paul Weyrich, Bob and Elizabeth Dole, Tom DeLay, Trent Lott, Oliver North, Jesse Helms, Ralph Reed, John Ashcroft, and virtually every presidential hopeful including Bob Dornan, Phil Gramm, Patrick Buchanan, Alan Keyes, and Steve Forbes all spoke at CWA conventions.

Again, the notion that political standing does not rely on mainstream media coverage is an important one. Social movement scholars often implicitly or explicitly argue that mainstream media coverage helps groups build credibility with politicians because it shows that they represent an active and visible constituency – one that politicians will want to mobilize for their own purposes. While mainstream coverage undoubtedly helps groups build their political muscles, the relative importance of this coverage likely varies by organization. Relatively new activist groups with leaders who have yet to be certified by mainstream media professionals are likely to gain more from media attention than established organizations with a leadership that is known on Capitol Hill. CWA's decision to cultivate conservative Christian media channels, in short, did not diminish the influence of the group. If anything, its ability to speak directly to and mobilize sympathetic audiences enhanced its standing with politicians.

CWA, in sum, initially was very critical of mainstream outlets and its ability to use these venues to disseminate organizational ideas and effect political change (Dilemma 1). This more adversarial understanding of mainstream media reflected its ideological assumption that mainstream journalists were secular humanists who were opposed – and therefore would not report on – the organization's Judeo-Christian points of view. As a result, CWA took the lack of coverage of organizational events personally and attributed the "media blackout" to bias rather than viewing it in the broader context of the news of the day. CWA's political clout was not affected by its perception of mainstream media. CWA used its most powerful resource, Beverly LaHaye's celebrity status, to build media programming that could be disseminated in sympathetic outlets and a radio station that could mobilize its listeners at a moment's notice.

MOVING INTO THE MAINSTREAM

Given CWA's investment and success in Christian media as well as its suspicion of "secular" media, it is not surprising that CWA was slow to target mainstream outlets (Dilemma 1). What is noteworthy is that CWA was critical of these venues even though it experienced mainstream media success in its early years. One of its first experiences with mainstream media involved its opposition to the Equal Rights Amendment (ERA). In its campaign, CWA pitched itself as the "anti-NOW," and directly refuted the group's claims that the ERA would improve women's lives. CWA specifically argued that the ERA would demolish differences between men and women by making "every person legally neuter in gender."[23] This, CWA posited, would put American women at risk because it would effectively erase legal protections from statutory rape and prostitution as well as the military draft and combat service. Likewise, the passage of the ERA would "destroy" the traditional family by legalizing homosexual marriages and adoptions as well as invalidating existing legal restrictions on abortion.[24] An ERA, it asserted, would do more harm than good and women would be better served by the political system if they addressed issues of wage inequality through the legislative process. A CWA activist argued:

> During its previous ten years of consideration, ERA was seen by many as an issue for equal pay and equal opportunity. This was the result of excellent propaganda ... Christians need to recognize what is happening in the feminist movement. There seem to be two segments: (1) the radical feminists who emphasize abortion on demand and related options; and (2) women who work for equal opportunities for women. Informed citizens who know Biblical principles can be a decisive factor in effecting the final demise of ERA as a Constitutional Amendment ... A better solution than a Constitutional Amendment is legislation. The Equal Pay Act of 1963, the Civil Rights Act of 1972 all give legislation and legal power to correct these kinds of injustices. There need [*sic*] to be better enforcement and appropriate legislation to guarantee equal opportunities in education, jobs and pay for women. We do not need the "evils" that may come with a loosely defined Constitutional Amendment. It is our task to search for fair and righteous laws to benefit every human being.[25]

CWA's anti-ERA campaign consisted of more than just rhetoric. The group aggressively targeted states where NOW was hard at work trying to pass the amendment. CWA employed two strategies to stymie NOW's ratification efforts. First, it used paid advertising to explain the negative consequences of the ERA on women's lives. CWA sponsored four 30-second advertisements, which were televised a total of 246 times at the cost of US$ 30,000. Second, LaHaye lobbied female politicians and invited them to stand with her publicly against the ERA. In Illinois, one of the states in which ratification was hotly contested (Staggenborg 1991), LaHaye appeared with representatives Betty Hoxsey, Mary Lou Sumner, Penny Pullen, and Mary Lou Kent at a press conference denouncing the ERA.[26]

CWA experienced mainstream media success beyond its anti-ERA campaign. In 1984, the group hired Victory Communications of Phoenix to publicize its first convention. A range of mainstream outlets produced stories on the event, including the Associated Press, CNN, CSPAN, and "The Rest of the News" (an international news program that airs on more than 300 radio stations worldwide). That same year, Beverly LaHaye appeared on the Phil Donahue Show. This success generated some enthusiasm regarding the ability of CWA to

[23] Michael, Caroline. "The Roots and Objectives of ERA." *CWFA Newsletter*, September 1983.
[24] Lyons, Barrie. "Vote on ERA Imminent." *CWFA Newsletter*, October 1983.
[25] Michael, Caroline. "The Roots and Objectives of ERA." *CWFA Newsletter*, September 1983.
[26] Unknown. "CWA Press Conference." *CWFA Newsletter*, June/July 1980.

effectively disseminate its ideas via mainstream outlets and the organization formed a communications department. However, the department, which was only staffed by secretaries, did little more than respond to media requests for information until Rebecca Hagelin, a "journalist and public relations professional," joined CWA in 1986. A press secretary for CWA explained:

> Until 1986, when Rebecca Hagelin was hired, there was not someone doing pro-active media outreach. They were responding to interview calls . . . [Then the leadership of CWA realized] that the secretary cannot handle all these calls anymore and we should have somebody to handle the [media] response.[27]

Hagelin tried to get CWA and its ideas into mainstream media coverage. She set aside the widespread suspicion of secular media and established relationships with mainstream journalists. These efforts paid off. LaHaye and other organizational spokespeople appeared on several television programs, including *Good Morning America*, *The Oprah Winfrey Show*, *The Macneil/Lehrer Newshour*, CNN News, *Nightline*, *Today*, and *Crossfire*, as well as numerous national newspapers. Hagelin also initiated programs that would teach regional and local activists how to sell CWA and its campaigns to local media as well as started the CWA Communications Coordinator Program, which handpicked activists from across the country to write press releases, feature stories, opinion pieces, and letters to the editor in order to promote local and state events. Finally, Hagelin convinced CWA to create a series of public service announcements featuring Beverly LaHaye. While these ads could not take on political issues directly, they provided CWA an opportunity to get media attention at no additional cost (other than the production of the advertisement). During Hagelin's tenure, CWA produced several thirty- and sixty-second public service announcements, which aired on stations throughout the country.[28] Hagelin cultivated opportunities for the organization to get media attention with mainstream journalists.

While Hagelin clearly was effective in this regard, the unwillingness of its leaders to target mainstream outlets meant that any serious efforts to get mainstream attention ended when Hagelin resigned. In fact, because the communications department consisted of only one paid activist during most of the 1980 to 2000 time frame, there were at least two several-month stretches where the department was unstaffed and completely inactive relative to mainstream outlets. The lack of consistent and adequate staffing had another implication as well. Each time a new communications director accepted the position she would have to begin the mainstream media efforts anew, assuming she had the inclination to do so. One former activist, who was hired as the communications director after the position was empty for several months and wanted to try to get

[27] Interview with a press secretary at CWA.
[28] Unknown. "Communications Department: Keeping CWA in the News." *CWFA Newsletter*, July 1989.

more mainstream coverage for the group, expressed frustration that none of Hagelin's programs or media contacts were maintained. She noted that she had to "start from scratch" and build media lists and networks while responding to media inquiries and addressing inaccurate media coverage across the country, which left little time for her to organize media training sessions for local activists.

When asked if CWA's belief that mainstream media were hostile to the group and its positions were behind the general lack of resources invested in the department, the former communications director implied that this indeed was a factor. She noted:

> Conservative groups did not understand media or its importance then [ten years ago] as much as they do now. [Now they understand that mainstream] media is the name of the game and whoever frames the issue wins the argument.[29]

The current communications director disagreed that there was a link between the amount of personnel and financial resources invested in the department and mainstream media coverage. Instead, she pointed to the skills and motivations of the individuals holding the position and the political ideologies of the newspaper editors.

> You kind of go through cycles of efforts. We had great newspaper outreach when Rebecca [Hagelin] was here. She wrote a column for UPI [and] regularly appeared in *USA Today*. At other times we found it very difficult to get placed anywhere. So, a lot depends on the person that's been here doing the job and the editors you're dealing with around the country.[30]

While individual connections and skill, as well as the particular interests and opinions of editors, do influence media coverage on the margins, organizational support is critical for groups to attract mainstream media (McCarthy and Zald 1977). CWA's suspicion of mainstream media made it reluctant to target these outlets and affected the amount of resources it was willing to put into its mainstream media efforts.

CWA changed its tune in the late 1990s after successfully reframing its opposition to gay rights (Dilemma 2). As the "anti-NOW," CWA has a long history opposing gay rights. Initially, the organization worked vigorously to "expose" NOW's support for gay rights to the Christian community. In 1984, CWA reported on a NOW Lesbian Rights Leadership Conference held in Milwaukee, WI, where, according to an undercover CWA member, activists met "to train and further radicalize lesbian feminists in overturning any laws which supposedly 'discriminate' against the 'lesbian lifestyle'" and to "actively campaign for the election of pro-homosexual candidates for Congress and the Presidency." The unidentified activist further revealed that NOW leaders encouraged "homosexual activists" to "cover up their activities by keeping a low profile in the press,"

[29] Interview with a former communications director at CWA.
[30] Interview with the current communications director at CWA.

because this would allow them to move their bills through the state legislature without attracting the attention of the public and the "Bible crazies," who were sure to oppose their efforts.[31]

Focusing on NOW's support for gay rights was a savvy tactic in the 1980s. CWA recognized that some feminist goals, particular those targeting wages and the workplace, would appeal to women and could swell NOW's ranks. In response, CWA identified wedge issues that conflicted with religious tradition and fed into larger political debates about gender and sexuality. It did not hurt that the nation was caught in the grips of the "AIDS crisis," which reached a fevered pitch in the 1980s. Because the medical and scientific aspects of the disease were downplayed in mainstream media, AIDS quickly became regarded as a problem within the homosexual community and the result of a socially and morally deviant lifestyle. Although the focus primarily was on gay men, emphasizing NOW's "lesbian agenda" on the heels of its ERA defeat represented an explicit attempt to diminish support among Christian women for the organization.

CWA cast NOW as one in a larger contingent of organizations that sought "to desensitize Americans into believing that 'it's OK to be gay'" – an attitude that clearly clashed with Judeo-Christianity and went against God's teachings.[32] This was clear in CWA's criticism of NOW in 1992 after its membership elected Patricia Ireland, a self-identified lesbian, president of the organization. Referencing Biblical warnings against homosexuality, Beverly LaHaye argued that NOW was trying to mainstream homosexuality:

> Rejecting these warnings from our Creator, NOW and its allies have dedicated themselves not just to promoting "gay rights" – but to making homosexuality morally acceptable. They want to break down the average person's innate sense that homosexuality is wrong and sinful – not to mention disgusting. When pressed by a CBS reporter, Ireland revealed this larger goal when she said that NOW's "battle" is to "take the sting out of being called a lesbian." And in her interview with *The Advocate*, the NOW president pledged close cooperation with the radical homosexual groups "Queer Nation" and ACT-UP, saying "Our enemies are clearly the same."[33]

CWA did not just couch its opposition to gay rights exclusively in moral terms, but also political and legal ones. CWA argued that homosexuality was an individual choice and did not warrant legal protection. At a 1991 "Day of the Family Celebration" rally in Sacramento, LaHaye stood with 3,500 Californians to oppose two bills before the legislature that would grant minority status to homosexuals and would legalize gay marriage. She argued, "homosexuals already enjoy the same rights and privileges granted to all other citizens ... The *preference* of homosexuals for an abnormal form of sexuality does not mean their desire is appropriate, normal, or should be legally

31 Unknown. "NOW Plans Lesbians' Strategy for 1984." *CWFA Newsletter*, March 1984.
32 Lussier, Elaine. "Gay Activists Press Teachers on 'Sexual Minorities.'" *CWFA Newsletter*, August 1991.
33 LeHaye, Beverly. *Family Voice*, April 1992.

protected [emphasis in original]."[34] Similarly, in an article opposing a conference in Maryland titled "Affirming Diversity for Sexual Minority Youth II," a CWA activist noted:

> The Maryland gathering illustrates another facet of the homosexual community's nationwide campaign to make its perverse sexual behavior a criterion for being considered a minority. The "sexual minority youths" that the conference hoped to "affirm" include bisexuals, homosexuals, and transsexuals. Events like this are an integral part of the effort by homosexual activists to desensitize Americans into believing that "it's OK to be gay." Until recent years, only ethnic groups and the disabled have been considered legal minorities. Members of these groups have no control over the factors that cause them to be a protected class. However, homosexuals, who *choose* to engage in unnatural behavior, are not considered minorities in any legal sense. But if they have their own way, that will change [emphasis in original].[35]

CWA also argued that legal protections for homosexuals created economic burdens for businesses by forcing corporations to financially support "unconventional relationships." Outlining the battles CWA faced in 1992, CWA activist Peter LaBarbera argued:

> Domestic partnership laws open up a can of worms for businesses and society in general as they provide disincentives for people to get married, and add a plethora of cost to businesses forced to support employees involved in unconventional "relationships." In this free land, there are few obstacles to people living as they choose, but that does not mean government should force businesses to reward them with insurance and other benefits.[36]

CWA's active opposition to gay rights had two important related consequences for the organization. First, it became a prime target of radical gay rights organizations, including Queer Nation and ACT-UP, which sent CWA faxes critiquing its stance on gay rights and protested outside its national conventions. Second, it positioned CWA as a legitimate opponent and, from the perspective of journalists, a source of information on opposition to gay rights. This is often an unintended consequence of movement campaigns. When working against their opponents, organizations inadvertently establish these groups as legitimate players and make them potential sources of information (Meyer and Staggenborg 1998). That is what happened here. In targeting CWA, gay rights organizations certified the group as an opponent and gave CWA credibility with journalists. This has not gone completely unnoticed by CWA. The press secretary for CWA at the time of this study guessed correctly that the group got far more coverage on their

[34] Unknown. "Families Rally Against Pro-Homosexual Bills." *CWFA Newsletter*, July 1991.

[35] Lussier, Elaine. "Gay Activists Press Teachers on 'Sexual Minorities.'" *CWFA Newsletter*, August 1991.

[36] LaBarbera, Peter. "What's at Stake in 1992?" *CWFA*, October 1992. CWA also challenged the validity of "special rights" for homosexuals under the "Employment Non-Discrimination Act of 1994."

opposition to gay marriage than it did on the abortion issue. She explained, "We [CWA] have definitely been a forefront player on issues dealing with homosexuality ... and gay marriage."[37]

Initially, CWA found its notoriety regarding its opposition to gay rights problematic because it often was vilified in mainstream media coverage (Dilemma 2). Don Feder, a syndicated columnist, explained to CWA activists at the organization's 1992 convention that mainstream journalists employ several conventions that cast pro-family groups in a negative light.[38] In his assessment, mainstream journalists: 1) ignored the media events of gay rights opponents whenever possible; 2) failed to include opposing views when homosexual groups were in the media spotlight; 3) stacked "the expert deck" so that there were three or four "pro-homosexual" sources for every pro-family opinion; 4) included the least articulate or most extreme representative to speak on behalf of the pro-family cause; and 5) presented the most forceful arguments for "pro-homosexual" advocates alongside the weakest responses of pro-family activists. In an effort to improve its image on the issue, CWA shifted its focus from opposing gay rights to showing homosexuals the pathway to salvation and admonishing its opponents for failing to respect the organization's right to free speech. These messages were clear in CWA's 1998 "Truth in Love" ad campaign, which appeared in newspapers across the country as well as national media outlets including *USA Today*, *The New York Times*, *The Washington Post*, and *The Washington Times*.[39] The ads largely featured individuals who had, "through the power of Christ," chosen to "come out" of homosexuality. Another advertisement defended baseball legend Reggie Jackson, who had publicly declared homosexuality a sin. CWA argued that Jackson had a right to publicly discuss his opinion and called for an open debate on homosexuality noting:

> True 'tolerance' allows Christians the right to free speech. *And recently, the only point of view covered in the media has been that of the radical homosexual activists.* We are in favor of a free and open debate on homosexuality. *Just because we disagree doesn't mean we're "homophobic." We simply believe our side is legitimate and deserves to be heard with an open mind* [emphasis in original].[40]

The ad campaign was a success. It enabled CWA to reframe its opposition to gay rights on its own terms, and in ways that resonated with democratic principles, and generated additional coverage for CWA in outlets across the country.

In the wake of this success, the CWA leadership decided that the group should increase its efforts to use mainstream outlets to disseminate its ideas to a broader audience (Dilemma 1). The press secretary reported that CWA became more "pro-active" in the late 1990s:

[37] Interview with a press secretary at CWA.

[38] Unknown. "'Overcoming Evil with Good.'" *FV*, November/December 1992.

[39] CWA tried to air a series of television advertisements, but stations rejected the ads, citing that they were too controversial.

[40] Unknown. "CWA is Making Headlines!" *FV*, September 1998.

[CWA] has taken a much more pro-active media stance [in terms of] making connections with praisers in the [network] TV world ... and secular radio. We already had a lot of good, regular connections in Christian media but I think we've moved forward a step even with those, being more pro-active, calling them, doing more to be a regular part of their shows, and trying to create real campaigns at times when it's necessary or helpful to us.[41]

She credited the strategic shift to CWA's revelation that the organization needed to be a visible part of the culture it sought to change.

One of the goals of CWA is education and educating people on issues. I think that as the issues CWA cared deeply about were debated and fought [over] in the [mainstream] media, there was a calling to be the voice for the kind of truth we were teaching our members ... [We] needed to be able to counteract the voice that was so strong in the public sphere. We still have a big emphasis on Christian media, but not everyone has access to or utilizes those tools – even if they might be someone we would consider part of our like-minded audience ... We needed to be a part of it. I think there was a growing sense that a part of our organization's role and education would have to include education through public, secular media.

CWA made three changes to its media strategy as a result of this experience. First, it reinstituted its media training programs at the state and local level and resumed its efforts to systematically communicate with the chapters. CWA established "Home Captains," whose job it was to send legislative alerts and press releases from the national to the state level. Second, CWA created a public role for its new president, Carmen Pate, and began to 'sell" her to mainstream venues. After serving as its leader for nineteen years, LaHaye stepped aside as the president in 1998 and became the chairman of the board of trustees. The move was made as part of a larger effort to attract a new generation of women to the organization. CWA also thought it might help the organization attract mainstream coverage. CWA recognized that NOW got a fair amount of coverage and that part of its success was the result of having an identifiable leader speaking on behalf of the organization. With its frequent turnover in the communications department, some due to activists accepting different positions within the organization, CWA lacked a public face relative to mainstream venues. Pate, it was decided, would be the "woman's face" of CWA.

Finally, CWA reorganized its communications department and began using a media consulting firm that represents several conservative organizations to promote its causes in mainstream outlets. In 2003, it restructured the communications department by creating a press secretary position. The press secretary generally does not provide statements to the press but arranges interviews with the appropriate policy expert in the organization. This strategy is designed to build credibility with journalists by giving them access to activists with the most expertise on a given issue. Likewise, the media consulting firm focuses on creating relationships between CWA activists and mainstream media

[41] Interview with a press secretary for CWA.

professionals. The press secretary noted that the firm has increased CWA's coverage:

> [The firm] expanded our contact base considerably. I think that is the number one thing that we are paying them for: access to the people that they know. As a firm, it is able to maintain a broader contact list and a more accurate list than I am as an individual operating alone here at CWA.

CONCLUSION

The mass media field is comprised of diverse outlets, and organizations do not have to focus on mainstream media in order to achieve their goals. CWA is an ideal example in this regard. CWA largely spurned mainstream media, other than paid advertising, and focused its efforts on conservative, Christian outlets instead. However, CWA did more than target sympathetic venues. It put substantial resources into cultivating programs, concerts, and, later, a radio station that would effectively showcase CWA and its issues. This strategy was quite successful. The group found that it could use these venues to mobilize sympathizers to action and grow its organization. Additionally, CWA found that its strong reputation in the conservative, Christian world gave it legitimacy in the political world. This is an important point. Organizations that make good use of paid media and alternative venues can build and maintain their legitimacy with like-minded politicians and, potentially, influence policy processes when their allies are in power. As such, scholars must be careful not to conflate mainstream coverage and political legitimacy. Although the two are related, organizations do not require the recognition of mainstream news outlets to be politically effective.

Not all organizations could achieve CWA's success using the same strategy. LaHaye was a prominent leader before founding CWA and had established networks with Christian media outlets. Her celebrity in Christian circles afforded her opportunities that are not necessarily available to other leaders. Additionally, CWA spent a fair amount of resources cultivating opportunities and formats that would highlight its issues. The political context also mattered. The growth of CWA corresponded with a changing political environment in which Republican candidates sought to establish relationships with Christian leaders and organizations. These relationships were mutually beneficial. Politicians reached out to leaders, who mobilized their members on behalf of Republican candidates. Once elected, leaders pressured politicians to honor their campaign promises and forward movement goals.

While CWA's strategy effectively built the organization's political clout among conservatives, it involved tradeoffs and affected how the organization responded to media dilemmas (see Table 7.1 for a summary of the organizations strategic choices). First, it affected CWA's reputation with mainstream journalists, which means it could not always weigh in on debates when and how it wanted (Dilemma 1). CWA was not regarded as a credible source of information on the abortion issue and, with so many other, more reputable

TABLE 7.1. *Summary of CWA's strategic choices*

Organizational Identity	Conservative Christian women's organization
Framing the Abortion Issue	Christian framework
Public Image	Judeo-Christian organization with a recognizable leader
Reputation in the Media Field	Strong in sympathetic outlets
Dilemma 1: Access External Media?	
Perception of Mainstream Outlets	CWA regarded mainstream journalists as hostile to its Christian ideas and focused its efforts on sympathetic outlets instead.
Examples	Yes, but not successfully on the abortion issue. It did not target mainstream outlets until the 1990s, at which point it built a media reputation on its opposition to gay rights.
Dilemma 2: Respond to Negative Attention?	
Example	Yes, pointed out that diverse points of view were part of a democratic society.
Dilemma 3: Weigh in on Losing Issues?	
Example	No, it was not regarded as reputable on the abortion issue, and gay rights was a winning issue during this time frame.
Tradeoffs	
	Resources for control over organizational presentation and messaging
	A strong reputation in mainstream outlets for a strong reputation in sympathetic venues and with conservative politicians

organizations vying for the media spotlight, it rarely received coverage. That said, the organization was not excluded from mainstream coverage altogether. Activists mobilizing around gay rights identified CWA as an enemy of their cause and, in doing so, credentialed the group as a legitimate opponent. CWA used this opportunity to get coverage and build its reputation with the mainstream. Its efforts were aided by its campaigns designed to "cure" individuals of their homosexuality and the fact that the number of actors competing to publicly oppose gay rights is far smaller than the number of groups looking to speak out against legal abortion. The CWA case illustrates that reputation can vary by issue, particularly when journalists want to include an opposing point of view. CWA never emerged as a leader on abortion, but did help lead the early charge against gay rights.

Second, it constrained how CWA responded to other media dilemmas and how it dealt with mainstream outlets. While opposing gay rights was not a losing issue in the 1980s and 1990s (a time frame in which, according to Gallup, 68 percent of those polled opposed same-sex marriage, and Congress passed and Clinton signed the Defense of Marriage Act), it is difficult to oppose civil liberties and get positive mainstream attention. Consequently, CWA initially received a fair amount of negative coverage for its position (Dilemma 2). What changed was how CWA discussed and promoted its position on the issue. Instead of focusing on the rights of the lesbian, bisexual, gay, and transgender community, CWA emphasized its right to speak freely about and defend its position in a democratic society. To ensure that freedom of speech became part of the broader debate, CWA reinforced its argument in paid advertising. However, given the changes in public opinion and legislation on same-sex marriage, this no longer is a winning issue for the organization. While CWA still "defends marriage," recent actions focus on the threat of same-sex marriage to "religious freedom" and publicly pressuring elected officials to uphold laws that define marriage as between a man and a woman. In February 2014, CWA held a press conference outside the district court house of Virginia demanding that Attorney General Mark Herring cease his attack on that state's (traditional) definition of marriage.

Finally, the CWA case reminds us that while strategies are path dependent, they are not static. Unexpected success (or failures) can cause a group to reevaluate and even change its media strategy. This transformation is apparent in each of the cases, but particularly striking here because CWA largely avoided mainstream media for a number of years. Although the organization is still suspicious of mainstream media professionals, CWA tries to use these venues to further its goals. The ability of CWA to achieve its new media goals – specifically to "speak to" a younger generation and establish itself as part of the mainstream – is not without obstacles. Ironically, the biggest obstacle in this regard has been LaHaye herself. LaHaye has been reluctant to hand over CWA's reins, which has prevented the group from creating a new public face for the organization. In September 1999, Julia Duin from *The Washington Times* argued that the organization was "undergoing an identity crisis of sorts" because LaHaye is unwilling to allow new leaders to change the organization.[42] In fact, CWA has had a fair amount of turnover in the president position since LaHaye stepped down in 1998. Carmen Pate, who took over the presidency, resigned in 2001 as a result of conflicts with LaHaye regarding the agenda and management of the organization. Pate was replaced by Sandy Rios, who resigned in 2004, citing "irreconcilable differences concerning the administration of the organization."[43] Long-time CWA activist Wendy Wright was

[42] Duin, Julia. "20-Year-Old CWA Struggles to Find, Retain New Leader." *The Washington Times*, September 1999.

[43] CWA website.

appointed to the position, but was replaced quietly by Penny Young Nance, founder of Kids First Coalition, in 2011. This tremendous turnover in leadership could have implications for the organization's political standing. While LaHaye remains a powerhouse in her eighties, a sudden departure after three decades could create an organizational void insofar as politicians, media professionals, and constituents question the viability of CWA without LaHaye at the helm. It remains to be seen whether CWA will continue to flourish without LaHaye's celebrity.

8

Conclusion

Activists want to remake the world to reflect their values, and media can help them do so. Media allow activists to introduce their ideas to a broader public, generate support for their positions, and mobilize people to action. Given the payoffs, it is not surprising that activists and scholars are interested in whether movement messages are included in media coverage. I have argued that the tendency of scholars to try to connect strategy to media outcomes – and mainstream media outcomes in particular – is short sighted insofar as it does not provide an accurate picture of how groups use mass media in their political efforts. Getting coverage is not always the goal. Sometimes an organization may think that another group is better suited to make the movement's case. PPFA, for instance, steered media professionals to allies that it felt would represent the movement well. Likewise, there are good reasons for groups to avoid media attention. While sometimes avoidance is a result of an organization's perception of external outlets (e.g., CWA), other times ignoring a media request is practical. NRLC had nothing to gain by associating itself with extremists such as Paul Hill. Similarly, PPFA decided to avoid the rancorous debate over partial-birth abortion while Clinton was in office.

The emphasis on mainstream outcomes also ignores the fact that these venues are not always the target of a group's efforts, nor is earned coverage always the goal. If an organization has the funds, it can use direct media to speak to audiences in moderated media directly. At one time or another, each of the groups used advertising to champion their ideas without the commentary or distractions of other actors. Likewise, organizations may find more utility in targeting sympathetic outlets with their ideas. CWA, for instance, virtually ignored mainstream venues and targeted Christian television and radio instead. This strategy did not drive the organization into obscurity, but allowed CWA to mobilize its constituents quickly and build its legitimacy with Republicans. In short, scholars need to move away from the idea that strategy is simply a more or less effective means to an end and focus more on the *choices* organizations make in a larger political and media context. A strategic choice approach does this by focusing attention on the three media dilemmas all groups face and identifying the tradeoffs they make.

THE MEDIA DILEMMAS ORGANIZATIONS FACE

The strategic choices a group makes matter. In the short term, the choices an actor makes can determine the success or failure of a campaign. NOW's decision to defend clinics and those accessing them gave it a much-needed membership boost and helped pave the way for legislative change. Choices, however, can have consequences over the long haul. NOW's decision to move the battle from the streets to the courtroom circumscribed its ability to weigh in on other issues for the next two decades. Decision points are rife with dilemmas, and the consequences of choosing one course of action over another are impossible to know. Here, I summarize the three media dilemmas groups face and underscore the general tradeoffs inherent to each (Table 8.1).

Dilemma 1: whether to engage external media outlets

Most scholars would regard this as a no-brainer and argue that movements should try to get their ideas in moderated outlets. The potential rewards of coverage are too great for movements to ignore. This perspective discounts the potential downsides of media attention. Poor or negative coverage can make a group seem unrealistic in its goals or dangerous, cause constituents and politicians to withdrawal their support from a cause, undermine the political inroads made by a movement, and provide opponents fodder in their efforts to derail movement progress. While the potential for poor-quality media coverage is particularly high for movement groups that use themes and tactics that fall outside the cultural and political norm, even activist organizations with good reputations will find it difficult to get their ideas picked up wholesale. Moreover, sympathetic outlets are not a panacea in this regard. Media professionals in alternative news venues are not obligated to give a complete or accurate description of an organization and its ideas, and, in fact, are likely to put their own ideological spin on the news of the day (Rohlinger 2007). Sympathetic venues are not without benefits. An organization that successfully harnesses alternative media may find that it can mobilize sympathetic audiences to action, and even move its ideas to more mainstream venues (Rohlinger and Brown 2013).

The obvious solution to the external media dilemma is for an organization to find ways to control how it is represented to the public. There are at least three ways an activist group can accomplish this. First, it can create formats and programming that allow an organization to represent the group and its issue without distortion. An organizational website, for example, can serve as a "brochure" for a group and make it easy for a web surfer to learn about a cause and join an organization (Earl and Kimport 2011). However, as illustrated

TABLE 8.1. *Central dilemmas and tradeoffs*

	Tradeoff	Examples
Dilemma 1		
Whether to access external media	Control for reach	CWA focused on sympathetic outlets and format creation to control its messaging. It had difficulty getting mainstream coverage on the abortion issue. PPFA created a brand and crafted different messages for different targets (mainstream and members).
Dilemma 2		
Whether to respond to negative coverage	Organizational public image for movement public image	NRLC remained silent on Operation Rescue's tactics so that it would not offend current or potential members. As a result, Operation Rescue became the new face of the movement.
	Movement's public image for political clout	NRLC remained silent on Operation Rescue's tactics and positions and gained members, money, and political clout.
Dilemma 3		
How to deal with losing issues	Opportunity to weigh in on the debate for potential marginalization	NOW vocally opposed popular parental involvement laws in all instances and was cast as a pro-choice extremist.
	Movement consensus for political opportunity	NRLC tried to change a losing issue (legislation without an exception) into a winning one by building consensus among prominent, mainstream groups. The consensus-building process was sufficiently long that pro-lifers missed the window to bring about sweeping political change.

in the CWA case, a group can produce concerts as well as radio, public access, and television programming to effectively spotlight its campaigns. Second, an organization can invest in direct media and use advertising to sell itself to a target audience without interference. All of the organizations in this research used advertising to control how their ideas and campaigns were relayed to a mass audience. NRLC mass-marketed the horrors of partial-birth abortion, PPFA peddled its organizational legacy, NOW sold the importance of the ERA, and CWA advocated its pro-family platform in advertisements. Third, a group may invest resources in its social media presence. Increasingly, organizations rely on Facebook, Twitter, Tumblr, Instagram, and YouTube to communicate with a geographically diffuse and technologically savvy public. However, as outlined in Chapter 2, the majority of social media platforms are oriented toward profit-making rather than political connection. Thus, some movements may have an easier time than others promoting themselves and their ideas, and finding support through commercial platforms.

While producing programming and paying for advertising allows a group to control how it is represented, there is a tradeoff. The potential audience that an organization can reach is fairly limited. Organizational websites are a great tool, but a web surfer has to be looking for the group or cause in order to be exposed to the information. Likewise, advocacy ads and content circulated on niche media venues reach relatively small audiences. Even when groups "go big" and pay for advertising in national news outlets, these expensive efforts may have a shelf life of one day and the potential effectiveness is limited to the number of people picking up the paper or tuning in at a given moment. In some cases, the tradeoff between control and reach may not be a problem. CWA targeted niche audiences in its media efforts and has lived to tell the tale. Moreover, for actors there will be events or moments that arise where staying out of media coverage and generally remaining silent makes a lot of sense. Most organizations, however, will walk the tightrope line and try to cull the benefits of news coverage and avoid some of its drawbacks with a mixed media approach – meaning they promote their ideas in earned coverage, organizational publications and websites, social media, and paid advertising.

Dilemma 2: whether to respond to negative media attention

Negative coverage is unavoidable. The dilemma is how to respond without sullying an organization's public image. The options available to an organization depend on the nature of the attack. Opponents are the easiest to deal with because audiences expect, and media thrive on, conflict. When negative coverage features the issues, tactics, and leaders of a movement, however, it is more difficult for a group to craft a reasonable response. An organization can directly respond to negative coverage and contact the media professionals responsible for the story. Both NRLC and NOW did this at different points. NRLC launched an "unending media campaign" that challenged mainstream media to quit covering pro-life extremists. Likewise, NOW responded to mainstream coverage that it found either terribly offensive. An organization also may decide to ignore unfavorable coverage. Strategic silence has its benefits. Silence can be interpreted different ways by different audiences, and these interpretations can favor the movement group. NRLC's strategic silence regarding the tactics of Operation Rescue indicated tacit approval to some audiences and repudiation to others. The organization benefited from both interpretations, and the group's coffers and membership swelled. Silence also can effectively distance an organization from a rancorous debate. PPFA did not want to get dragged into the public debate over partial-birth abortion and remained silent on the issue through much of the Clinton era. When the organization did publicly comment on the issue, PPFA took issue with the terminology used in the debate rather than defending the procedure.

The first potential tradeoff an activist group faces involves protecting its public image rather than the movement's. Choosing to protect the group's image makes a lot of sense. Survival is an organizational imperative and a group will try to minimize tactics, statements, and other activities that might result in its demise.[1] While a principled response, rather than a dramatic one, and strategic silence can protect the public image of an organization, the movement's image is likely to take a blow. Once radicals become the visible public face of a social movement, an issue may get more media attention, but the coverage is unlikely to be positive. This can undermine movement support.

This tradeoff is not always cut and dried. Sometimes an organization will take a media opportunity knowing that it will get negative coverage because it does not feel like better opportunities are forthcoming. Both NOW and CWA found themselves in this position. NOW responded to pro-life extremists and CWA took on gay rights groups because their media opportunities on the abortion issue were limited. Likewise, even when more moderate groups decide to weigh in on issues, they may find it difficult to do so. Moderate voices in a shrill debate are too muted to attract the media spotlight. This was true for NRLC. The rhetoric and actions of pro-life extremists were too enticing to be ignored by the mainstream, and, in this context, NRLC's pleas were not nearly dramatic enough to warrant media attention. Again, this does not mean that these efforts are without value. NRLC's messages may not have gotten covered, but its efforts let supporters know that the organization was trying to counter the messages of extremists. Similarly, NOW used its continual, negative coverage as a rationale for changing what and how it used mass media to share its ideas. The point here is that sometimes the tradeoff a group prefers is not the one it can take.

A second potential tradeoff involves sacrificing the movement's public image for political legitimacy and clout. The likelihood that this tradeoff will be an option for a moderate activist group depends, in part, upon the composition of a movement. Movements that consist of a range of organizations using different kinds of tactics to forward their goals are more likely to have radical groups that employ direct action as means to an end. The fiery rhetoric and uncompromising tactics of the radical flank attract media attention, put politicians on edge, and provide moderate actors a chance to extend their influence in politics

[1] This is true of radical groups as well. Operation Rescue temporarily closed its doors after it lost the lawsuit and its leadership. However, it quickly reformed under a new leader and slightly different name (Operation Rescue America).

(Haines 1988). However, this does exact a public relations cost. As radicals come to represent the movement, moderate supporters may flee, bystanders may express distaste, and opponents may "tar and feather" the movement. NRLC experienced some of these public relations problems as a result of its informal cooperation with (and public silence on) Operation Rescue. Dramatic images of activists blocking clinic entrances and Terry's insistence that abortion providers were mass murderers doomed to spend eternity in Hell reinforced stereotypes that the pro-life movement was largely white, male, and focused on religious doctrine rather than women's health. Pro-choice groups were quick to emphasize this stereotype in their efforts to mobilize support.

Dilemma 3: how to publicly deal with losing issues

Issues are rarely framed to the liking of movements and the abortion issue is not an exception in this regard. Generally speaking, framing is a consistent challenge with which an organization must contend. This is particularly true of losing issues. How a group handles losing issues is important because a group will have difficulty distancing itself from its position once a policy goes into effect. When a political loss is imminent, a group must choose its position wisely, as it will have lasting consequences. Organizations have three options, each of which involves a tradeoff. First, a group can accept a frame and challenge it on its merits. The tradeoff is that if the frame and proposed policy have widespread support, the group will be marginalized in coverage. This is what happened to NOW when it tried to defend the rights of minors in the debate over parental involvement laws. NOW argued that all women, including minors, had a right to an abortion. This argument fell on deaf ears and the group was branded with the extremist label – a tough position for an organization already struggling with the feminist backlash.

Second, a group can work to reframe the debate, but do so in ways that protect its public image. The tradeoff is that the organization will likely lose political ground, but maintain their reputation in the media field and political clout. This was the route PPFA chose in the debate over parental involvement laws. Because PPFA knew this was a losing issue, it simply tried to mitigate the "extreme" rhetoric of NOW and pull members of the "mushy middle" to the pro-choice camp with arguments that focused on government's interference in the lives and decisions of citizens. Although PPFA may not have gotten much return on its investment, it crafted frames that reinforced its brand and position as a mainstream organization – which protected its brand equity and positioned it for the next battle.

Finally, an organization can try to change a losing issue into a winning one by altering how it is regarded by its allies. The tradeoff, however, may be costly. While a group works to convince its allies to change its perspective, disputed proposals may languish (or die) in the process or the opportunity to effect change may disappear. This happened in the pro-life movement. Policy proposals that eliminated legal abortion, but did not include an exception for the life of the mother, were often considered political losers. Rather than accept a competing frame or reframe the debate, NRLC built consensus around its political proposal. Consensus-building is not an easy task and requires a lot of resources. By the time consensus was built within the pro-life movement, the opportunity to effect political change had passed. While building consensus may have a high political price tag, it plays an important public relations role. A movement that is united around a policy is less vulnerable. Even as clinic violence was on the rise in the early 1980s, the moderate middle of the pro-life movement presented a united front in its struggle to find balance between the rights of women and unborn children. This dividing line was important because it distinguished the politically legitimate pro-life organizations from the illegitimate and made it difficult for opponents to paint the entire movement as extreme.

Organizations face strategic dilemmas and must decide what tradeoffs they are willing to make as they work to push forward their goals. Strategic decision-making is not always clear or straightforward. Dilemmas are not mutually exclusive and resolving one dilemma may create another. While sometimes a group engages media knowing this is the case, often it does not. This is true of tradeoffs as well. The implications of organizational choice are not always clear, especially over the long term. A group, for instance, may decide to use mass media in their political efforts and intentionally trade off control for reach. While this decision may pay off for the organization, how a group can engage mainstream outlets in the future is circumscribed by this choice. Similarly, a group may trade off its or the movement's public image for political clout without fully understanding the ramifications of this decision. Dilemmas, in short, are recurring and not easy to resolve. This is particularly true when we consider the organizational, institutional, and movement contexts in which they are made.

ORGANIZATIONAL DYNAMICS: THE BUILDING BLOCKS OF STRATEGY

Organizations are the foundation for collective challenges. It is not surprising, then, that scholars have focused on the importance of organizational structure to strategy as well as political and media success. In terms of the latter, groups with a formalized organizational structure have an easier time building their credibility with mainstream journalists and have more opportunities to shape news coverage. While having a formal organizational structure can help an organization get media attention, it is by no means the only factor that affects media strategy. In fact, the importance of structure in facilitating the ability of organizations to attract media attention may be overstated. As illustrated by CWA, having a communications department means very little when the organization does not make the effort to staff the department on a consistent basis and it is suspicious of mainstream media. The influence of organizational characteristics on media strategy is more complex than structure alone. In this book, I highlight three additional characteristics that play a critical role in determining a group's media strategy: identity, public image, and resources.

Organizational identity affects strategy at a basic level. It specifies perceptions about American institutions and culture and how change occurs. These perceptions are important because they affect organizational decision-making. NOW identified mainstream media as an avenue through which it could influence political debate and crafted a media strategy to support its efforts early in its history. Similarly, NRLC recognized the ability of mainstream news to shape political debates and steadily built its organizational capacity so that it could use mass media more effectively. However, not all organizations regard mainstream media as a means through which they can effect change. CWA viewed mainstream journalists as hostile to its issues and goals and focused on conservative outlets instead. Organizational identity, in short, provides the scaffolding for strategic decision-making, which means it constrains how it uses mass media to forward its goals.

Of course, a group's perceptions regarding the utility of particular outlets can change over time. NOW, for instance, viewed mainstream media as generally hostile to feminism by the mid-1990s. As a result, the group looked to alternative and cable news and direct media to disseminate its ideas. Likewise, in the mid-1990s, CWA decided that it needed to take mainstream media seriously. Although it remained suspicious of secular outlets, CWA realized that it could use mainstream media to shape cultural perceptions of political issues.

As discussed in Chapter 1, organizational identity shapes media strategy in two related ways. First, it circumscribes how a group ascribes meaning to its issues, campaigns, and activities. A group must craft frames that effectively sell its ideas and campaigns to a broader public. However, its frames must be consistent with the beliefs, claims, and stated intent of the organization. Organizational identity determines the kinds of ideas that a group can champion with legitimacy while maintaining the support of existing members. Second, organizational identity affects a group's public image. Again, public image and organizational identity are related, but may be understood as the "front stage" and "back stage" of an organization respectively. On the "front stage," organizations try to gain acceptance and support, and they do so by casting themselves and their campaigns in the most appealing ways possible. While the "back stage" does not fundamentally break from the "front stage," organizations can step out of character and speak to their supporters in more polemical ways. This is something PPFA did fairly often, using internal newsletters to speak passionately to its base.

Whether an organization's identity is restricted or elaborated shapes how a group frames its issues. NOW's restricted identity as a feminist organization circumscribed its ability to tailor its frames to a mainstream audience. This was clear in the 1990s when NOW adopted an uncompromising message on parental involvement legislation just as the backlash against feminism reached a frenetic pitch. This was not true for PPFA, which has an elaborated identity. PPFA sidestepped the thorny debate over minor women's rights and framed its opposition to parental involvement laws in terms of government interference on familial life. While arguably this was not a strong rebuttal to abortion restrictions, it drew on familiar rhetoric to draw attention to the implications of restrictions.

Financially well-heeled organizations may spend a great deal of time and money on their public image and even craft a brand for an organization. As I illustrate in Chapter 6, a brand is different from a public image. The latter is a crafted interpretation of organizational ideas that is circulated to a broader public. While a good public image can help an organization achieve its goals, it is not regarded as indispensible to an organization – nor does it drive organizational choice regarding campaigns or strategies. NRLC was quick to choose political leverage over public relations. One might argue that NRLC leaders would have chosen differently had they known that OR would dominate the public scene for so long. I would disagree. NRLC knew that this was a risk and made the tradeoff anyway. As NRLC respondents note, activists were displeased by Terry's media antics. NRLC, however, was in no position to change what OR did or said and took a calculated risk. A brand, in contrast, is consistently leveraged across a broad range of media platforms (e.g., social and direct media) and affects organizational decision-making. This is why PPFA stayed out of the partial-birth abortion debate as long as possible – it was a losing issue that threatened the PPFA brand.

Brands do have benefits. An effective brand makes it easier for an organization to navigate media and politics simultaneously. PPFA's response to parental involvement laws and the partial-birth abortion debate are good examples in this regard. While the organization worked behind the political scenes to stymie these measures, publicly it weighed in on the debates when and how it chose to. Sometimes, this involved reframing the debate in different terms. For example, PPFA tried to reframe the parental involvement debate by emphasizing what these laws represented – a government intrusion on individual rights. While this line of argumentation ultimately failed, it did counter its opponents' efforts to paint pro-choicers as embittered, out-of-touch activists. Similarly, PPFA publicly avoided the rancorous debate over partial-birth abortion while Clinton was in office. When the organization did comment on the procedure, PPFA focused on the terminology being used in the debate.

Organizations that have the financial resources to craft and maintain a brand face different media challenges and have different media strategies than groups that do not. An organization with an established brand will have an easier time distinguishing itself from its allies and developing a strong reputation in the media field. As a result, it is less concerned about its ability to access media and shape discourse and more concerned about when, if, and how to weigh in on controversial issues and events – and the effects of weighing in on its brand. In this regard, media strategy primarily focuses on developing frames that test well in market research and disseminating them across the media field. These efforts do not guarantee that an organization will be able to diffuse the battle or reframe public debate; nor are they intended to do so. The purpose of these efforts is to buttress the legitimacy of an organization and set it apart from its allies as a group that has political connections and public support. Groups without a brand face more commonplace challenges such as trying to attract media attention as well as building and maintaining credibility with journalists.

The ability of an organization to craft a brand is greatly dependent upon its resources. Creating an effective public image (let alone a brand) requires tremendous amounts of time, energy, and money, which, for many groups, are already in short supply. Thus, some organizations will be quickly priced out of these kinds of media ventures. Of course, resources affect organizational decision-making more generally. Human and financial resources determine whether an organization can respond to an issue or event. NOW had so many human and financial resources tied up in its campaign and lawsuit against pro-life extremists that it had difficulty taking up other issues. While it expanded its campaign to include violence other than that taking place at abortion clinics, it was still forced to sit on the sidelines in other debates. Likewise, resources affect the more routine media efforts of an organization. Resources determine how well a media department is staffed (if at all), which shapes the kinds of media work they are able to accomplish during any given day.

Leadership is another resource. As discussed in Chapter 1, leader effectiveness is related to organizational structure. A structure that facilitates open communication, holds leaders accountable to constituents, and provides a foundation for broad-based networks increases the "strategic capacity" and effectiveness of leaders (Ganz 2000). There also are characteristics specific to leaders that can help organizations in the media field. Leaders who are institutionally credentialed can help set an organization apart from its allies. NRLC leaders, for example, stood apart from the pro-life movement as a whole because of their medical credentials. Their experiences as doctors, nurses, and researchers allowed them to speak authoritatively to journalists on the science of fetal development and the abortion procedure. Likewise, leader celebrity can help an organization garner media opportunities. CWA's figurehead, Beverly LaHaye, found it easy to build an empire of programming in conservative, Christian outlets because of her celebrity status as an author, public speaker, and the wife of conservative powerhouse, Tim LaHaye. The same is true of NOW's first leader, Betty Friedan, who was not just known as an activist, but also a seasoned journalist.

Being unique also has benefits. While it is beyond this book to analyze whether PPFA leader Faye Wattleton was a charismatic leader, she was unique insofar as she was the only African-American female leader of a national organization – a status she strategically exploited to help build PPFA's reputation and brand. It is worth noting that leaders have pull in the mass media field long after they leave an organization. Both Friedan and Wattleton publicly criticized the groups that they once ran. Friedan lamented NOW's narrow agenda, buttressing the broader criticism that the organization was losing touch with the average woman. Wattleton accused her successor of avoiding the abortion debate in favor of less controversial issues. While these very public criticisms by no means crippled the organizations, they definitely did not help the movement groups manage already difficult moments in their respective histories.

THE COMPLICATIONS OF CONTEXT

Organizations do not make strategic decisions in isolation. The broader political and movement environments provide the contexts in which groups' strategies are crafted. This book considers institutional, opposing movement, and intra-movement dynamics and their effect on strategic choice.

Groups operate in a political environment that is more or less receptive to their goals. In this regard, political allies are extraordinarily important because they can focus public and governmental attention on an issue and increase the access organizations have to political and policy processes. However, elites have their own agendas and this affects how they frame their support for (or opposition to) an issue. Because politicians consider constituencies, rather than movement groups, when they frame policy issues, some organizations will find it more difficult than others to use mainstream media to shape public discourse on a particular debate. For example, PPFA was in a much better position than NOW to respond to Clinton's Health Security Plan, which shifted the abortion debate way from whether the procedure should be legal to whether it should be universally available. As both a reproductive health care service provider and a political organization with mainstream backing, PPFA could reframe its support for abortion to focus on accessibility relatively easily and advocate on behalf of Clinton's plan via mainstream media. Even if NOW had not been bogged down in the legal battle over clinics protests and violence, it would have had difficulty crafting a campaign that championed universal health care *and* got picked up by mainstream media in a culture generally hostile to feminism. By proffering frames, elites shape the political opportunities available to an organization and its opportunities to use news media to shape discourse.

Elites also make it possible for some organizations to avoid divisive debates. If it is clear to a group that their elite allies will thwart the political efforts of their opponents, then it may avoid publicly commenting on a particular debate. This strategy is practical because it both protects the public image of the organization and it allows the group to sink its resources into institutional politics (or reserve its resources for another battle). This was the strategy of PPFA on the partial-birth abortion issue while Clinton was in office. Rather than engage in the debate, PPFA let Clinton carry the water and veto the ban. Political elites are not simply competitors vying with organizations for media attention. While this is true for groups that are reluctant to pass up any opportunity to comment on the news of the day, other organizations will strategically play off their political allies.

Opposing organizations are an important component of the political environment. Opponents can introduce new issues, find new avenues through which to pursue their goals, and frame debates in ways that are consistent with their point of view. Opponents are beneficial for groups that seek media attention. Stories involving conflict are a staple in mainstream news and, therefore, visible opponents can help organizations attract the media spotlight. CWA benefited from the opposition to its programs and goals involving gay rights. There are two other, arguably just as important, lessons highlighted in this book about opposing movements and media strategy. First, groups do not always capitalize on conflict with their opponents in order to get mainstream media coverage. In fact, a group may avoid media attention in an effort to make an issue less newsworthy or, simply, to keep themselves out of a debate. Second, whether or not a group engages its opponent in the media field depends, in part, on its reputation. Organizations with a strong reputation have more frequent and better opportunities to shape coverage. Groups that are not so well positioned will be reluctant to pass up opportunities to get their ideas and organizations in coverage, even when the coverage promises to be less than favorable.

Finally, intramovement dynamics play an important role in media strategy. Cooperation and competition shape whether and how an organization uses media to forward its goals. During moments of political threat, organizations will cooperate with one another in both the political and media arenas in an effort to stave off losses, even if they are not in complete ideological agreement (Rohlinger 2006; Staggenborg 1986). This is not necessarily the case during moments of political opportunity. In these moments, generally allied organizations will compete to push forward their own particularistic goals. As seen in the case of NRLC, savvy groups can mitigate some of this competition by engaging their allies in consensus-building. This not only helps focus movement attention on a shared political strategy, but also conveys a unified front to the broader public. If consensus-building involves prominent groups, this strategy can go a long way toward undermining opponents' efforts to demonize the movement in media.

Cooperation may be far less public. A group can work informally with allied organizations that it generally respects but cannot support in public. As seen in the relationship between NRLC and OR, cooperation involves tradeoffs. NRLC benefited from the "radical flank effect," gaining additional political leverage (Haines 1988). There was a public relations tradeoff, however. Randall Terry became the spokesperson for the movement and reinforced unflattering stereotypes regarding its composition and goals. This is an important point. NRLC absorbed the blow to its public image in order to enhance its political influence. In other words, while getting media attention and shaping how the public sees political issues are essential, many groups regard political leverage as more important.

Cooperation is not always possible. Personal animosities as well as ideological differences can make competition the only option. In these instances, an organization must decide how to respond to its allies without undermining its public image. Ignoring an ally's attacks can buttress an organization's efforts to cast itself as mainstream and politically powerful. However, an organization will eventually be forced to respond in kind. In some cases, allies are so extreme that renouncing them altogether is the best strategy a group can employ. NRLC did all of these things when dealing with its allies. NRLC blithely responded to ALL's attacks largely through correspondence until ALL's attacks extended beyond its newsletter. Once ALL publicly criticized the group, NRLC pushed back publicly. Likewise, NRLC condemned the violent acts of pro-life extremists.

A group often engages in cooperation and conflict with allied movement organizations simultaneously and, consequently, adopts different strategies for dealing with different groups. Although decisions to engage in cooperation or conflict are not static, it is clear that two considerations influence how it responds to its allies. First, it considers the costs and benefits of publicly distancing itself from (or renouncing the activities of) an ally. If openly criticizing an ally may have adverse consequences for an organization, it is unlikely to do so. Likewise, if an organization can garner additional political leverage as a result of its ally's position or campaigns, it is likely to exploit this opportunity, even if it potentially means bad publicity for the movement and organization. Second, a group considers the political environment in which its strategic decisions are made. An organization is much more likely to take a hit to its public image in a political environment receptive to its cause because political/legislative change is a possibility. Conversely, a group is less likely to make such a tradeoff in a political environment hostile to its goals because political change is the unlikely and, therefore, nothing would be gained by enduring a period of negative publicity.

Organizational, institutional, and movement dynamics interact and influence the strategic choices of groups. This means that media strategy is far more complicated than previous research suggests. Scholars are myopic when they think about media strategy as simply a means to mainstream news. While coverage has benefits, it is only one aspect of a larger strategic calculus in which the choices available constantly change. A group faces dilemmas and makes tradeoffs that are not just a function of organizational assets or deficits, but also a reflection of the positions of elites, allies, and opponents. However, there is a final component of this equation that matters – the mass media field itself.

THE MASS MEDIA FIELD: RECONCEPTUALIZATION AND REPUTATION

Another key contribution of this book is the reconceptualization of mass media in order to highlight how an organization's reputation affects its ability to use mass media for its own purposes. While the time frame of the analysis necessitates a focus on print and broadcast media, my conceptualization of the media field, which highlights the importance of reputation, has utility beyond these cases. An organization whose identity corresponds with the institutional logic of the field as well as the more particularistic goals of the media outlet it is targeting has a stronger reputation than a group whose identity does not. Early in the book, I distinguish reputation from standing and argue that reputation provides additional leverage in scholarly efforts to understand the movement–media relationship. Reputation explains how a group's opportunity to use media to forward their goals varies across the field. The mass media field is composed of three layers – moderated media, social media, and direct media – that differ in their form, function, and the extent to which they are oriented to the heteronomous and autonomous poles. As such, a group's reputation in one outlet may be very different to how it is viewed in another – and these variations can affect whether and how an organization uses a venue to forward its goals. A group with a weak reputation in mainstream media outlets may be well regarded by an alternative journalist who is sympathetic to the organization's cause and not bound to be objective in news coverage. Not only is such an outlet inclined to cover movement issues at higher frequency, in more depth, and with an eye to diversity of opinion on an issue, but an organization can use these venues to speak directly to their constituents, mobilize sympathetic audiences to action, and even cross their ideas over to larger, more mainstream venues. The same group may also find a following on social media and occasionally try to attract new supporters through direct media efforts. Reputation helps illuminate when and which outlets a social movement does or does not target.

Reputation explains the media efforts of an organization more generally. A group with a strong reputation may focus its media efforts primarily on mainstream venues. This is largely because it has many more options available to it than a group with a weak reputation. For instance, organizations with a strong reputation do not have to get media attention to acquire coverage, but can do so behind the scenes. Likewise, groups with a strong reputation can get their ideas in coverage, even if they diverge from the contemporary debate. In contrast, movement groups with a weak reputation will enter the mainstream fray even if the results promise to be less than desirable. Not surprisingly, the media efforts of these organizations will be different insofar as they will rely more heavily on direct and social media outlets to forward their goals. Reputation can vary by outlet. As seen in the CWA case, organizations can build their political muscles with politicians on one side of the aisle using sympathetic outlets alone. A smart organization understands that reputation circumscribes how it will be able to use media and will play to its strengths in the field.

Reputation provides a more nuanced account of media outcomes. While it is important to observe whether a group gets mainstream attention, this is not the only relevant media outcome. Whether coverage helps a group accomplish its goals is arguably more important than the coverage itself. An organization with a strong reputation is more likely to regard mainstream media coverage as a goal, which may entail everything from shaping political debate to reasserting its position as a moderate movement group. This is less true of groups with a weak reputation, which are more likely to regard mainstream attention as a means to an end, and try to find ways to connect the audience with their organizations. NOW, for example, used its media conflict with the Promise Keepers to draw thousands of visitors to its website, which fully outlined its opposition to the group. Organizations also target different media venues for different reasons, and the outcomes in these outlets are no less important. If an organization with a weak reputation in mainstream venues opts for outlets with sympathetic audiences, it is important to discern whether their ideas are covered and whether a group is meeting its goals.

Reputation is sensitive to movement and political dynamics. An organization's reputation varies according to the composition of the movement and broader culture. Media professionals determine the reputation of an organization, in part, by comparing it to its allies. Because movements can vary dramatically in their organizational composition, some groups may find it more difficult to maintain a strong reputation than others. Some movements are largely comprised of national organizations that employ a professional staff to shape legislative debate and policy (e.g., the pro-choice movement). Others may be segmented insofar as they have different areas of specialization and, consequently, have fewer formal organizations working to effect policy change (e.g., the pro-life movement). In these movements, professional organizations will stand apart from their allies and have a relatively strong reputation with a range of outlets in the media field. NRLC is a good example. It stood out to journalists in a movement composed of organizations with diverse – often religious – aims, most of which had little to do with institutional change.

Again, scholars cannot simply focus on moderated media if they are to understand strategic choice as it relates to mass media. Groups use news media, newsletters and websites, concerts, games, social media, talk radio, and, even, create radio and television broadcasts in order to achieve their media goals. These diverse efforts should not be considered as fundamentally different or separate from one another. On the one hand, this makes studying strategy demanding work. It takes time and tenacity to provide a relatively comprehensive account of a group's media efforts. On the other hand, it presents an opportunity to build interdisciplinary bridges and better leverage the findings of one discipline on another. Technology moves at an astounding rate, and, just as quickly, activists find new ways to exploit it for their own purposes. If scholars want to keep up and understand the movements around us, we need to work across the disciplinary divides.

Afterword: abortion politics in the twenty-first century

The battle over abortion continues. Over the last two decades the pro-life movement has continued to gain legislative ground, pushing the limits of what constitutes on "undue burden" on women. Mandatory waiting periods (required in twenty-six states), abortion counseling (required in thirty-five states), and ultrasounds (required in twelve states) as well as the ability of individual health care providers and institutions to refuse to participate in or provide abortion services (in forty-six and forty-three states respectively) have increased the costs of the abortion procedure. Depending on the number and type of restrictions as well as TRAP (Targeted Regulation of Abortion Providers) laws, which require facilities that provide abortions to meet the same standards as ambulatory surgical centers or abortion providers to be affiliated with local hospitals, women may find that they have to cross state lines multiple times in order to obtain an abortion. For some women, the costs of gas, hotel bills, a required ultrasound, and the procedure are simply too high.[1]

Legislative efforts, particularly those aimed at defunding Planned Parenthood, gained momentum in 2010 with the influx of Tea Party politicians at the state level. As I discuss elsewhere (Rohlinger et al. 2014; Rohlinger and Klein 2014), Independents, Libertarians, and some disgruntled Democrats quickly learned that the "smaller government" mantra of political candidates was little more than a campaign promise. Much to the chagrin of supporters, once Tea Party politicians took state office they championed a socially conservative legislative agenda. In Florida, where Republicans hold a super-majority in Congress and are led by Tea Party-favorite Governor Rick Scott, the legislature quickly introduced eighteen additional restrictions to abortion access as well as

[1] For the most recent trends regarding abortion legislation, see the Guttmacher Institute's State Center at http://www.guttmacher.org/statecenter/abortion.html.

state-mandated drug testing of welfare recipients and state employees (elected officials were excluded from the latter). Recent pro-life legislative gains have been, in part, a result of social conservativism's new Tea Party package.

Likewise, mainstream pro-life groups have done an excellent job shifting the debate away from women's health as a whole. Debates over taxpayers' rights, parental rights, practitioner and pharmacist rights, and the rights of the unborn have narrowed concerns regarding women's health to topics such as whether abortion is linked to breast cancer and whether abortion negatively affects women's mental health. These efforts have been aided by groups such as Women Exploited by Abortion, which feature anecdotes from women who regret their abortions and campaigns that compare abortion to genocide. While these projects are controversial, they have largely gone unanswered by pro-choicers. This relative silence fuels the sense of stigma around the procedure and legitimizes the interpretations of the few women who are willing to discuss their abortion experiences publicly.

Most recently, the abortion debate has been subsumed in the partisan fight over the Patient Protection and Affordable Care Act (ACA). The battle over abortion coverage in the ACA took center stage in 2009 when pro-lifers contended that the bill forced pro-life Americans to pay for other people's abortions. This tactic proved successful in the 1990s when pro-life Republicans used the abortion issue to squelch Clinton's attempt at health care reform. Anticipating the firestorm, Obama issued Executive Order 13585 – Patient Protection and Affordable Care Act's Consistency with Longstanding Restrictions on the Use of Federal Funds for Abortion, which extended the Hyde Amendment restrictions to the new state health insurance exchanges, on March 24, 2010. Although Republicans occasionally return to this issue, conservatives now include contraception and sterilization in their criticism of the ACA and are challenging the law on religious grounds. In fact, at the time of this writing, a divided Supreme Court recently ruled on the *Sebelius v. Hobby Lobby Stores, Inc.* and *Conestoga Wood Specialties Corp. v. Sebelius* cases. The consolidated cases challenged the ACA's "contraceptive mandate," which requires employers to cover all federally approved contraception methods at no additional cost to their employees. The Christian owners of the two companies successfully argued that contraception is synonymous with abortion and is in violation of their religious beliefs.

Progressive groups and respected scholars are quick to point out that conservatives put forward a nearly identical health care plan in 1993 (see Quadagno 2005, 2011, 2014 for a comprehensive discussion of health care reform in the United States). Democrats and feminists are less charitable in their characterization and argue that Republicans are waging a "war on women." The description found political legs among some American women, who were appalled by the violent gang rape of an Indian woman on a New Delhi bus, political-hopeful Todd Aiken's comment that victims of "legitimate rape" rarely got pregnant, and, more recently, the Supreme Court ruling that struck down a Massachusetts law that created buffer zones prohibiting protestors from blocking abortion clinic entrances and walkways (*McCullen v. Coakley*). It remains to be seen whether these rulings motivate American women to vote on election day.

The pro-choice movement has changed as well over the last two decades. Pro-choice groups have been working to connect abortion to a broader reproductive justice agenda – and the movement's efforts to reframe how inequality affects reproductive options and decision-making are coming to fruition. These efforts have gained steam in the wake of national health care reform. However, dissention among pro-lifers has helped as well. Radical groups are intent on pushing "personhood" legislation, which defines a fertilized human egg as a legal person. Mainstream groups such as NRLC distance themselves from this unpopular legislation, arguing that it cannot withstand legal scrutiny and could affect the availability of contraception, which, in turn, could mobilize the citizenry against the movement. Unmoved by these arguments, radicals once again argue that NRLC is not really pro-life and urge activists to withdraw financial and moral support from the organization.

These internal debates have been further complicated by the Catholic Church, which has seemingly backed off the abortion issue. Nuns associated with the Leadership Conference of the Women Religious made national news in 2012 when they challenged what it means to be Catholic and pro-life in the twenty-first century. Speaking to Terry Gross on NPR's Fresh Air, Sister Pat Farrell responded to the Church's criticism that the Leadership Conference of the Women Religious didn't push the pro-life position enough by connecting the right-to-life cause with social justice more generally. She noted:

> I think the criticism of what we're not talking about seems to me to be unfair ... Our works are very much pro-life. We would question, however, any policy that is more pro-fetus than actually pro-life. If the rights of the unborn trump all of the rights of all of those who are already born, that is a distortion ... We have strongly spoken out against the death penalty, against war, hunger. All of those are right-to-life issues.

While Pope Benedict XVI strongly disagreed, Pope Francis has not taken a hard line approach on social issues, including abortion and gay marriage. In fact, Pope Francis urged Catholics to back away from their "obsession" with abortion, contraception, and homosexuality and focus on the social justice example set by Jesus instead. This conceptualization of "pro-life" advocates for policy solutions that redress social, political, and economic inequality and clearly shares common ground with activists fighting for reproductive justice.

While I cannot predict what will happen next in the battle over abortion, the trajectories of the movements may look quite different in the coming decade. Pro-lifers clearly are prepared to stay the course that has brought them success in the past – arguing that other rights such as religious and free speech trump those of women's right to contraception and abortion. Pro-choicers, however, look ready to explore a new path, one that could create new coalitions and energy around women's issues as a whole. Change, of course, is never easy. It remains to be seen if pro-choice groups, particularly ones who have made their political reputations championing legal abortion, are ready to turn their social justice discourse into sustained action.

Works cited

Aaker, David. 1991. *Managing Brand Equity: Capitalizing on the Value of a Brand Name*. New York: Free Press.

Amenta, Edwin. 2006. *When Movements Matter: The Townsend Plan and the Rise of Social Security*. Princeton, NJ: Princeton University Press.

Amenta, Edwin, Beth Gharrity Gardner, Amber Celina Tierney, Anaid Yerena, and Thomas Alan Elliott. 2012. "Set in Stories: Standing and Demands in the Newspaper Coverage of SMOs, and the Townsend Plan." *Research on Social Movements, Conflicts & Change* 33.

Amenta, Edwin, Neal Caren, Sheera Joy Olasky, and James Stobaugh. 2009. "All the Movements Fit to Print: Who, What, When, Where and Why SMO Families Appeared in the New York Times in the Twentieth Century." *American Sociological Review* 74:636–656.

Andrews, Kenneth. 2004. *Freedom is a Constant Struggle*. Chicago: University of Chicago Press.

Andrews, Kenneth, and Neal Caren. 2010. "Making the News: Movement Organizations, Media Attention, and the Public Agenda." *American Sociological Review* 75:841–866.

Armstrong, Elizabeth. 2002. *Forging Gay Identities: Organizing Sexuality in San Francisco: 1950–1994*. Chicago: University of Chicago Press.

Armstrong, Elzabeth, and Mary Bernstein. 2008. "Culture, Power, and Institutions: A Multi-Institutional Politics Approach to Social Movements." *Sociological Theory* 26:74–99.

Atton, Chris. 2001. *Alternative Media*. Thousand Oaks, CA: Sage Publications Ltd.

Atton, Chris, and Emma Wickenden. 2006. "Sourcing Routines and Representation in Alternative Journalism: A Case Study Approach." *Journalism Studies* 6:347–359.

Baker, C. Edwin. 2002. *Media, Markets, and Democracy*. New York: Cambridge University Press.

Barasko, Maryann. 2004. *Governing NOW: Grassroots Activism in the National Organization for Women*. Ithaca, New York: Cornell University Press.

Barker-Plummer, Bernadette. 2002. "Producing Public Voice: Resource Mobilization and Media Access in the Nation." *Journalism and Mass Communication Quarterly* 79:188–205.

Benford, Robert. 1993. "Frame Disputes within the Nuclear Disarmament Movement." *Social Forces* 71:677–701.
Benford, Robert, and David Snow. 2000. "Framing Processes and Social Movements: An Overview and Assessment." *Annual Review of Sociology* 26:611–639.
Bennett, Lance. 2003. "Communicating Global Activism." *Information, Communication & Society* 6:143–168.
Bennett, Lance, Regina Lawrence, and Steven Livingston. 2007. *When the Press Fails: Political Power and the News Media from Iraq to Katrina*. Chicago: University of Chicago Press.
Bennett, Lance, and Alexandra Segerberg. 2013. *The Logic of Connective Action: Digital Media and the Personalization of Contentious Politics*. New York: Cambridge University Press.
Benson, Rodney. 2005. "Mapping Field Variation: Journalism in France and the United States." Pp. 85–112 in *Bourdieu and the Journalistic Field*, edited by Rodney Benson and Erik Neveu. Malden: Polity Press.
2006. "News Media as a "Journalistic Field": What Bourdieu Adds to New Institutionalism, and Vice Versa." *Political Communication* 23:187–202.
Benson, Rodney, and Daniel Hallin. 2007. "How States, Markets and Globalization Shape the News: The French and US National Press, 1965–97." *European Journal of Communication* 22:27–48.
Benson, Rodney, and Erik Neveu. 2005. *Bourdieu and the Journalistic Field*. Malden, MA: Polity Press.
Benson, Rodney, and Abigail Saguy. 2005. "Constructing Social Problems in an Age of Globalization: A French-American Comparison." *American Sociological Review* 70:233–259.
Berlet, Chip. 1998. "Who's Mediating the Storm? Right-Wing Alternative Information Networks." Pp. 249–273 in *Media, Culture, and the Religious Right*, edited by Linda Kintz and Julia Lesage. Minneapolis: University of Minnesota Press.
Bimber, Bruce, Andrew Flanagin, and Cynthia Stohl. 2012. *Collective Action in Organizations: Interaction and Engagement in an Era of Technological Change*. New York: Cambridge University Press.
Blackett, Tom. 2009. "What is a Brand?" Pp. 13–25 in *Brands and Branding*, edited by Rita Clifton. Hoboken, NJ: Bloomberg Press.
Blanchard, Dallas. 1995. *The Anti-Abortion Movement and the Rise of the Religious Right*. New York: Twayne Publishers.
Bob, Clifford. 2005. *The Marketing of Rebellion: Insurgents, Media, and International Activism*. Cambridge: Cambridge University Press.
Bourdieu, Pierre. 1998a. *On Television*. New York: New Press.
1998b. *Practical Reason: On the Theory of Action*. Stanford, CA: Stanford University Press.
2005. "The Political Field, the Social Science Field, and the Journalistic Field." Pp. 29–47 in *Bourdieu and the Journalistic Field*, edited by Rodney Benson and Erik Neveu. Malden, MA: Polity.
Bowker, Deborah. 2009. "The Public Relations Perspective on Branding." Pp. 143–155 in *Brands and Branding*, edited by Rita Clifton. Hoboken, NJ: Bloomberg Press.
Brymer, Chuck. 2009. "What Makes a Brand Great." Pp. 65–76 in *Brands and Branding*, edited by Rita Clifton. Hoboken, NJ: Bloomberg Press.

Burns, Gene. 2005. *The Moral Veto: Framing Contraception, Abortion, and Cultural Pluralism in the United States*. New York: Cambridge University Press.

Chesler, Ellen. 1992. *Woman of Valor: Margaret Sanger and the Birth Control Movement in America*. New York: Simon & Schuster.

Clemens, Elizabeth. 1993. "Organization Repertoires and Institutional Change: Women's Groups and the Transformation of U.S. Politics, 1890–1920." *American Journal of Sociology* 98:755–798.

1996. "Organizational Form as Frame: Collective Identity and Political Strategy in the American Labor Movement, 1880–1920." Pp. 205–226 in *Comparative Perspectives on Social Movements: Political Opportunities, Mobilizing Structures, and Cultural Framings*, edited by Doug McAdam, John McCarthy, and Mayer Zald. New York: Cambridge University Press.

1997. *The People's Lobby: Organizational Innovation and the Rise of Interest Group Politics in the United States, 1890–1925*. Chicago: University of Chicago Press.

Costain, Anne. 1992. *Inviting Women's Rebellion: A Political Process Interpretation of the Women's Movement*. Baltimore: The John Hopkins University Press.

Critchlow, Donald. 1999. *Intended Consequences: Birth Control, Abortion, and the Federal Government in Modern America*. New York: Oxford University Press.

Curtis, Russell, and Louis Zurcher. 1973. "Stable Resources of Protest Movements: The Multi-Organizational Field." *Social Forces* 52:53–61.

1974. "Social Movements: An Analytical Exploration of Organizational Forms." *Social Problems* 21:356–370.

Deephouse, David. 1999. "To Be Different, or to Be the Same? It's a Question (And Theory) of Strategic Balance." *Strategic Management Journal* 20:147–166.

Diamond, Sara. 1995. *Roads to Dominion: Right Wing Movements and Political Power in the United States*. New York: The Guilford Press.

DiMaggio, Paul, and Walter Powell. 1983. "The Iron Cage Revisited: Institutional Isomorphism and Collective Rationality in Organizational Fields." *American Sociological Review* 48:147–160.

Downey, Dennis, and Deana Rohlinger. 2008. "Linking Strategic Choice with Macro Organizational Dynamics: Strategy and Social Movement Articulation." *Research on Social Movements, Conflicts and Change* 28:3–38.

Dugan, Kimberly. 2004. "Strategy and 'Spin'": Opposing Movement Frames in An Anti-Gay Voter Initiative. *Sociological Focus* 37: 213–233.

Duval, Julien. 2005. "Economic Journalism in France." Pp. 135–155 in *Bourdieu and the Journalistic Field*, edited by Rodney Benson and Erik Neveu. Malden: Polity Press.

Earl, Jennifer. 2006. "Pursuing Social Change Online: The Use of Four Protest Tactics on the Internet." *Social Science Computer Review* 24:362–377.

Earl, Jennifer, and Katrina Kimport. 2011. *Digitally Enabled Social Change: Activism in the Internet Age*. New York: MIT Press.

Einwohner, Rachel. 2002. "Bringing the Outsiders In: Opponents' Claims and the Construction of Animal Rights Activists' Identity." *Mobilization: An International Quarterly* 7:253–268.

Ellingson, Stephen. 1995. "Understanding the Dialectic of Discourse and Collective Action: Public Debate and Rioting in Antebellum Cincinnati." *American Journal of Sociology* 101:100–144.

Eyerman, Ron, and Andrew Jamison. 1998. *Music and Social Movements: Mobilizing Traditions in the Twentieth Century*. Cambridge: Cambridge University Press.

Feldwick, Paul. 2009. "Brand Communications." Pp. 127–141 in *Brands and Branding*, edited by Rita Clifton. Hoboken, NJ: Bloomberg Press.

Ferree, Myra Marx. 2003. "Resonance and Radicalism: Feminist Framing in the Abortion Debates of the United States and Germany." *American Journal of Sociology* 109:304–344.

Ferree, Myra Marx, William Gamson, Jurgen Gerhards, and Dieter Rucht. 2002. *Shaping Abortion Discourse: Democracy and the Public Sphere in Germany and the United States*. New York: Cambridge University Press.

Fetner, Tina, and Carrie Sanders. 2012. "Similar Strategies, Different Outcomes: Institutional Histories of the Christian Right of Canada and of the United States." Pp. 245–262 in *Strategies for Social Change*, edited by Gregory Maney, Rachel Kutz-Flamenbaum, Deana Rohlinger, and Jeff Goodwin. Minneapolis: University of Minnesota Press.

Flanagin, Andrew, Cynthia Stohl, and Bruce Bimber. 2006. "Modeling the Structure of Collective Action." *Communication Monographs* 73:29–54.

Fligstein, Neil. 2001. "Social Skills and the Theory of Fields." *Sociological Theory* 19:105–125.

Fligstein, Neil, and Doug McAdam. 2012. *A Theory of Fields*. New York: Oxford University Press.

Friedland, Roger and Robert Alford. 1991. "Bringing Society Back In: Symbols, Practices, and Institutional Contradictions" Pp. 232–263 in *The New Institutionalism in Organizational Analysis*, edited by W. Powell and P. DiMaggio. Chicago: University of Chicago Press.

Gamson, Joshua. 1994. *Claims to Fame: Celebrity in Contemporary America*. Los Angeles: University of California Press.

"Messages of Exclusion: Gender, Movements, and Symbolic Boundaries." *Gender & Society* 11:178–199.

Gamson, William. 1990. *The Strategy of Social Protest*. Homewood, IL: Dorsey Press.

Gamson, William, David Croteau, William Hoynes, and Theodore Sasson. 1992. "Media Images and the Social Construction of Reality." *Annual Review of Sociology* 18:373–393.

Gamson, William, and David Meyer. 1996. "Framing Political Opportunity." Pp. 275–290 in *Comparative Perspectives on Social Movements: Political Opportunities, Mobilizing Structures, and Cultural Framings*, edited by Doug McAdam, John McCarthy, and Mayer Zald. Cambridge: Cambridge University Press.

Gamson, William, and Gadi Wolfsfeld. 1993. "Movement and Media as Interacting Systems." *The Annals of the American Academy of Political and Social Science* 578:104–125.

Gans, Herbert. 1979. *Deciding What's News: A Study of CBS Evening News, NBC Nightly News, Newsweek, and Time*. New York: Pantheon Books.

Ganz, Marshall. 2000. "Resources and Resourcefulness: Strategic Capacity in the Unionization of California Agriculture, 1959–1966." *American Journal of Sociology* 105:1003–1062.

Gerlach, Luther, and Virginia Hine. 1970. *People, Power, and Change*. Indianapolis: Bobbs-Merrill.

Gitlin, Todd. 1980. *The Whole World is Watching: Mass Media in the Making and Unmaking of the New Left*. Los Angeles: University of California Press.

Goffman, Erving. 1959. *The Presentation of Self in Everyday Life*. New York: Anchor.

Haines, Herbert. 1984. "Black Radicalization and the Funding of Civil Rights: 1957–1970." *Social Problems* 32:31–43.

1988. *Black Radicals and the Civil Rights Mainstream, 1954–1970*. Knoxville, TN: The University of Tennessee Press.

Haney, Eleanor Humes. 1985. *A Feminist Legacy: The Ethics of Wilma Scott Heide and Company*. Buffalo: Margaretdaughters, Inc.

Harcup, Tony. 2003. "'The Unspoken – Said': The Journalism of Alternative Media." *Journalism* 4:356–376.

Hathaway, Will, and David Meyer. 1997. "Competition & Cooperation in Movement Coalitions: Lobbying for Peace in the 1980s." Pp. 61–79 in *Coalitions and Political Movements: The Lessons of the Nuclear Freeze*, edited by T. Rochon and D. Meyer. Boulder, Colorado: Lynne Rienner Publishers.

Hensmans, Manuel. 2003. "Social Movement Organizations: A Metaphor for Strategic Actors in Institutional Fields." *Organization Studies* 24:355–381.

Hermida, Alfred. 2010. "Twittering the News: The Emergence of Ambient Journalism." *Journalism Practice* 4:297–308.

Hilgartner, Stephen, and Charles Bosk. 1988. "The Rise and Fall of Social Problems: A Public Arenas Model." *American Journal of Sociology* 94:53–78.

Hoff, Derek. 2010. ""Kick that Population Commission in the Ass": The Nixon Administration, the Commission on Population Growth and the American Future, and the Defusing of the Population Bomb." *Journal of Policy History* 22:23–63.

Jamieson, Kathleen Hall, and Joesph Cappella. 2010. *Echo Chamber: Rush Limbaugh and the Conservative Media Establishment*. New York: Oxford University Press.

Jasper, James. 1997. *The Art of Moral Protest: Culture, Biography, and Creativity in Social Movements*. Chicago: The University of Chicago Press.

2004. "A Strategic Approach to Collective Action: Looking for Agency in Social-Movement Choices." *Mobilization* 9:1–16.

Jasper, James. 2006. *Getting Your Way: Strategic Dilemmas in the Real World*. Chicago: University of Chicago Press.

Jasper, James. 2012. "Choice Points, Emotional Batteries, and Other Ways to Find Strategy Agency at the Microlevel." Pp. 23–42 in *Strategies for Social Change*, edited by Gregory Maney, Rachel Kutz-Flamenbaum, Deana Rohlinger, and Jeff Goodwin. Minneapolis: University of Minnesota.

Johnson, Victoria. 1997. "Operation Rescue, Vocabularies of Motive, and Tactical Action: A Study of Movement Framing in the Practice of Quasi-Nonviolence." *Research in Social Movements, Conflicts and Change* 20:103–150.

Keller, Kevin Lane. 1999. "Managing Brands for the Long Run: Brand Reinforcement and Revitalization Strategies." *California Management Review* 41:102–124.

King, Brayden, and Sarah Soule. 2007 "Social Movements as Extra-institutional Entrepreneurs: The Effect of Protest on Stock Price Returns." *Administrative Science Quarterly* 52:413–442.

Kintz, Linda, and Julia Lesage (Eds.). 1998. *Media, Culture, and the Religious Right*. Minneapolis: University of Minnesota Press.

Klandermans, Bert. 1988. "The Formation and Mobilization of Consensus." Pp. 173–196 in *International Social Movement Research: A Research Annual Volume I*, edited by Bert Klandermans, Hanspeter Kriesi, and Sidney Tarrow. Greenwich, CT: JAI Press Inc.

1992. "The Social Construction of Protest and Multiorganizational Fields." Pp. 77–103 in *Frontiers in Social Movement Theory*, edited by Aldon Morris and Carol McClurg Mueller. New Haven: Yale University Press.
Koopmans, Ruud, and Susan Olzak. 2004. "Discursive Opportunities and the Evolution of Right-Wing Violence in Germany." *American Journal of Sociology* 110:198–230.
Lader, Lawrence. 1955. *The Margaret Sanger Story and the Fight for Birth Control.* New York: Doubleday.
Lasorsa, Dominic, Seth Lewis, and Avery Holton. 2012. "Normalizing Twitter: Journalism Practice in an Emerging Communication Space." *Journalism Studies* 13:19–36.
Lievrouw, Leah. 2011. *Alternative and Activist New Media: Digital Media and Society.* New York: Polity.
Lo, Clarence. 1982. "Countermovements and Conservative Movements in the Contemporary U.S." *Annual Review of Sociology* 8:107–134.
Luker, Kristin. 1984. *Abortion and the Politics of Motherhood.* Los Angeles: University of California Press.
Marchetti, Dominique. 2005. "Subfields of Specialized Journalism." Pp. 64–82 in *Bourdieu and the Journalistic Field*, edited by Rodney Benson and Erik Neveu. Malden, MA: Polity Press.
Marshall, David. 1997. *Celebrity and Power: Fame and Contemporary Culture.* Minneapolis: University of Minnesota Press.
Martin, John Levi. 2003. "What Is Field Theory." *American Journal of Sociology* 109:1–49.
Maxwell, Carol. 2002. *Pro-Life Activists in America: Meaning, Motivation, and Direct Action.* New York: Cambridge University Press.
McAdam, Doug, John McCarthy, and Mayer Zald. 1996. *Comparative Perspectives on Social Movements: Political Opportunities, Mobilizing Structures, and Cultural Framings.* New York: Cambridge University Press.
McCammon, Holly. 2003. ""Out of the Parlors and into the Streets": The Changing Tactical Repertoire of the U.S. Women's Suffrage Movements." *Social Forces* 81:787–818.
2012. *The U.S. Women's Juy Movement and Strategic Adaptation: A More Just Verdict.* Cambridge: Cambridge University Press.
McCammon, Holly J., and Karen Campbell. 2002. "Allies on the Road to Victory: Coalition Formation Between The Suffragists and the Woman's Christian Temperance Union." *Mobilization* 7:213–251.
McCarthy, John, Clark McPhail, and Jackie Smith. 1996. "Images of Protest: Dimensions of Selection Bias in Media Coverage of Washington Demonstrations, 1982 and 1991." *American Sociological Review* 61:478–499.
McCarthy, John, Jackie Smith, and Mayer Zald. 1996. "Accessing public, media, electoral, and governmental agendas." Pp. 291–311 in *Comparative Perspectives on Social Movements: Political Opportunities, Mobilizing Structures, and Cultural Framing*, edited by Doug McAdam, John McCarthy, and Mayer Zald. New York: Cambridge University Press.
McCarthy, John, and Mayer Zald. 1977. "Resource Mobilization and Social Movements: A Partial Theory." *American Journal of Sociology* 82:1212–1241.
McManus, John. 1994. *Market Driven Journalism: Let the Citizen Beware?* Thousand Oaks, CA: Sage Publications.

Meyer, David. 2004. "Protest and Political Opportunities." *Annual Review of Sociology* 30:125–145.
Meyer, David, and Joshua Gamson. 1995. "The Challenges of Cultural Elites: Celebrities and Social Movements." *Sociological Inquiry* 65:181–206.
Meyer, David, and Debra Minkoff. 2004. "Conceptualizing Political Opportunities." *Social Forces* 82:1457–1892.
Meyer, David, and Suzanne Staggenborg. 2012. "Thinking About Strategy." Pp. 3–22 in *Strategies for Social Change*, edited by Gregory Maney, Rachel Kutz-Flamenbaum, Deana Rohlinger, and Jeff Goodwin. Minneapolis: University of Minnesota Press.
1998. "Countermovement Dynamics in Federal Systems: A Comparison of Abortion Politics in Canada and the United States." *Research in Political Sociology* 8:209–240.
1996. "Movements, Countermovements, and the Structure of Political Opportunity." *American Journal of Sociology* 101:1628–1660.
Meyer, David, and Sidney Tarrow. 1998. *The Social Movement Society: Contentious Politics for a New Century*. New York: Rowman and Littlefield Publishers, Inc.
Minkoff, Debra. 1993. "The Organization of Survival: Women's and Racial-Ethnic Voluntarist and Activist Organizations, 1955–1985." *Social Forces* 71:887–903.
1997. "The Sequencing of Social Movements." *American Sociological Review* 62:779–799.
1999. "Bending with the Wind: Strategic Change and Adaptation by Women's and Racial Minority Organizations." *American Journal of Sociology* 104:1666–1703.
Mohr, James. 1978. *Abortion in America: The Origins and Evolution of National Policy*. Oxford: Oxford University Press.
Mottl, Tahi. 1980. "The Analysis of Countermovements." *Social Problems* 27:620–635.
Noonan, Rita. 1995. "Women Against the State: Political Opportunities and Collective Action Frames in Chile's Transition to Democracy." *Sociological Forum* 10:81–111.
Oliver, Pamela, and Gregory Maney. 2000. "Political Processes and Local Newspaper Coverage of Protest Events: From Selection Bias to Triadic Interactions." *American Journal of Sociology* 106:463–505.
Oliver, Pamela, and Daniel Myers. 1999. "How Events Enter the Public Sphere: Conflict, Location, and Sponsorship in Local Newspaper Coverage of Events." *American Journal of Sociology* 105:463–505.
Olzak, Susan, and Emily Ryo. 2007. "Organizational Diversity, Vitality and Outcomes in the Civil Rights Movement." *Social Forces* 85:1561–1591.
Piven, Frances Fox, and Richard Cloward. 1977. *Poor People's Movements*. New York: Basic Books.
Quadagno, Jill. 2005. *One Nation, Uninsured: Why the US Has No National Health Insurance*. New York: Oxford University Press.
2011. "Interest Group Influence on the Patient Protection and Affordable Care Act of 2010: Winners and Losers in the Health Care Reform Debate." *Journal of Health Politics, Policy and Law* 36:449–454.
2014. "Right-Wing Conspiracy? Socialist Plot? The Origins of the Patient Protection and Affordable Care Act." *Journal of Health Politics, Policy and Law* 39:35–56.
Raeburn, Nicole. 2004. *Changing Corporate America from Inside Out*. Minneapolis: University of Minnesota Press.
Rao, Hayagreeva, Calvin Morrill, and Mayer Zald. 2000. "Power Plays: How Social Movements and Collective Action Create New Organizational Forms." *Research in Organizational Behaviour* 22:237–281.

Reger, Jo. 2002a. "More Than One Feminism: Organizational Structure and the Construction of Collective Identity." Pp. 171–184 in *Social Movements: Identity, Culture and the State*, edited by David Meyer, Nancy Whittier, and Belinda Robnett. New York: Oxford University Press.

2002b. "Organizational Dynamics and the Construction of Multiple Feminist Identities in the National Organization for Women." *Gender & Society* 16:710–727.

Rindova, Violina, Ian Williamson, and Antoaneta Petkova. 2005. "Being Good or Being Known: An Empirical Examination of the Dimensions, Antecedents, and Consequences of Organizational Reputation." *Academy of Management Journal* 48:1033–1049.

Risen, James, and Judy Thomas. 1998. *Wrath of Angels: The American Abortion War*. New York: Basic Books.

Rochon, Thomas, and David Meyer. 1997. *Coalitions and Political Movements*. Boulder, CO: Lynne Rienner.

Rohlinger, Deana. 2002. "Framing the Abortion Debate: Organizational Resources, Media Strategies, and Movement-Countermovement Dynamics." *The Sociological Quarterly* 43:479–507.

2004. "Getting into Mass Media: A Comparative Analysis of Social Movement Organizations and Mass Media Outlets in the Abortion Debate." Dissertation in *Sociology*. Irvine: University of California.

2006. "Friends and Foes: Media, Politics, and Tactics in the Abortion War." *Social Problems* 53:537–561.

2007. "American Media and Deliberative Democratic Processes." *Sociological Theory* 25:122–148.

Rohlinger, Deana, JoEllen Pederson, and Giuseppina Valle. Forthcoming. "Inclusive Discourse? Local Media Coverage of the Terri Schiavo Case." *Sociological Spectrum*.

Rohlinger, Deana, Leslie Bunnage, and Jesse Klein. 2014. "Virtual Power Plays: Social Movements, Internet Communication Technology, and Political Parties." Pp. 83–109 in *The Internet and Democracy in Global Perspective* vol. 31, edited by B. Groffman, A. Trechsel, and M. Franklin. New York: Springer.

Rohlinger, Deana, and Jordan Brown. 2013. "Mass Media and Institutional Change: Organizational Reputation, Strategy, and Outcomes in the Academic Freedom Movement." *Mobilization: The International Quaterly Review of Social Movement Research* 18: 41–64.

Rohlinger, Deana, Ben Kail, Miles Taylor, and Sarrah Conn. 2012. "Outside the Mainstream: Analyzing Coverage of Social Movement Organizations in Mainstream, Liberal/Left and Conservative News Outlets." *Research on Social Movements, Conflicts & Change* 33:51–80.

Rohlinger, Deana, and Jesse Klein. 2014. "From Fervor to Fear: ICT and Emotions in the Tea Party Movement." Pp. 125–148 in *Understanding the Tea Party Movement*, edited by N. Van Dyke and D. Meyer. Burlington, VT: Ashgate.

Rohlinger, Deana, and Jill Quadagno. 2009. "Framing Faith: Explaining Cooperation and Conflict in the U.S. Conservative Christian Political Movement." *Social Movement Research* 8:341–358.

Ryan, Charlotte. 1991. *Prime Time Activism: Media Strategies for Grassroots Organizing*. Boston: South End Press.

Ryan, Charlotte, Michael Anastario, and Karen Jeffreys. 2005. "Start Small, Build Big: Negotiating Opportunities in Media Markets." *Mobilization* 10:111–128.

Sanger, Margaret. 1938. *An Autobiography*. New York: Cooper Square Press.

Schudson, Michael. 2003. *The Sociology of News*. New York: W.W. Norton & Company.

Scott, Richard. 2001. *Institutions and Organizations*. Thousand Oaks, CA: Sage Publications.

2003. *Organizations: Rational, Natural, and Open Systems* Englewood Cliffs, NJ: Prentice Hall.

Sigelman, Lee. 1973. "Reporting the News: An Organizational Analysis." *American Journal of Sociology* 79:132–151.

Silliman, Jael, Marlene Fried, Loretta Ross, and Elena Gutierrez. 2004. *Undivided Rights: Women of Color Organizing for Reproductive Justice*. Cambridge, MA: South End Press.

Smith, Jackie, John McCarthy, Clark McPhail, and Boguslaw Augustyn. 2001. "From Protest to Agenda Building: Description Bias in Media Coverage of Protest Events in Washington, D.C." *Social Forces* 79:1397–1423.

Smith, Shaun. 2009. "Brand Experience." Pp. 97–111 in *Brands and Branding*, edited by Rita Clifton. Hoboken, NJ: Bloomberg Press.

Snow, David, and Leon Anderson. 1987. "Identity Work among the Homeless: The Verbal Construction and Avowal of Personal Identities." *American Journal of Sociology* 92:1336–1371.

Snow, David, E. Bruke Rochford Jr., Steven Worden, and Robert Benford. 1986. "Frame Alignment Processes, Micromobilization, and Movement Participation." *American Sociological Review* 51:464–481.

Sobieraj, Sarah. 2010. "Reporting Conventions: Activists, Journalists, and the Thorny Struggle for Political Visibility." *Social Problems* 57:505–528.

2011. *Soundbitten: The Perils of Media-Centered Political Activism*. New York: New York University Press.

Soule, Sarah, and Brayden King. 2008. "Competition and Resource Partitioning in Three Social Movement Industries" *American Journal of Sociology* 113:1568–1610.

Sparrow, Bartholomew. 2006. "A Research Agenda for an Institutional Media." *Political Communication* 23:145–157.

Staggenborg, Suzanne. 1986. "Coalition Work in the Pro-Choice Movement: Organizational and Environmental Opportunities and Obstacles." *Social Problems* 33:374–390.

1988. "The Consequences of Professionalization and Formalization in the Pro-Choice Movement." *American Sociological Review* 53:585–606.

1991. *The Pro-Choice Movement: Organization and Activism in the Abortion Conflict*. Oxford: Oxford University Press.

Sternheimer, Karen. 2011. *Celebrity Culture and the American Dream: Stardom and Social Mobility*. New York: Routledge.

Street, John. 2004. "Celebrity Politicians: Popular Culture and Political Representation." *The British Journal of Politics & International Relations* 6:435–452.

Tarrow, Sidney. 1998. *Power in Movement: Social Movements and Contentious Politics*. New York: Cambridge University Press

Till, Brian. 1998. "Using Celebrity Endorsers Effectively: Lessons from Associative Learning." *Journal of Product & Brand Management* 7:400–409.

Tuchman, Gaye. 1972. "Objectivity as Strategic Ritual: An Examination of Newsmen's Notions of Objectivity." *American Journal of Sociology* 78:660–669.

1978. "The News Net." *Social Research* 45:253–276.

1987. "Representation and the News Narrative: The Web of Facticity." Pp. 331–344 in *American Media and Mass Culture: Left Perspectives*, edited by David Lazere. Los Angeles: University of California Press.

Turner, Kathleen. 1980. "Ego Defense and Media Access: Conflicting Rhetorical Needs of a Contemporary Social Movement." *Central States Speech Journal* 31:106–116.

Turner, Ralph, and Lewis Killian. 1987. *Collective Behavior*. Englewood Cliffs, NJ: Prentice-Hall, Inc.

Turow, Joseph. 1997. *Breaking Up America: Advertisers and the New Media World*. Chicago: University of Chicago Press.

2006. *Niche Envy: Marketing Discrimination in the Digital Age*. Cambridge, MA: The MIT Press.

Van Dyke, Nella, and Holly McCammon. 2010. "Strategic Alliances: Coalition Building and Social Movements." Minneapolis: University of Minnesota Press.

Vliegenthart, Rens, Dirk Oegema, and Bert Klandermans. 2005. "Media Coverage and Organizational Support in the Dutch Environmental Movement." *Mobilization* 10:365–381.

Warf, Barney. 2007. "Oligopolization of Global Media and Telecommunications and its Implications for Democracy." *Ethics, Place and Environment* 10:89–105.

Warner, Judith 1993. "Where is Pamela Maraldo Taking Planned Parenthood." *Ms. Magazine*, pp. 21–35.

Wattleton, Faye. 1996. *Life on the Line*. New York: Ballantine Books.

Whetten, David. 2006. "Albert and Whetten Revisited: Strengthening the Concept of Organizational Identity." *Journal of Management Inquiry* 15:219–234.

Whetten, David, and Alison Mackey. 2002. "A Social Actor Conception of Organizational Identity and Its Implications for the Study of Organizational Reputation." *Business & Society* 41:393–414.

Wolfsfeld, Gadi. 2004. *Media and the Path to Peace*. Cambridge: Cambridge University Press.

Zald, Mayer, and John McCarthy. 1987. "Social Movement Industries: Competition and Conflict Among SMOs." Pp. 161–180 in *Social Movements in an Organizational Society: Collected Essays*, edited by Mayer Zald and John McCarthy. New Brunswick: Transaction Publishers.

Ziegler, Mary. 2009. "A Framing of a Right to Choose: Roe v. Wade and the Changing Debate on Abortion Law." *Law and History Review* 27:281–330.

Zucker, Lynne. 1987a. "Institutional Theories of Organization." *Annual Review of Sociology* 13:443–464.